SEVENTY YEARS OF BIRDWATCHING

H. G. ALEXANDER
Seventy Years of Birdwatching

With drawings by
ROBERT GILLMOR

T. & A. D. POYSER
Berkhamsted

© 1974 by H. G. ALEXANDER

First published in 1974 by T. & A. D. Poyser Limited
281 High Street, Berkhamsted, Hertfordshire

All rights reserved. No part of this Book may be reproduced, stored in a retrieval system, or transmitted in any form or by any means, electronic, mechanical, photocopying or otherwise, without the prior permission of the publisher

Text set in Monotype Bembo and printed and bound in Great Britain at The Pitman Press, Bath

ISBN 0 85661 004 6

Contents

	Preface	9
I	Beginnings	11
II	Some British Ornithologists, 1907–1940	22
III	The First of January	40
IV	The Kentish Weald: Population and Territory	49
V	Firecrests, Willow Tits, Water Pipits	70
VI	Migration	100
VII	Dungeness and Romney Marsh	123
VIII	West Midland Reservoirs	154
IX	Peveril Point, Dorset	163
X	Winter Birds in the Mid-Atlantic States of North America	176
XI	Some Indian Birds	191
XII	Do Birds Migrate over the Himalayas?	214
XIII	Rare birds	222
XIV	Some Problems and Notions	239
	Index	259

List of Illustrations

The author's uncle, James B. Crosfield
Jack Tart, R.S.P.B. 'watcher' at Dungeness
The Austen family, Dungeness   *facing page* 16

The Hoppen Pits and lighthouse at Dungeness, 1912
Dungeness today   *facing page* 17

T. A. Coward
Miss E. L. Turner   *facing page* 32

F. C. R. Jourdain and Harry Witherby   *facing page* 33

The author with W. B. Alexander and companions at Blakeney
Point   *facing page* 112

A. W. Boyd
Bernard Tucker   *facing page* 113

The Alexander brothers at Dungeness, c.1951   *facing page* 128

The author and his wife with Bert and Joan Axell, Swanage
With Salim Ali, Bombay   *facing page* 129

MAPS

'Section of Country near Tunbridge Wells, showing pairs of Certain Species of Birds in their Nesting Areas, 1907-14.'
                                                52 *and* 53
Migrant birds near Tunbridge Wells, from *British Birds* 1909   58
The Upper Bittell Reservoir area   156
The area South of Granchester, Cambridge   157
The Mid-Atlantic States of USA   177
The Indian sub-continent and adjoining countries   192

Preface

When I began to write these chapters of autobiography a few years ago, it was due largely, I suppose, to the pleasure an old man gets in dreaming himself back into his youth. I thought it unlikely that any publisher would care to publish what I was writing. True, I did rather want to get the main facts of the mapping of summer migrants in parts of the Kentish Weald into print, somewhere, in the hope that, perhaps in the nineteen-seventies or eighties, some Kentishman might be able to survey some of the ground again to see what changes there have been after sixty or seventy years. And those are, perhaps, just the chapters that the 'average reader', if such an animal exists, may find less readable.

The later chapters will show, I believe, that I enjoy birdwatching in my eighties just as much as I did in my teens. Birds become more and more fascinating, not less, the more you watch them. Today's Baltimore Oriole seen just outside our window in Swarthmore, Pennsylvania, is as fascinating as the first Hawfinches outside our window at Tunbridge Wells, Kent, in March 1898.

It would have been difficult to negotiate successfully with a publisher in England whilst still in the United States without most generous assistance from Bruce Campbell. Both Michael Rowntree and his sister Tessa Cadbury, who married across the Atlantic before I did the same thing, have nobly carried heavy scripts in their baggage across the ocean; and they and Jack Cadbury have given me a lot of encouragement to keep me going until the script was finished and the publisher found. So I have much reason to thank them for their help; and, of course, most of all my wife for the kind of help that cannot be put into words.

To some extent this is a family biography of three brothers who all found birdwatching an absorbing operation, but inevitably it becomes personal to myself from quite an early time. Christopher went to Rome in 1911, Wilfrid to Australia in 1912. Christopher was killed in Flanders in 1917. Wilfrid had gone off birds for the years from about 1905 till he went to Australia. When he returned to England in the nineteen-twenties I was delighted to find that birds were his main hobby. We were able to go birding together from time to time in the remaining forty years of his life; but most of his work was done from Oxford, whilst I was living in Birmingham—or in India. So the work that made his fame does not come into these pages.

When you have lived as long and have travelled as much as I have done you meet plenty of birdwatchers in many different countries. Some of my birdwatching friends come into these pages; others do not. It depends on the places and occasions that I happen to have written about. Anyway, I hereby apologise to those who might fairly have expected to find themselves here, but who are absent. If I had written a few more chapters, covering other events, especially in various parts of Europe, their pleasant companionship would have been acknowledged.

I must, however, record my thanks to Robert Gillmor whose drawings have long given me pleasure, but never more so than in the pages of this book.

H. G. A.

Swarthmore, Pennsylvania

CHAPTER I

Beginnings

On my eighth birthday, 18th April 1897, my eldest brother, Gilbert, gave me a book called *The Naturalist's Diary: A Day Book of Meteorology, Phenology and Rural Biology*. We lived at Tunbridge Wells on the borders of Kent and Sussex; the book's author was Charles Roberts, a meteorologist, who also lived at Tunbridge Wells. The book, I believe, was published by Peltons of Tunbridge Wells and no doubt it was bought from their shop nearly opposite the (then) South-Eastern Railway Station. Probably my mother had spotted it, and had suggested to Gilbert that he should give it to me. However that may be, the book was, I am sure, his present to me; so that this book, which had a decisive influence on the family natural history development, came from the one brother who was not interested in natural history and who must sometimes have been driven almost to distraction by his three younger brothers' obsession.

In this book, one page was devoted to each day. The left half of the page was divided into sections covering Weather, Plants flowering,

Birds nesting, singing or migrating, Insects appearing and so forth. The second half of each page was left blank for the owner-recorder of the book to enter his own observations. I used this book for some forty years but I unwisely took it on a journey to India in 1946, when conditions of travel were still abnormal after the war. The suitcase in which it was packed disappeared in Bombay, so what I write about the book now is based on memory. Happily, I was always such a voracious note-maker or recorder that most of what was recorded in my *Naturalist's Diary*, at any rate concerning birds, was transcribed in one or two other places.

Charles Roberts had culled the literature for early or average dates on which things might be expected to appear. Some of these were based on the records kept by Gilbert White at Selborne in the eighteenth century; others were taken from the Marlborough College Natural History Society records, kept for many years in the nineteenth century. Both of these localities are in the south of England, so they were good for comparison with our observations at Tunbridge Wells—or Reigate in Surrey where we often stayed. In fact, except during our schooldays at York, all our early life was spent in the three south-eastern counties of Kent, Sussex and Surrey.

A few weeks earlier, in the same year, 1897, we had been staying at my uncle James Crosfield's house at Reigate. His brother Herbert, not yet married, still lived with his brother and sister, and always came down to eat a solitary breakfast after the rest of us had finished. Then he would rush off down the hill to catch his train to London (perhaps the 8.45 or so, whereas Uncle James always hurried down the hill in time to make the 8.03 or whatever it was). On the morning of 25th March Uncle Herbert had just shut the front door when he came back again and called out: 'Horace, there is a Chiffchaff singing in the front garden,' and off he ran a little faster than usual. For the next hour or so I wandered round the front garden, listening in high rapture to that Chiffchaff, watching the slender brown warbler flitting from tree to tree. Once at least it came very close to me in a low bush. Still in memory I can see it dashing out after insects, its tail gently wagging, the song coming fitfully as it flitted hither and thither. The 25th of March was surely an unusually early date. I did not think either of my older brothers, Wilfrid and Christopher, had ever heard one so early. So when Gilbert gave me *The Naturalist's Diary* on 18th April, I proudly entered my March Chiffchaff as the first entry in the book. Also, I had by then seen my first Swallow for the year, and on that day a Nightingale sang to us from the 'Nightingale copse' as we called it, a mile or two to the east of Tunbridge Wells. I was well away with regular recording.

We were four brothers. I was the youngest. Gilbert was seven years older, Wilfrid (known later in ornithological circles as W.B.) four years older, Christopher (C.J.) two years older. Where did our craze for natural history come from? The simplest answer, and possibly the truest, would be 'from our Quaker ancestry'. All through the eighteenth and nineteenth centuries, the Quakers denied themselves any full appreciation of the arts. There were occasional Quaker painters and poets, but music and drama were strictly forbidden in nearly all Quaker households, whether in England, Ireland or the 'American colonies'. So, by way of compensation, Quakers became students of natural history, of the world of nature; and they got a great deal of pleasure from this pursuit. All our ancestors, on both sides of the family, had been Quakers for at least two centuries. Our maternal great-grandfather, James Backhouse, undertook extensive 'missionary' travels in Australia and South Africa in the 1830s, where he mixed his religious activities with extensive botanical researches. His son, James Backhouse of York, was also a botanist of distinction, who helped to discover the botanical wealth of Teesdale, in north Yorkshire, destined now (1970) to be ruined for ever. He was also one of the first landscape gardeners in England, and he managed to create a rock-garden with cascades and surrounded by many rare trees on the Acomb side of York, in a part of England that looks most unpromising for the creation of a minor montane woodland. When we brothers were at school at Bootham, the Quaker boarding school in York, his daughter, Mary Louisa Backhouse, lived alone in the house at West Bank. There we spent almost every Sunday afternoon of our schooldays. There I found a Goldcrest's nest suspended from a deodar tree. There I watched a party of Siskins feeding within a few feet of me under a conifer. There I once almost trod on a Jack Snipe. And so on. Louie Backhouse died when she was only fifty, and I discovered to my amazed delight that she had left me, in her will, her copy of Dresser's *Birds of Europe*. Wilfrid in his schooldays was primarily a botanist, and he had explored Teesdale with Cousin Louie. Christopher, in his Bootham schooldays, appeared to be chiefly an entomologist. Birds were always my dominant passion. Anyway, whether I deserved it or not, she left those seven noble quarto volumes to me, and they have been a priceless possession for over sixty years.

The Backhouse heritage was no doubt the original source of our natural history urge; but it came directly from 'Uncle James', my mother's eldest brother, whose full name was James Backhouse Crosfield. He was a good all-round naturalist, with special knowledge of plants and birds. Once he arranged his summer holiday so as to see the total eclipse of the sun in Spain—and, incidentally, the Azure-winged Magpie, a bird confined to the Iberian peninsula and only scantily distributed there. Birds were his first love. For many years he was chairman of Harrisons and Crosfield, Tea Merchants, a firm founded by his father Joseph Crosfield, in partnership with two Harrison brothers. They started business in the forties in Liverpool, but Joseph Crosfield moved to London in the early 1850s, and built a house at Reigate. Uncle James spent all but the first four or five years of his long life at Reigate. Until he was well over fifty, I doubt if he ever took a full working day off from the London office, certainly not for 'fun'. Moreover, his Sundays were filled with attendance at an Adult School and two Quaker meetings. So his only free time for nature walks was Saturday afternoon, and from the earliest time I can remember he took one free Saturday every month. Our visits to his house, Undercroft, where he lived with his youngest sister after the rest of the family were married, were frequent. We always hoped that, if a week-end appeared, it would be Uncle James's free Saturday. When we were old enough, this might mean a whole day's outing to the Frensham ponds and the heaths of south-west Surrey. This would require a very early start by train to Guildford or Godalming, then a long walk by lanes and over the heath to Frensham; tea at an inn near Frensham ponds (our lunch sandwiches we always took with us; and Uncle James's two-course lunch consisted of sardine sandwiches and sugar sandwiches). Then a brisk four-mile walk along the dusty road to Farnham, at rather over four miles an hour, where we caught a train back to Guildford and so to Reigate.

But I am anticipating. At the age of eight I was much too young for a day out with a fifteen-mile walk. A Saturday afternoon on or below Reigate Hill, or round Park Hill and over Reigate Heath, or perhaps down to the river Mole, occasionally by train to Dorking and then up to Leith Hill and back, was our boyhood idea of heaven—in the company, of course, of Uncle James. In the summer he would occasionally get up really early, I suppose at 5.30 or 6.00, for an hour's walk before breakfast. I have an early memory of envying Wilfrid, who had been allowed to get up early and join Uncle James. At breakfast Wilfrid was full of excitement because they had seen a Green Woodpecker. A Green Woodpecker, thought I; what a marvellous bird to see! Should I ever be old enough to go out before breakfast to see a Green Woodpecker?

In childhood, the time you have to wait before you are old enough to do the things the older ones are doing seems like eternity. But being the youngest has its compensations. In course of time the older brothers have all gone off to boarding school. I can now go walks all alone with Uncle James. The 1897 Chiffchaff belongs to this halcyon period. And on 19th February 1898, Uncle James took me for a Saturday afternoon walk through Gatton Park and then up under the beech trees by the road that came to the top of Reigate Hill near the Suspension Bridge. We came on a flock of birds feasting on the beech mast in the road. No motor cars or other disturbances of avian peace in those days. Among the Chaffinches Uncle James detected a few Bramblings. I was able to watch them through his telescope. At that time in my life I had hardly heard of a Brambling and I was sure neither Wilfrid nor Christopher had ever seen one.

A few years later (probably 1907) Christopher and I decided to get specially bound books for recording the dates of arrival and departure of summer and winter migrants, year by year. When we went back over our existing records, we found that my 1897 Chiffchaff was in fact the earliest date that any of us had recorded. So 1897 became our starting year. In that year we had nine arrival dates, five of them mine, three of them Christopher's and one seen by both of us. Next year we had thirteen, and Wilfrid was responsible for two of them. It is not till 1901 that there is anything like a complete record of the commoner regular British summer migrants: 21 of them. That year gives the first recording for Redstart, Wood-Wren (now of course Wood Warbler), Red-backed Shrike and Nightjar. It is singular now to notice that one of the nine in 1897 was a Corncrake, heard by Christopher near Dover. In the whole series, we recorded an early Corncrake (or at least a passing spring migrant) in no less than 25 years. The last was one heard by Wilfrid in April 1949 near Oxford; and that was the first since 1937. The Corncrake list becomes irregular after 1926. But again I have jumped far ahead. There will be more to be said on these migrant dates in a later chapter.

Very early we all became avid list makers: lists for our lives, the year's list, county lists and so on. Probably Wilfrid set the example here. He certainly was the first to make a complete list of all European birds in a note-book. One Christmas holiday, probably 1901, we spent at Reigate. Wilfrid had had a small operation on his foot, so he had to lie up on a couch all day. Uncle James's copy of Dresser was an endless resource on such occasions. That Christmas, while Wilfrid lay on the couch, I took down one volume after another (my hands had to be examined by an adult to see that they were clean each time I took out a volume). I read out the list from Dresser and Wilfrid wrote it down. A few months later Christopher copied Wilfrid's list; and then I copied Christopher's. I never noticed that Dresser had listed the birds by number at the beginning of each volume. I laboriously went through each big volume, admiring every picture in turn. Of course, this was much more fun. Not quite all the birds were illustrated, so I made two mistakes, and Wilfrid made one. I missed the Black-bellied Dipper, Dresser's number 17; so from there on all the numbers were one out, up to 499. Then Wilfrid jumped from 499 to 501, so we were all right again up to the Herring Gull at 586. Then I missed two gulls Dresser does not illustrate, so the rest are two out, and Dabchick, the last, is 621 in our list, not 623.

I have referred to this because, soon after, Christopher began to learn the numbers by heart—at least all those that normally occur in England—and I quickly followed him in this. For the rest of our lives we constantly used these numbers as shorthand for all our daily bird lists. Curiously, Wilfrid never learnt them, although he had made the original list. When Christopher was staying with H. F. Witherby in London in 1909 or 1910, he discovered that Witherby also used the Dresser numbers—but accurately, of course.

As far as I remember, it was Christopher who first made regular daily entries, not only of birds, but equally of flowering plants and of insects, in a diary. He was given a Letts' diary, with a full page for each day, in perhaps 1904. Within a year or two I followed his example, and bought myself a one-page-a-day Letts' diary every year for many years. It was a very misguided thing to do; and I cannot imagine why I was so slow—nearly fifty years in fact—to realise how unsatisfactory it was. True, the actual lists of 'firsts' or 'lasts' were transcribed into other note-books in ink; but all the notes taken on the spot, including the day's list of birds seen and heard singing, were entered in the diary of fixed size, one page per day, no more, no less, every day *in pencil* (the pencil sold with the diary). If there were two days in succession with very full notes—days spent, for instance, at Dungeness or exploring the South Downs—by the end of the year the two pages were

Above, the author's uncle, James B. Crosfield, c.1890. *Right*, Jack Tart, R.S.P.B. 'watcher' at Dungeness, c.1924. Note 'backstays' for walking on shingle. *Below*, the Austen family at the door of their home, Dungeness, c.1914. Left to right, Fred Austen, Nelson Freathy (son-in-law), Mrs Mills (mother-in-law), Edith Freathy (daughter), Mrs Austen.

Faded photographs by Miss E. L. Turner of The Hoppen Pits and of the lighthouse in 1912. *Below*, Dungeness today, with atomic power station, old and new lighthouses and pylons. Photo Jim Flegg.

smudged, and the very notes most worth preserving were illegible. It is only in the past few years that I have had the sense to buy open note-books, where I can expand to two or three pages if necessary, and compress three days into one page when that is sufficient, and all in ink. Nevertheless I still believe in the value of the daily record.

A few years ago, an old school and college friend, Philip Noel-Baker, on a more or less public occasion, declared that I had kept a note of every bird I had seen every day of my life. That was a slight exaggeration; but only slight. Until my ears began to give way, in my late sixties, I did record every bird song I heard every day of the year, at any rate when I was in Europe. So the bird-song charts that I have published in *British Birds* and in the Witherby *Handbook* are based on records covering well over forty years.

Until I was over sixty, my ears were as good as my eyes, that is, they were exceptionally acute. One day, perhaps about 1908, Christopher and I were taking one of our usual short walks round Bishopsdown, Tunbridge Wells, when we were aware of hearing a very distant Yellowhammer song. We knew where it must be as we already had them charted on our six-inch maps. It was at least a quarter of a mile from us. We were amazed and delighted to find that we could both hear at such a distance. The loss of such a faculty is not easy to accept. One day in 1950 or a little later, I was walking by myself in the Himalayan forest, near Dalhousie, when I came on a party of tits in the trees. I was puzzled that they were silent. I did not think I had ever in my life, in either Europe or Asia, observed a wandering party of tits that were not vocal as they moved and fed. A few weeks later I was in the Lickey Woods, Birmingham, with Duncan Wood. He heard a party of Coal Tits in the trees. We soon came up with them. I could not hear a thing. Then I knew. I suppose I have never since heard that charming little conversational twitter of the tits, sweet music to the ear of every bird lover.

One day, probably in 1905, a well-known Quaker, Neave Brayshaw, who at one time taught at Bootham School, was staying at our house. Some special bird or other, a Nuthatch or Lesser Spotted Woodpecker, perhaps, had suddenly appeared while we were at breakfast and we had all rushed to the window. Neave Brayshaw commented: 'You boys ought to start a journal of natural history.' 'Oh yes,' I said eagerly, 'Wilfrid will be in charge of the botany, Christopher the insects and I will do the birds.' 'Oh,' said Christopher, 'so you will keep the best part.' I was astonished. He had just left school, and was beginning work at the South-Eastern Agricultural College at Wye, between Canterbury and Ashford in mid-Kent. But I still thought his main interest was in butterflies and moths. Here he was announcing that birds were his first choice. From that moment dated an intimate association, involving a voluminous correspondence, with no detail of observation too trivial to record or share, beginning in 1905 and ending with his death in Flanders in October 1917. Recently I have re-read all those letters again; and I shall be quoting them. Memory registers our first walk together under the new circumstances. I had just returned home from school at the end of July 1905. We went a short walk round the area we knew as Bishopsdown. At the bottom of the hill there was a small wood, and here we saw a family of newly fledged Spotted Flycatchers. As we watched, one of the parents brought a Meadow Brown butterfly to feed its young. This butterfly is specifically mentioned as in the range of flycatcher food by Jourdain in the *Handbook of British Birds*, but I think it is unusual.

Wilfrid's early interest in birds must have been a great delight to Uncle James. He never married, so his interests and enthusiasm could best be shared by nephews. His oldest nephew, Anthony Wallis, became an enthusiastic botanist, but the next four nephews, including Gilbert, showed no particular interest in nature study of any kind. Then came Wilfrid. Not unnaturally, Uncle James, who was always generous and intelligent in his choice of Christmas presents for all of the younger generation, began to give him bird books. First came

Johns' *British Birds in their Haunts*, for which Wilfrid was destined to prepare a new edition fifty years later. In 1899, he had the second edition of Howard Saunders' *Manual of British Birds*, which remained the standard British bird book till Witherby got going in the nineteen twenties. Uncle James also gave him Wilfrid Bucknill's *Birds of Surrey*, when it was published in 1900. This contained a number of notes on Surrey birds from the note-books of both James and his younger brother Albert Crosfield. Nor was Christopher forgotten. At Christmas 1896, Uncle James gave him the newly published *British Birds* by W. H. Hudson. Its few coloured plates by Archibald Thorburn, and the numerous black and white illustrations by G. E. Lodge, some of them full page pictures of a number of birds together, all very much alive, as one could expect to see them on next Saturday's walk across the countryside, made a strong appeal to me then, and still do. That book is now in my possession, and it takes me into the heart of the country whenever I open it. For his twenty-first birthday, 24th March 1908, Christopher got the four volumes of Yarrell's *British Birds* from Uncle James: the fourth edition, published through the seventies and eighties of the nineteenth century, the first two volumes edited by Alfred Newton, the third and fourth by Howard Saunders. So he too was well supplied with authoritative books. By contrast, my own early gifts were of much lower calibre. In 1898 Uncle James gave me a book, *Birds of the British Isles*, by John Duncan. Neither the letterpress nor the black and white illustrations by the author are of any special merit. With the sensitiveness of a child, I somehow felt that, deeply as I loved Uncle James, he had not really found the right bird books for me. But of course all this was forgotten when the astonishing bequest of Dresser came from Louie Backhouse in 1907.

It will be seen that, as a family, we were well supplied with good reference books on British and European birds. There is one book of that period that I regret never having known, namely Seebohm's *British Birds*. Seebohm was a remarkable man who had travelled widely, so that he wrote from rare first-hand experience; I suspect that, even today, his work remains full of original matter, by no means out of date. So, indeed, are Saunders, Newton and Dresser. 'There were giants in those days,' but how they fought one another!

As a schoolboy I went on acquiring bird books, some from prize money, others as gifts; some of these took my mind far beyond the mere knowledge of bird systematics. First among these was Warde

Fowler's *A Year with the Birds*, which I have lately re-read with immense satisfaction. I find it as fresh as ever. So too with his two other bird books, which I never knew as a boy. Then I began to learn about American birds and beasts from Ernest Seton Thompson's books: *Wild Animals I have known*, and others (he became 'Thompson Seton' some years later). But who remembers the books of William J. Long? *Beasts of the Field, Fowls of the Air*, and *A Little Brother to the Bear*. How I found these American books in a York bookshop I cannot say. Presumably they had a fair sale in England at the turn of the century. Anyway, they made such birds as the chickadees, the Bald Eagle, the 'Golden-winged Woodpecker' (which we always call the Flicker today), and several more North American birds, familiar to me, although I was to wait over forty years before I saw any of them in the wild.

Then there were the Kearton books of early bird photography. It seemed almost incredible that anyone should go all the way to remote St Kilda to photograph the Fulmar Petrel. If Uncle James had disappointed me with some of the earlier bird books, this was amply compensated when, at Christmas 1905, he gave me Edmund Selous' *Bird Watcher in the Shetlands*. Christopher, by this time, had become a thorough W. H. Hudson addict; but here was a new type of book altogether. Now I learnt that the most exact field observation had scientific value. It was not necessary to be a museum man if you were to make a contribution to ornithological science. None of our uncles ever used a gun. But Uncle James had a collection of eggs, and Wilfrid followed his example. At first I wanted to do the same; but my parents discouraged the idea. By the time I acquired his book, Selous, supporting Hudson, confirmed me in accepting this way of bird study as the best.

A further comment needs to be added about that word 'phenology' which appears in the title of Charles Roberts' *Naturalist's Diary*. It was a word commonly used fifty years ago in the age of 'Natural History and Philosophical Societies', when elderly people with leisure were eager to assist in the post-Darwinian search for the truth about natural phenomena: in other words, the animals and plants of the countryside around them. 'Phenological' means 'the science of appearances'. Is there such a science? Perhaps not, at least in the sense understood by the 'phenologists'. The Royal Meteorological Society had a Phenological Section; and its aim was to relate the annual occurrences in the world of nature to the data of weather and temperature. The

Roberts book gave the average temperatures throughout the year, and other such meteorological data. The observer was encouraged to keep records of maximum and minimum temperatures, to record the daily rainfall, and so on. For some years we regularly did this. Indeed, I have made a point of recording the daily weather, and as a rule the maximum and minimum temperatures, in my bird diary until this day. It helps to give a background to one's observations.

But some of the assumptions of the phenologists seem to be unsound. My brother Christopher pointed out, long ago, that it was absurd to suppose that, at midnight on the night of 31st December, suddenly, the whole of the natural world was given the word 'go'. As if all the plants in the earth were lying dormant up to that moment and then began to stir. So many degrees above freezing from 1st January onward would cause the first snowdrop to flower. So many more degrees the first primrose, and so on. Such and such an accumulation of temperatures and sunshine would evoke song from the Skylark, or the Chaffinch. But what about the daisies that were already flowering in the grass in December, or, to take a better example of a wild flower, as daisies seem to go on flowering in southern England nearly all the time, what about such a plant as the annual mercury with its curious greenish flowers, that begins to flower in mid-December? And what about the Robin, that has been singing all through the autumn? Or the Song Thrush, that has sung intermittently, in fine weather as a rule, but sometimes in the most miserable weather conditions (cf. Thomas Hardy's poem, 'The Darkling Thrush') all through December?

Obviously, there is a relationship between weather conditions and the appearance of flowers, insects, birds in song and all the rest. But it is a very complex and subtle relationship, which cannot be exactly correlated with meteorological data, however carefully and fully recorded.

But if 'Phenology' fails as a science, it is still a fascinating amusement or occupation for those who enjoy the world of nature and who have time and inclination to keep records of what they see and hear in the world around them. I am a life-long 'phenologist', but I prefer to drop the long word, and simply say that I have always enjoyed keeping records of what I see. As the rest of this book may show.

CHAPTER II

Some British Ornithologists: 1907—1940

As already recorded, our early birding was due to the influence of our uncle James Crosfield and his brothers. Their brother-in-law, H. M. Wallis, lived rather further away, in Reading to be exact, so we did not see so much of him; but he was always available for aid if necessary. He was the only one of that generation in our family who was at all widely known as an ornitholgist. He was a member of the British Ornithologists' Union for some fifty years, and often attended the monthly dinners of the British Ornithologists' Club in London. He was still active when Witherby was preparing his *Handbook of British Birds*, for which he did some effective diagnostic sketches of the commoner European raptors. He was a man of vivid personality and lively imagination, who in the intervals of an active business life found time to write half a dozen novels. He enjoyed coining ingenious phrases. Of the learned German-born Dr Ernst Hartert, whom Walter Rothschild had lured to Tring, where he had charge of the vast collections of bird skins, H.M.W. would say: 'What Hartert doesn't know about birds you could put inside a homoeopathic pill, and even then it would rattle.'

Outside the family, Dr Norman Ticehurst of St Leonards was the first ornithologist I came to know. In November 1907, Christopher and I each received a printed letter from Ticehurst, explaining that for fourteen years he had been collecting material for a book on the Birds of Kent. He was now getting it into shape, but he was first anxious to get fuller information from all over the county. He attached a long 'schedule', listing his main needs, and invited our assistance. Christopher, then a student at Wye, no doubt sent him information from that district. With Christopher's help, I sent him material from Tunbridge Wells. He asked for information on sixteen locally distributed breeding species. I sent him information on all these except two owls (I have never been much of a nightbird myself, so I tend not to see the owls). I also sent comments on several other matters he raised, such as the occurrence on migration of Ring Ouzel, Pied Flycatcher and some more, and 'rarities', where I told him of Firecrests and a Woodchat Shrike. In reply he wrote me a letter of two long pages, full of warm appreciation. My 'splendid series of notes . . . cover an area about which very little has hitherto been written and which will consequently be of the utmost value to me'. A letter in such a tone naturally captivated a shy youth of 18, and I was his man for life.

From 1907 to July 1914 I received no less than forty letters or briefer notes from him. The first seven letters, covering the first eighteen months, are all addressed to 'Dear Sir'; I suppose that sounds fantastic to anyone accustomed to the 'first name only' habit of the later years of this century; indeed, when I turned up these old letters the other day, I could scarcely believe it myself. In 1909 I became 'Mr Alexander'. At last in 1910 he suggested that it was about time for us to drop the 'Mr'. Although his home was less than an hour's distance by train, in fact at the end of our line from London to the coast, and although we spent holidays or even an occasional single day at Rye and on Romney Marsh, which meant travelling past his home, we did not meet till July 1909, when he invited me to lunch. I was in a panic at meeting such a distinguished stranger; but I had been seeing some puzzling birds in Romney Marsh, which I hoped he could elucidate, so once we got onto that all was plain sailing.

Exploring Romney Marsh by bicycle, looking for the good places for waterfowl, which I knew still existed, I had stumbled on a wonderful spot, close to an old church, where there were a lot of ducks on the marshes, and some waders which, with my small telescope, I could not identify. I had not dared to approach any nearer to them, for I saw a bicycle standing there and assumed that some other man might be watching the birds; so I must not disturb him or them. N.F.T. put various questions to me, and elucidated that it was Fairfield Church and the famous Fairfield Brack that I had stumbled on. Which day was I there? I told him. His eyes gleamed. 'I must not put the leading question,' he said, 'but did you see anything else that was strange?'

He had already assured me that my strange birds were Ruffs. I probably told him I had noticed some Herons. 'Well,' he said, 'my brother Claude was there that day. It was his bicycle. He saw the Ruffs; and while you were wondering if you dared to approach nearer, he was watching a Stork.' The date was 19th July.

Several of his early letters refer to the possibility of Ruffs breeding in Romney Marsh. Indeed, he was almost sure that they were doing so. But, even as early as 1910, he found that the pumping of Fairfield Brack had begun. In April the water level was as low as it had usually been at mid-summer. He urged me to go at once if I wanted to see the multitude of ducks that had been there earlier in the month. The pumping continued, year after year; so that Fairfield, where Claude Ticehurst had watched Ruffs in full plumage a year or two earlier, and had even seen them courting, was ruined ornithologically, and was only of interest in the winter.

Norman Ticehurst was the secretary of the B.O.C. Migration Committee, which investigated spring and autumn migration year by year from 1906 to 1914. During the first year or two, it confined itself to the spring migration of some 34 species of birds that breed in Britain but all, or nearly all, of which leave for more southerly countries in the autumn. The first report was criticised in *Nature* as being a mere repetition of an enquiry carried out some years earlier by the British Association for the Advancement of Science. Even the first report did not deserve that criticism; for the B.A.'s investigation was confined to migrants observed at lighthouses and lightships. The B.O.C., from the beginning, had numbers of inland observers who filled in weekly schedules.

As the years went by, the B.O.C. extended its coverage. It included autumn as well as spring migration; and it encouraged its observers to send in reports of every migratory movement of every species of bird—not only arrivals, but also increases, passage movements and departure—of the 34 'scheduled' species.

All this suited me wonderfully. Year by year I filled in the weekly schedules. Year by year I was more and more aware of the complexity of migration, and the number of species involved. A good proportion of Ticehurst's letters to me relate to these migration enquiries. One year I saw so much additional migration that I sent some of the extra observations on a single sheet of paper. This produced an indignant protest from Ticehurst; so apparently I did them over again on separate sheets—anyway, I hope I did.

I was not altogether content with the reports. Although inland observers provided a mass of information, it seemed to me that the committee was still disposed to think that the coastal observations were the most important. In other words, any strong migratory movement was sure to be noted at the lighthouses; if they had nothing to report, there could not have been much of a movement. But this is now recognised to be a fallacy. Migrants returning to their breeding grounds in such a small country as Britain may, in many cases, make the journey to their nesting ground from some place in France, perhaps even in Iberia, in a single flight. In fine weather, which is their preferred weather, this is most likely to happen. Large coastal movements may indicate a hold-up of migration rather than a strong normal movement.

Thus, a single inland observer, if he is free to cover a fair amount of ground—woodland, fields and hedgerows and whatnot—day by day, may be able to give a better picture of the arrival times of the Willow Warblers, the Whitethroats, the Swallows and the Cuckoos, than half a dozen lighthouse keepers. As it happened, during most of the years of the B.O.C. enquiry, I was able to do this, and I did it. So when, a year later, I found that the committee's reports did not fit the picture my observations had built up of the main arrival periods of some of the commoner birds I protested strongly, too strongly in fact. Ticehurst took it very well, but I doubt if I made any impression. It was T. A. Coward, I think, who noted that the 'waves' of immigration in the committee's reports had a suspicious tendency to fit the week-end observations of a large number of the observers. In those days there were no professional field ornithologists able to be out and about every day of the week. The few R.S.P.B. Watchers were in coastal areas, so they were not in a position to tell when the main arrivals took place, except in the case of a few species, such as Wheatears and the Terns. I suspect that Christopher and I were among the very few who were observing almost every day of the week.

Ticehurst was for many years the accepted authority on British migration; and deservedly so. He had a careful, scientific mind, ever ready to accept new facts. For many years, even after I was in close touch with Witherby, I reported first to him any interesting birds I saw, and more especially any special migratory phenomena; and he always found time to write a full letter in reply. Reading through those letters now, I am amazed that a busy doctor could find time to write at such length in longhand. And this was on top of the work he undertook for many years as one of the joint editors of *British Birds*. He was so modest that his contribution to British ornithology has not been adequately recognised.

After I left Kent for the Midlands, I had far less occasion to write to him. But from time to time we did exchange letters, especially if I saw some unusual birds on visits to Romney Marsh and Dungeness. He could rarely get away from his work to meet me on the marsh. The last time we met was a chance meeting at the Midrips, which he was exploring with his son, then a medical student. He held out his hand with the words: 'After many years,' as indeed it was. Unfortunately I never managed to visit him in his retirement at Tenterden, the country town where he had grown up.

I had no opportunity to discuss the so-called 'Hastings rarities' with him. Although I am convinced that a good many of them were frauds, any careful reader of Ticehurst's own book will, I think, conclude that some, such as the Black Larks and some of the rare sandpipers, were almost certainly genuine. It is no doubt too late now to disentangle the good from the bad.

The launching of *British Birds* magazine by H. F. Witherby in June 1907 was an exciting event for Christopher and me. Before that we had sent a few bird notes to the *Zoologist*, but *British Birds* was from the beginning much to our taste. The first note either of us published was a record of a Woodchat Shrike that I saw at Tunbridge Wells that year, published in the December number. And my first letter from Witherby was an acknowledgment of this note, expressing some scepticism. My reply must have satisfied him. In May 1908, the last number of volume one, we published a joint article on 'Song-Periods of Birds'. I had kept records of song-periods for several years; Christopher had begun to do the same when he went to Wye College. It was his idea that we should publish what he had done at this rather early stage. Leonard Gill, well-known later as the author of a Guide to South African birds, had published an article on the song-periods of British birds in the *Zoologist* a few years before this, and he had sent me a copy of this article; but already in some respects we had gone beyond what Gill had recorded. Christopher undertook the correspondence with Witherby on this and later joint articles that we published. Moreover, he stayed with Witherby in his London home, and did some beautiful paintings of the races of European titmice from some of Witherby's skins.

My correspondence with Witherby continued right down to 1939. Three letters from different periods seem to demand quotation, for very different reasons. Already in 1914 Witherby was keen to encourage the serious study of ecology. Possibly we had a preliminary talk about this at a B.O.C. dinner; but letters written in connection with the article that I wrote will show his approach.

On 2nd September 1914, he wrote: 'I think the best thing as a start certainly would be to give a short article suggesting some methods for the observer to employ, as you suggest. I want to work up an interest in the subject first, of course, before we can do anything practical. No doubt you saw the article by S. E. Brock in the July number, but this was far too heavy and theoretical to be of much value in working up a practical interest.' A long letter, hand written on the 10th October, reveals the workings of his mind in this field quite admirably.

He wrote: 'Many thanks for your letter and article. I think the latter is very good as an introductory article and I can see many branch lines in it which might be developed in future articles with more detail! If you could do this I mean in a future article or two sketching out in some detail certain points for investigation I feel sure it would have practical results.

'E.G. Why is the Starling increasing and the Swallow decreasing? The number of young per brood hatched and reared might be counted. Nesting sites and possible nesting sites carefully examined in view of their suitability or otherwise, food, enemies, etc. People say Starlings are increasing in their neighbourhoods—they don't inquire what the broods are, whether food has increased, whether more nesting sites are available, etc, etc, they merely look at the birds. I don't think it is sufficient to recommend accurate counting—a good many do this already and you want to take them further. The surrounding circumstances must be investigated and I think this should be more insisted upon in your article. For instance it does not teach us a great deal to study a flock of tits and observe exactly over what ground they travel each day and how many there are unless we are told why they do it and that cannot be discovered without a searching enquiry into the environment, say insects depending on certain vegetation depending on certain physical or geological features.

'Now here is an engrossing task for someone: a flock of tits: observe how it is built up of families: mark the trees it chiefly affects: the chief food: whether that food depends upon those particular trees: whether the food is difficult to find: whether it is more easily found by a flock than singly: whether the flock is an advantage against enemies if any: etc, etc: then the breaking up of the flock into pairs: do the old birds separate first, i.e. do the father and mother remain paired although in the flock (not quite impossible to observe in Blue Tits): does food become more plentiful and hasten on pairing etc, etc.

'Perhaps I have rambled on but please excuse. I had a dream to work out flocks of Tits in that sort of way years ago but drifted off it chiefly because I am not enough in the country. I have, however, seen flocks of Tits gradually form by families uniting, this meeting between the families apparently by chance.

'Also I have watched flocks break up in spring and this process is gradual and I have observations to indicate the possibility that the older birds whose affairs are more or less settled break off first. Anyone who could work out such a problem with the aid of entomology and botany would beat G.W. [Gilbert White]. He was a saint in ornithology far far in front of his time but why should we not beat him—Howard for example might if he were not so infernally theoretical.

'Well now I think you might touch up the paper by expanding it a little here and there keeping the definition of ecology more to the front and giving an illustration or two—elaborate the flock of Tits in some way as I have suggested if it appeals to you at all.'

The rest of this letter is concerned with Willow Tits, on which he and I had much correspondence.

My article was duly published, but we did not go ahead at that time with the further plans he had outlined. Why? I suspect that the chief reason was the war. The slaughter of the innocents in Flanders dried me up, and I had little heart for such efforts. To go out and forget for a few hours, as one watched birds, was very comforting; but serious ornithological work, whether in the field or in the study, was too difficult.

Witherby's proposed thorough study of tit behaviour was not

carried out for another forty years or so; and a study of Lack's book on *Ecological Isolation in Birds*, published in 1971, which summarises the latest studies of British tits, and which is discussed at some length in another chapter of this book, suggests that even today some aspects of the work that Witherby outlined in 1914 have still not been attempted.

I cannot resist quoting the brief letter Witherby wrote to me when Isent him the news of Christopher's death in Flanders in 1917. This book is, in part, a family history, so such a letter seems appropriate.

He wrote: 'Your sad letter just received comes as a great shock. I had a great admiration for your brother who was doing splendid work in his quiet and unassuming way. I deeply sympathize with you in your terrible loss. I am very very sorry and I know what good friends you two were. Personally I feel it very much.'

The last letter I had from him, dated 11th February 1939, is of a very different kind. Over the years, Witherby, as editor of *British Birds*, had the unenviable job of rejecting a number of records of rare birds that were sent to him. He had several times rejected records I sent. Of course, in the days before his own remarkable *Handbook* was published, field observers often had great difficulty in deciding what bird they had seen if it was a bird in some rather unusual plumage. The books simply did not tell you what you needed to know; and one could not habitually go and examine the skins at South Kensington. I recall, for instance, a winter sandpiper at Cambridge sewage-farm, with strikingly dark central tail-feathers. I thought this was diagnostic of the Solitary Sandpiper. So, in fact, did Ticehurst, when I first reported it to him. Witherby soon persuaded me that it was only a Common Sandpiper.

What he had rejected in 1939 I cannot now recall, but I must have written him an unexpectedly reassuring letter, to judge from his reply:

'It is very nice of you to write me such a charming letter. I can assure you that I greatly appreciate what you say. I never feel happy about a thing until I have had really good evidence that it is right, and for this reason I had an idea that I must have offended hundreds of people by doubting their accuracy and it is delightful to know that there are so many who are generous enough to be appreciative rather than offended. It is often a very difficult job as you know and doubting people's conclusions is not a job I like at all: but it has to be done!'

In the later years of his life, when he lived out in the country at

Gracious Pond Farm, Chobham, Surrey, I several times visited him there. In those days you had a good chance of hearing Woodlarks singing as you stood on the doorstep. On the common there were Curlews, Grasshopper Warblers and sometimes Dartford Warblers—all gone now, I fear.

When did I first meet Miss E. L. Turner? She was a near neighbour, living only three miles from Tunbridge Wells, at Langton Green. She published photographs in the first volume of *British Birds*. I think I first met her after she had given a lecture to the Tunbridge Wells Natural History Society in 1908. Christopher cannot have been at home. Anyway, she invited me to visit her on Hickling Broad, and I spent a delectable week there in May 1909. Christopher went to Rome, to work in the International Institute of Agriculture that summer, so he never knew her well. Thereafter, with Christopher abroad, if I wanted a companion for a morning's walk round Tunbridge Wells, I would get onto my bicycle, ride to Langton and see if Miss Turner could make herself free for a morning's walk round the Groombridge sewage-farm and the open stretches of Broadwater Forest.

During the next twenty years, I often stayed with her on her island in the middle of Hickling Broad; and when she moved to Cambridge, her house was only five minutes' walk from the home of my parents-in-law; so we often explored Cambridge sewage-farm together—a much more profitable place for ornithologists than the sewage-farms near Tunbridge Wells. One of our last adventures together was the discovery of a Lesser Yellowlegs at Cambridge sewage-farm on 29th March 1934. It remained there for nearly a year and was seen by many observers, including all the Oxford people available, such as my brother Wilfrid and Bernard Tucker: more about that in another chapter.

In the early days of bird photography, almost all bird photographs were taken at the nest. Even that was often difficult enough, with the equipment then available. One day, perhaps in the cold spring of 1917, when I was staying with Miss Turner on Holy Island, I told her that I was tired of all these nest photographs. Wasn't it possible to photograph birds away from the nest? So we got busy on what she called 'wait and see photography'. There was a spot beside the Holy Isle pond where Jack Snipe liked to feed. She set up her tent hide there, and I walked away. As she began to look around, she soon noticed a Jack Snipe that had not bothered to fly up as we put the tent up four

Some British Ornithologists: 1907-1940

feet from it. So that was her first 'wait and see' photograph. During the next two or three days a Heron and a Redshank came walking past within camera range. There was a patch of sandy beach, beloved by Sanderlings, Turnstones and other waders, where at high tide they fed quite near to the sandhills. Miss Turner established herself with her camera partly hidden at the outer edge of the dunes. I then took a walk round behind, came out at the far end of the bay, and slowly walked the birds along towards her. The result was quite successful.

A few years later, one cold winter's day when she was at Hickling, a herd of Whooper Swans arrived on the Broad. She went out in her boat, with a local assistant to row her, and in the course of some two hours she did in fact achieve some quite remarkable photographs. But she confessed that she had never been so nearly frozen.

Her last years were sad. She saw the coming of colour photography; and so she concluded that her life's work would be out of date in a few years. Then she had an unsuccessful operation for cataract. That, she said, broke her heart. She died soon after. But, although for some reason her name is not often mentioned today among the British pioneers of bird photography, her books seem to me to be among the best written books of bird photography that I know. She was a careful observer, and a good writer; and although I am no expert in photography, many of her photographs still strike me as extremely good. I recall how pleased and amused she was when, at a photographic exhibition to which she had sent some of her work, a judge commented: 'Miss Turner is very clever with her backgrounds.' Well, she was!

Miss Turner was a close friend of the Witherbys; and from the first volume of *British Birds*, hers were among the most frequent illustrations. When the B.O.U. agreed to elect a few 'honorary lady members', the obvious first names were Miss Turner and the Duchess of Bedford. The Misses Rintoul and Baxter, of Scottish fame, were of a slightly younger generation. So were Miss Haviland and Miss Best, both of whom did some of their early work with Miss Turner. Miss Annie Jackson, who became Mrs Meinertzhagen, completes the list of those early women ornithologists in Britain.

I joined the British Ornithologists' Union in 1911. Christopher joined at the same time. But he was off to Italy that year so I do not think he ever attended a meeting of the B.O.U. I attended a good many of the monthly dinners in the years before the 1914 war: but very rarely after.

When I first attended, the dinners were still presided over by Philip Lutley Sclater, about ninety years old, and the sole survivor of the founders of the B.O.U., which had just been celebrating its jubilee. He sometimes had to call unruly members to order, when he would rise from his chair with some difficulty, ring his bell and call 'Order, order' in as loud a voice as he could manage. It was probably Jourdain whom he thus called to order. In those days there was no separate oologists' club; and one of the members, Percy Bunyard, often had some rare eggs to exhibit; and usually Jourdain challenged the identification, for most of Bunyard's eggs were obtained through dealers. Bunyard was deaf, so he could hardly hear Jourdain's cruel quips. When he did, he had some reply ready, which I found less than convincing. All the same, I was inclined to sympathise with him, for Jourdain's comments were hardly in the language that I should have expected from a priest of the Church of England.

Apart from this, the early meetings of the Club were very pleasant, informal occasions. At my first meeting, I found myself watching a very large, heavily built man, with florid face and a beard, who during an interval walked around talking to several other members. My first impressions of him were not at all favourable. But outside appearances can be misleading. I soon found that this man was Walter Rothschild, and learnt that he was one of the kindest of men.

Witherby introduced me to Hubert Lynes, then Captain, a little later Admiral. He too was very friendly; and as his main interests included warblers (he did an enormous research into the Genus *Cisticola*, which appeared as a special supplement to *The Ibis*) and migration across the Mediterranean, I found plenty of common interest with him.

My one letter from Lynes, only dated 1st May (?1913) is chiefly concerned with what we now call leaf warblers, on which I had sent him various notes. I had also told him that on a recent winter visit to Hyères, on the French Riviera, I had found Chiffchaffs plentiful on the low-lying ground near the marshes. He commented: 'Re the Riviera—I thought it must be a normal winter habitat for Chiffchaff— the only time I'd ever been there at Marseilles 20th November last—on my way out to Sudan and actually before I sent my paper in—On that occasion I heard and saw a Chiffchaff singing in the Zoo gardens. I might have concluded from this as proved that the species was a winter visitor but the fact is I rather wanted to emphasize the utter barrenness of proper records on the subject in the mass of writing

T. A. Coward. Photo John Armitage, FRPS.

Miss E. L. Turner, c.1925. Frontispiece photograph by Mrs T. E. Hodgkin from Miss Turner's *Bird Watching on Scolt Head*.

F. C. R. Jourdain and Harry Witherby at Calvi in Corsica, June 1937. Photo John Armitage FRPS.

contained in the 55 years of *The Ibis* and all the modern standard works on European birds.' Quoting from memory, he notes that J. H. Gurney in a paper on the Riviera had not mentioned it at all; and Eagle Clarke had given the Willow Wren (now Willow Warbler) as wintering in the Riviera, but not Chiffchaff. 'H. Saunders and/or some other great authority draws attention to absence of Chiffchaff thereabouts in winter time.'

Such strange lack of observation of common small birds leads one to ask whether any of the leading ornithologists of the nineteenth century ever really looked at a small bird. Birds of prey were their first interest. Wildfowl and game-birds followed. The rest were mostly forgotten and overlooked. When Witherby sent one of Christopher's first letters from central Italy to Jourdain, his comment was: 'Why doesn't he spend his time finding the nests of his strange "eagles" [they proved to be Marsh Harriers] instead of wasting his time on the small birds?' When A. H. Evans gave a lecture at Cambridge on Birds of Shetland, he concluded by saying that he thought he had dealt with all the Shetland birds. As he had not mentioned a single passerine bird, I asked him if there were no Wrens in Shetland. With obvious annoyance he said he thought there were some. When I asked about pipits, he did not answer. Young upstarts should not put such questions to their elders.

Two fellow Kingsmen from Cambridge sometimes attended these dinners: H. W. Richmond, mathematician, Fellow of Kings, who was one of my supporters when I joined the B.O.U. and with whom I explored the Cambridge countryside. I have a painful memory connected with him, though he never held it against me. One summer he visited Shetland, and used his camera. He was particularly proud of a plate he had taken of a Red-throated Diver on its nest. He brought his plates to show me one day in my room. To my horror, this beautiful picture slipped from my hand and broke on the floor.

The other Kingsman was A. F. R. Wollaston, who had led the Jubilee expedition to New Guinea, and who told me how, after a fever had forced him to stay behind, he followed the main party through the jungle. Several times he saw the back of a man some way in front; but then it vanished again. It was some time before he overtook the others, none of whom fitted the back he had seen. This back remained a mystery, till, one day after he got home, he happened to see his own back in a mirror. That was what he had seen in the New Guinea jungle!

None of these men seem to be remembered today; but both Lynes and Wollaston made important contributions to ornithology in their day.

Charles Oldham was a frequent diner at the B.O.C.; and especially in the period after the first world war, any question of field identification was referred to him; usually he had some shrewd comment. When, in the twenties, I once visited the Severn geese with him (long before Sir Peter Scott's Wildfowl Trust days), I was amazed to find that he did not recognise the different call notes of the pipits: Meadow and Rock seemed to him to be indistinguishable; and he professed ignorance of the call note of the Tree Pipit. But his eyes were as good as those of any of us younger men.

Meade-Waldo was another frequent attender; and I soon discovered that he was a near neighbour, living at Edenbridge, only some twenty miles from Tunbridge Wells. He gave me a lot of help when I undertook to write an account of the birds of that part of the Weald for a volume published in 1916 on *Tunbridge Wells and Neighbourhood* for the South-Eastern Union of Scientific Societies. From time to time I visited him at his home, and learnt to know another section of the Kentish Weald.

The B.O.C. of those days, apart from the Jourdain–Bunyard controversies, seemed to me a friendly place, where everyone was on good terms with the rest. It may not have been so really. But if there were the usual jealousies and controversies among the men of weight, they were kept in the background. According to H. M. Wallis, there had been bitter feuds among the 'giants' of an earlier day: Dresser, Saunders, Newton, Seebohm, Sharpe; but all these had died, and the next generation seemed to be gentler and more tolerant. When, in the twenties, I learnt more about Jourdain from Witherby and Tucker, I began to like him too: respect one was bound to have, for his knowledge was second only to that of Ernst Hartert. Hartert himself was as regular at the Club meetings as Rothschild. One or other usually had some communication to make, or specimens of some new species or race to exhibit. If any man was accepted as the oracle, it was surely Hartert.

Among my prized possessions from the early years are a letter from Warde Fowler, to whom I had written about birds seen in Switzerland in the spring of 1907, and one from Edmund Selous, whose *Bird Watcher in the Shetlands* I had devoured when I was at school. This was written in 1908, in reply to a letter I had written to him also about that Swiss visit, when I had watched a Great Spotted Woodpecker carrying cones from a spruce tree to a convenient fork in a fruit tree, where it proceeded to feed on the seeds. He encouraged me to send a note on it to the *Zoologist*. He wrote: 'The bird's carrying the spruce-cone, if of any size, seems to dispose of some of my theory, but the many unused or hardly used ones is in favour of some of it.' Alas, I have no idea what his theory was; no doubt the *Zoologist* of 1908 would reveal. At least his letter shows the honest man, ready to see his theory partly undermined.

In July, 1919, I received a letter from one J. P. Burkitt, from Enniskillen, Northern Ireland. He explained that he had been investigating such matters as song periods, nesting periods and territory of some of the birds of his area; and he had published some of the results in the *Irish Naturalist*. Lately he had become a subscriber to *British Birds*, and Witherby had told him of some of my writings, which he thought might interest him, so he wrote to find out if I had any spares. He went on as follows:

'I was led to pursue this point [the relationship of song to the breeding cycle] by the rather interesting discovery I made ... last year, that the reason of the prolonged singing of Greater Whitethroats in end of May and on through June to first days of July is that every one of these songsters is a lonely male who builds away at a series of nests, complete except for finer lining and who (if not before) is pretty sure to get a mate and have her occupy one of his nests in the first days of July. The Whitethroat stops singing practically as soon as female sits if not before. The Garden Warbler follows the same line and the lonely male builds a number of foundations of nests near the occupied one. The Grasshopper Warbler also sings little after nesting begins. Of course this only holds true of a certain number of birds. I have been taking notes of Chiffchaff, Sedge Warbler and Willow Wren this year.'

We continued to correspond for several years. When I sent him our song-period articles, based on observations made chiefly in the south-east of England, he pointed out that the north Irish birds in some cases had much shorter periods. Thus: 'English Chaffinch continues a fortnight later than here. Blackbirds at least a month later (probably 1½ months). Song Thrushes at least a month later.' In Kent we heard Hedge Sparrows singing in every month. Burkitt commented: 'Your Hedge Sparrows are wonderful. This year and last year my last song was 2nd July. You have a regular list to 13th August.' He had found after extracting his notes that the two years he had covered showed an extraordinary similarity. The last letter of his that I have reports that he had now 'caught and marked six of my Robins'. This was the beginning of his wonderful work on Robins, which David Lack singled out as one of the outstanding pioneer activities of the earlier generation of field workers in the British Isles. He apparently told Lack that he had had no correspondence with British ornithologists. He seems to have overlooked the correspondence he had with Witherby and myself over several years.

T. A. Coward was surely one of the great field ornithologists of the early years of this century. I knew his writings long before I knew the man. He was a northerner who did not come to London to B.O.C. meetings or anything else. Fortunately the *Manchester Guardian* was already a national paper so his frequent articles published there were available to any southerner who liked to read a Liberal newspaper. Miss Turner knew the Cowards well, and I expect it was through her that I had my first correspondence with Coward, when he visited Dungeness, as recorded in another chapter. He had gone south to see the first authentic nests of Black Redstarts (1923-5), which had been privately reported to him by the finder. The nest was on the cliffs near Hastings; but it was Coward the northerner who was invited to confirm it. Why, I do not know. He considered himself free to tell me of it as soon as he had confirmed it. As a member of the R.S.P.B. Council, with special interest in that part of the country, I suppose I was considered safe. Soon after that, he visited Birmingham, and I was able to take him round the Bittell reservoirs and the Lickey Woods. He was an excellent field companion.

The first letter of some sixteen that I have kept from Bernard Tucker is dated 14th January 1926, but as he begins by acknowledging one from me I am not quite sure how we first discovered one another. But what brought us together is clear. He had been doing postgraduate work at the Marine Laboratory in Naples, and was writing up his ornithological observations for that part of Italy. Very little work had been done on Italian ornithology, either by Italians or by Britishers. Giglioli's local lists (published in 1890) were variable in quality, but the Neapolitan list, said Tucker, was 'hopeless'. He had read Christopher's two Italian articles published in *British Birds* just before his death; possibly he knew that I was still working on the remainder of his Italian diaries, the results of which I published in *The Ibis* in 1927. Anyhow, Tucker wrote at length about the birds of

Naples, and we soon got going. He invited me to speak at a meeting of the Oxford Ornithologists, still a very young society, and wrote me a long letter afterwards about the possible origins of bird migration, a topic on which I seem to have made some rather rash speculations in the course of my lecture. This I will quote, but first a little more about Tucker the man and the ornithologist.

The obituary written for *British Birds* by Max Nicholson and Duncan Wood, in February 1951, after his tragic death from cancer at the early age of forty-nine, is so perfectly done that everyone who wants to know him at second hand should read it whenever they can. Here I can add a little by quoting some of his letters and by paying my tribute to one whom I regarded as an intimate friend for twenty-five years.

First, what he wrote about the original causes of migration, in a letter dated 28th February 1926, when he was twenty-four. Although a great deal has been written and published on bird migration in the near fifty years that have passed since, I doubt if he would have wished to modify much of what he then wrote. In any case, the letter illustrates the clarity of his thought. I wish it could be reproduced photographically, for his writing was always a model of beautiful penmanship. Here is the bulk of what he wrote:

'I cannot help thinking that the habit [of migration] must confer some ... definite and specific advantage on the species, or to put it another and more forcible way that the habit must be one which is absolutely necessary to the species for some reason or other. That migratory birds *are* migratory in the face of so many risks suggests to my mind very strongly that migration must be so vital to the species that the cessation of migration (if one for purposes of argument imagines such a thing) would mean not a contraction of range, but complete extinction. I think it may be taken as an axiom that any species of animal will tend to occupy the maximum area that the environmental conditions permit, in other words that it will tend to spread until something in the conditions it meets with or in its own constitution prevents it from going further. This being so it seems to me that if extension of range and utilisation of surplus energy were the primary causes of migration then one would expect some kind of general post movement or something of the sort, having the effect of populating with breeding birds not only the breeding area which they now occupy but the winter quarters as well. The fact that the birds don't breed in their winter quarters seems to me conclusive that breeding is not possible there. I still feel that considerations connected with food and reproduction are probably at the back of the whole thing, though I do not at all suggest that they are the only factors involved. But to admit that food-shortage is not the stimulus which causes the individual bird to begin its migration is not necessarily to deny that food supply may be one of the ultimate causes of the development of the habit of migration. Again one would like to know more about the temperatures at which the reproductive organs of migrating birds function. It would be very interesting to know whether in a bird of a migratory species compelled to remain in its winter quarters through the summer the development of the reproductive organs is in any way retarded. Of course things like this will not account for everything in migration, nor will one factor cover all cases, but they may account for a part. Personally I believe that if the causes of migration are ever definitely elucidated (which I think doubtful, since they are probably largely bound up with conditions prevailing in the geological past, which we cannot adequately reconstruct) they will be found to involve a number of factors of which no one can be isolated as the primary or principal one, and all interacting closely with one another.'

Our earlier letters are largely concerned with Italian birds. Tucker tried to persuade me to join him on one of his later journeys to Naples, but unfortunately I could not manage it. Later, we made various plans for a holiday in Scotland together, and in 1948 I nearly joined him in Shetland; but that fell through too, so I never had the pleasure that I had constantly hoped for—a real holiday with this prince of birdwatchers. We had some good walks together round Oxford and Birmingham. Reading through his letters gives me the surprise that he was asking me to help him with Willow Tits. My recollection was that it was he who showed me the importance of the wing-patch formed by the pale edges to the secondaries. I think the truth is that he had detected that, but was still uncertain of some of the call-notes. So I helped him there and he helped me with the wing-patch.

When Witherby asked Tucker to undertake the Field Identification paragraphs for the *Handbook*, he asked me to help him. Charles Oldham had contributed brief, but in the main very good, field identifications for the *Practical Handbook* of 1912, and at first I was not clear what additional material was required, but it very soon did become clear. As the preface to Vol. I of the *Handbook* (published in 1938) explains, Tucker provided three distinct paragraphs, on Habitat,

Field-Characters and General Habits, and Voice. For several years, month by month, a small budget would appear, containing astonishingly complete, precise and clear accounts of all these aspects of the life of a number of birds, all written in Tucker's beautiful script, so that their arrival gave aesthetic pleasure as well as an ever-growing admiration for their author. Witherby himself and Max Nicholson also saw all these paragraphs in their first draft. The only response that I have kept to some of my comments is a letter discussing some suggestions I made about the ducks: I do not think he really accepted any of my suggestions on this, but the way he discussed them was so disarming that I could not have been better content if he had incorporated them all. On some other birds—the field identification of the three British divers in their difficult winter plumage is one case—I recall that we had quite a lively correspondence, and he made use of some of my experience.

When I went to see him in hospital in Oxford, I had no more idea than, I suppose, he himself had that his disease was mortal. His unexpected death was for me, as indeed for many others, a crushing blow. He had often shared his editorial secrets with me, during his years as editor of *British Birds*—the first breeding of Little Ringed Plovers in England at Tring in 1938, for instance; but he shared much more than that—his intense joy in bird life and the glow of a very open and direct friendship.

Most of my other bird letters have been from people who are still alive, so they need not be quoted. I find William Thorpe writing to me as long ago as 1926. David Lack (just recently and so sadly dead) wrote several letters while he was at work on *The Birds of Cambridgeshire*, which he published in 1934. His letter about Water Pipits is included in a later chapter.

Perhaps enough has been quoted here to show that in the first half of this century, ornithologists were still finding time to write at length on matters of serious bird study. Although some of the letters from those here mentioned were typed, all those I have quoted were written in longhand. Perhaps it makes a difference.

CHAPTER III

The First of January

Many ornithologists keep yearly lists of the birds they see. We brothers began this business early. Moreover, once Christopher and I had started our 'fraternal partnership' (not that we ever either called it that or thought of it in such high-falutin' terms) we always tried to begin with a good list on 1st January. This became for us nearly the equivalent of what is very widely practised in America today—a Christmas bird count. There were, however, three differences; first, it was always the 1st January, the start of the new year's list. Second, though we certainly did our best to get a good list, we did not go to the extreme lengths of rising before dawn and searching for owls, or continuing after dark. Indeed, for some years we did not even take a sandwich lunch out with us. Having eaten a normal family breakfast, we would set off soon after 9 a.m. and return home for lunch at one o'clock, with the possibility of going out again for a short walk before darkness fell.

The first year's list that survives for me is from 1905. In that year I was not in company with Christopher. Fifteen birds were seen from the windows of our Kentish home, and by going a short walk I added Wren and Goldcrest. That was all. Redwing was the only bird that was not an obvious common garden bird. I was then nearly sixteen.

The 1st January 1906 was the first New Year's walk we took together. On that day we followed a route which became the regular walk for the first day of the year. Starting out through Bishopsdown, we crossed Rusthall Common, then walked down the hill past Coldbath Farm to the Kent and Sussex boundary stream, just below the High Rocks. Here we turned in by a footpath through what we called the *Cardamine bulbifera* wood (a local plant, Coralroot, *C. bulbifera*, grew there in profusion, as I hope it still does). Thus we continued through this small wood and by the county boundary stream till we reached the Groombridge sewage-farm. Here we crossed the stream, and came off the sewage-farm into Broadwater Forest. There were several ways of crossing the forest. Then we usually chose another path behind the High Rocks, which brought us down across what was then the Brighton Railway to a point below Hungershall Park. So up the road to Tunbridge Wells common and ultimately back to our house at the bottom of Boyne Park—a good three-to four-hour walk through varied country, but with very little water: woodland, some meadow, some heath. In those days Tunbridge Wells's extensive common was almost entirely covered with heather or gorse. When I saw it in 1960 I was astonished to find that it was almost entirely grown over with trees.

In 1906 we had scored 15 birds before we set out, the most surprising being a Herring Gull that flew over the garden. At that time gulls of any sort were rare birds round Tunbridge Wells, which is some twenty-five miles from the sea. By the time we reached the High Rocks, we had added eight more, mostly small woodland birds, such as Goldcrest, Long-tailed Tit, Tree Creeper and Nuthatch. Along the boundary stream we found a party of Siskins in the alders, and as we came out of the wood we both saw a Kingfisher fly off suddenly down the stream. In those days Christopher had binoculars; I had none until I was given a pair for my twenty-first birthday in 1910. Christopher would whip his binoculars off in a split second so that I could see the vanishing bird. We omitted the sewage-farm that day.

On this first joint walk to start our year's list, we reached a total of 33. It seems strange to realise that I then thought this a good total. It included no water bird apart from the Kingfisher, not even a Moorhen.

In 1907 we followed the same route, but included the sewage-farm. By the time we got there, already the list was 28; the sewage-farm gave us Meadow Pipit, Greenfinch, Pied Wagtail, Fieldfare, Moorhen and Snipe. The day's total was 37. Year by year the total rose, though only to 38 in 1908. That year was a Brambling year, and we had the luck to walk up a Woodcock, possibly the only time I have seen one on New Year's Day. In 1908 there were Tree Sparrows at the sewage-farm. We may have overlooked them in earlier years. From that year on, we could count on finding a party of Tree Sparrows at the Groombridge sewage-farm every winter. They did not breed anywhere near Tunbridge Wells.

Each year I followed Christopher's example by making a number of additional lists: of the date when each bird was first heard singing—a list that rose quite soon to over sixty species in the year. Then dates for arrival and departure of summer and winter migrants, and some dates also for passage migrants; nests found with eggs or young (I was never much of a nest finder). Then lists of mammals, of reptiles and amphibians, of butterflies and from 1908, for the first time, I made a list of flowering plants, including trees and grasses. Christopher taught me most of these. This flower list, which I continued up to 1921, sometimes exceeded 300. I am not sure that it is wholly accurate. Some of the grasses and umbellifers, even more the hawkweeds, I did not learn too well in the few years before Christopher left England. Now I have forgotten nearly all of them.

In 1909 Willow Tit appears for the first time among the New Year's Day birds. After that, it is generally there. We shall come back later to this bird and its discovery in Britain.

In 1910 we decided to vary our New Year's Day activity. We took a mid-morning train by Tonbridge and Ashford to Appledore and so to Lydd and Dungeness. In those days the Southern Railway ran trains to within a few yards of Dungeness lighthouse, but this journey involved us in four changes of train even though the connections were good. The day's total was only 39, and 20 of these were seen before we left Tunbridge Wells. The sensation of the day was a Green Sandpiper, which luckily we both saw. It flew from a ditch half a mile out of Ashford. Only once since then have I seen a Green Sandpiper on New Year's Day. In 1940 Miss C. K. James of Barnt Green and I spent the last night of December at Shepherds Patch, close to what is now Sir Peter Scott's Wildfowl Trust area. Next morning we put up a Green Sandpiper from a ditch which must now be part of the Trust's ground. Returning to 1911, we saw Red-throated Diver, Common Scoter and Guillemot from Dungeness point; indeed we saw all these before we saw our first Herring Gull of the day. Then, as we walked westwards to catch a train from Rye home by Hastings to Tunbridge Wells, we added a few species before darkness fell, such as Grey Plover, Stonechat, Rock Pipit and Great Black-backed Gull. In those days I regarded Great Black-backs as somewhat uncommon birds. Hooded Crows, on the other hand, were still plentiful. We saw the first of the day from the train before we reached Ashford, and no doubt we saw some more on the marsh and Dungeness beach. But I did not see a Carrion Crow on New Year's day until 1915.

Of course, there were plenty of common woodland birds that we missed on 1st January 1910, so that the year's total went up fairly rapidly, and it was 65 by the 8th—this seemed a lot in those days, but not much by comparison with what I found could be done when woodland and water birds were seen all in one day. Nineteen hundred and eleven was special, in that there was a wintering Chiffchaff near the Groombridge sewage-farm—a typical *collybita* Chiffchaff, very different from the *tristis* Chiffchaff that spent some weeks near Tunbridge Wells two years later. I had to wait fifty-four years before seeing another Chiffchaff on New Year's Day, at Studland in Dorset (1965).

By 1912 Christopher was in Rome, and New Year's Day was an Italian holiday, so he was able to make a good New Year's Day list each year. He was at home on holiday at Christmas and over the 1st January in 1912-13, so we had one more New Year's Day together. For the rest, we exchanged letters about our walks on the 1st January in 1912, '14, '15 and '16. By the beginning of 1917 he was in the army in Flanders and he was killed on the Somme before the end of that year. My first year alone (1912) I took a train from Tunbridge Wells to Rye, via Hastings, and walked from there to the sea at Camber, along the coast to the Midrips, and across the marsh to Appledore. For the first time I exceeded 50—total 51. This included Snow Buntings in the saltings at Camber, Great Crested Grebe and Scoters on the sea, and several waders; but the duck count was poor, with nothing more than Mallard and Wigeon on the Romney Marsh fleets. A walk at Tunbridge Wells the next day brought the year's list up to 65.

On our last such walk together, on 1st January 1913, we saw Hawfinch for the first time. A Firecrest was spending the early part of the winter in the 'Firecrest field' at the end of Hurst Wood, and this we duly saw in the afternoon. The morning's walk was remarkable in giving us all three species of British woodpecker (Green, Great Spotted and Lesser Spotted) and the three south of England gamebirds—two partridges and a pheasant. The list of small woodland birds was also unusually complete: all six tits, Tree Creeper and Nuthatch, and the two Reguli (Goldcrest and Firecrest) and Wren. We also had both Siskin and Redpoll. On the other hand, the sewage-farm was very unproductive, apart from a Herring Gull that flew over. We saw no Snipe, and no Moorhen till near the end of the walk. Yet the day's total was 49, which is, I think, a remarkable total for mid-winter in England when almost no water-birds are included. Tunbridge Wells is also poor for birds of the open country. We never saw either Corn or Cirl Bunting.

In 1914 I was at the Lizard, Cornwall, and I got a list of 57, including, naturally, a number of birds I had never seen on 1st January before: such as Raven, Black Redstart, Turnstone, Purple Sandpiper, Shag, Gannet, Merlin, Cirl Bunting, Corn Bunting. That was the first year when I reached 100 before the end of January. The list was already 90 before we left Cornwall; on the 15th, stopping in Plymouth on our way east, I had the luck to find a wintering Common Sandpiper. My total was 98 before I went to Dungeness for a few days at the end of the month. Those three days gave me eleven more species, including Hooded Crow, Short-eared Owl, Pintail, Twite and two species of grey goose on the marshes—Pink-footed and White-fronted. On the last day of the month I was at Frensham Great Pond in south-west Surrey, where I saw my only Great Crested Grebe for the month, making a total of 110.

In 1915, for the first time, I used my bicycle for the 1st January 'walk'. Starting from Tunbridge Wells, I made my way past the Groombridge sewage-farm to Ashdown Forest. There, in spite of much rain, I managed to find a Dartford Warbler. At that time they were to be found in several places in Ashdown Forest but they were no more to be relied on to show themselves when wanted than they are today in Dorset. Another new species for these walks was a Carrion Crow. In those days Ashdown Forest was the only place near Tunbridge Wells where one had any reasonable prospect of seeing Carrion Crows. It was a scarce bird all over the south-east of England. Jack Tart, for many years one of the R.S.P.B. Watchers at Dungeness, told me that the first time he saw a Carrion Crow on the beach there, he thought it must be a Raven. By the 1960s, thirty years after his death, Carrion Crows were abundant on the beach, and Hooded Crows were rare.

Not much needs to be said about the next few years. They were all spent by me at Tunbridge Wells. On 1st January 1916 the list included a Water Rail and a Hawfinch. The fifth species that morning was a Redpoll seen from the window. In 1917, using my bicycle again, for the first time I included a visit to Eridge Lake, which gave me a few water birds, but only Coot, Dabchick, Tufted Duck and Mallard, besides Moorhen. However, I again got all the tits and both Redpoll and Siskin, and such uncertain species as Hawfinch, Sparrow Hawk and Stonechat, with a Kingfisher as climax, bringing the day's total to 51. I did not get to Hurst Wood, where again there was a 'wintering' Firecrest, which I saw next day. With five days at Dungeness and Romney Marsh the year's total rapidly grew, so that it was 91 by the 10th.

In 1918 I was back at the old walk, and only achieved a total of 38. Bad weather, I think. It had no special features, except that Long-tailed Tits had been nearly wiped out by the prolonged severe weather of 1917 and I did not see one until 30th January. Goldcrests were also scarce, and my first was seen on 9th February.

In 1918 I left Kent for the Midlands. My home for the next thirty years was in Selly Oak, south Birmingham. The obvious way to get a good score on New Year's Day there was to take a bus out to the Lickey Hills, walk through the extensive public woods there, and so across country to the Bittell reservoirs; and then catch another bus home again—a very nice three or four hours' walk for a winter's day. In fact I only did this five times, for when Ralph Barlow and Duncan Wood became available for joining the New Year's day walk we became more ambitious and took a bus (later we went by car) to the mid-Staffordshire reservoirs—Gailey and Belvide—and the woods and meadows near them. Twice we achieved a total of 63.

Also, during the twenty years between the wars, I spent ten New Year's Days at Dungeness. Romney Marsh and Dungeness beach are, of course, devoid of woodland; so the total for the day was not as high as on the best Staffordshire days. I used to comb the Lydd gardens for Robin, tits and thrushes, but even so, I did well to get over 50, especially if the weather was unfavourable. One year I woke up to fog, so the list of sea-birds was low. Later the fog lifted, and I was able to find most of the usual winter wading birds on Littlestone sands. Of course, at Dungeness anything might turn up. The winter of Little

Auks, unfortunately I had to be in London on the morning of the 1st; so I saw Little Auks on 31st December, but not on 1st January. On New Year's Day 1929, when Ralph and Duncan were with me, we saw what must have been an immature Long-tailed Skua (*Stercorarius longicaudus*). It was the beginning of a cold spell coming in from continental Europe, and many birds, chiefly Kittiwakes, were passing the point and flying down Channel. With several Kittiwakes came a dark skua, hardly larger than they. It passed us quite close to the beach, and we all saw it well, so I do not see how we can have been mistaken.

Rather than attempting to detail the fifty-odd New Year's Days since 1920, some of them spent in India, one in the Mediterranean, one in mid-Atlantic, where my only species was Kittiwake, and latterly several in the United States, let me single out a few specially memorable days.

In 1944, having just returned from India, I spent the New Year with the Yendells at Longdown, near Exeter. The 1st January was an exceptionally balmy winter day. I walked across country, through the woods and so to the Exe estuary, and reached the remarkable total of 73—ten more than my previous highest in England (in India over 100 is not difficult to achieve). This included Greenshanks on a flooded meadow at Powderham, and a Little Stint in full winter plumage on the mud by the Exe, among a mass of Dunlins. Fortunately it was close to the bank; the tide was just right.

When we came to live in Purbeck, I found that even my Devon total could be exceeded. On 1st January 1965 Trev Haysom and I managed a total of 84 (I missed two of them). The most remarkable feature, perhaps, of that day was a small party of birds close to the Studland ferry-toll. Trev heard a Long-tailed Tit—still a scarce bird after the severe winter of 1963. So we plunged down through the scrub to try to see it. It was solitary; but with it were two Goldcrests, a Firecrest and a Chiffchaff.

In 1967, the last bird of the list of 75 was, I suppose, the most improbable of all my New Year birds. Towards sunset we arrived at Durlston, above the cliffs, where the 'famous' Brown Thrasher from America had been in residence for some weeks. A Firecrest declared itself in the Evergreen Oaks (74), but at first there was no sign of the Thrasher. It was a sunny Sunday afternoon, so there were plenty of binoculars on the alert for the stranger. Suddenly it began calling, very loud and clear and unmistakable. At times it must have been within three yards of us, but confronted with such an audience, it preferred to remain hidden in the scrub.

In the course of nearly fifty years, I seem to have seen (or heard) 137 different species on 1st January in England. It is definitely a south of England list. Staffordshire is the most northerly point; my one Welsh day gave me nothing I have not since seen in Devon or Dorset. I have never been in Dipper country on New Year's day, still less in grouse country. And the only grey goose I happen to have seen is White-front. No doubt a few other possibilities could be suggested—Lapland Bunting for instance, or Shore Lark, not to mention Bearded Tit and Bittern; or even Avocet, if I had ever in recent years crossed to Brownsea Island on 1st January. So it could be 150.

It is not in my nature to start before dawn and rush around, trying to tick off every possible bird in the neighbourhood. Nor have I ever made a serious effort to achieve a hundred in the day, as some years ago first some young Scots near Edinburgh did, and then, just to prove that England is as good as Scotland, some other young men in Suffolk. Probably it could be done also in Dorset or Devon. If the daylight were longer, it might be as easy to do in mid-winter, when water-fowl and waders are plentiful, as in late May, at the tail end of the spring migration. On a good migration day, September might be the best month of all for making long lists. My first day's list of over 80 was at Dungeness and Romney Marsh, over fifty years ago, on a late September day, when the bushes at Dungeness were full of small migrants. But this takes us far from 1st January.

Although I never got up in the dark to prowl about for owls or other night birds on New Year's day, I have always been up in time to look for the first bird that might appear in the semi-darkness. Of common garden birds in England, Song Thrush and Blackbird are usually the first to get moving, with Robin soon after. On the coast the gulls are awake and astir soon after dawn if not earlier. Of forty-seven 1st Januarys spent in England, my list has started with Blackbird twelve times, Song Thrush ten times, Robin once, Carrion Crow three times, House Sparrow twice (one of these in London), Blue Tit once (we were staying with the Pickards at Reading), Jackdaw once, Skylark once. On the coast Black-headed Gull four times, Herring Gull three times, Great Black-backed Gull three times, Common Gull once. Recently I have included birds heard in the list at the moment of first hearing them. This has resulted in Tawny Owl leading off four times, all, I think, at Swanage. My first American list also began with an owl. We returned from a New Year party at about 12.30 a.m. As we drove in to the drive of my host's house, there were two Screech Owls, one red, one grey, on two posts beside the drive. My most recent American lists have begun with White-throated Sparrow, Blue Jay and Cardinal (1973).

Screech Owl

CHAPTER IV

The Kentish Weald: Population and Territory

I cannot remember quite how Christopher and I began to map birds in their breeding territories. As we went on our daily walks in the woodland round Tunbridge Wells, we began to note the singing quarters of the newly arrived migrants, first of all in the spring of 1907, and I suppose it was Christopher who suggested that we should buy some six-inch to the mile Ordnance Survey maps, and enter on these maps the singing males of the summer migrants. The 'Dresser' numbers were very convenient for this purpose. So we began; and for the next ten years we mapped birds, not only round Tunbridge Wells, but also in a number of other localities that we knew well: some round Reigate, Surrey, and Croydon; Christopher mapped a fairly extensive area round Wye, Kent, and in 1908 we mapped a large part of Romney Marsh, including most of Dungeness. I did quite a lot of mapping at Cambridge, in the years 1909 to 1914. Later, when I was teaching for two years at Cranbrook, also in the Kentish Weald, I did some fairly thorough mapping there; and later still, when I settled in south Birmingham, I got six-inch maps of that area, including the Lickey Hills and Bittell reservoirs, and for many years I attempted to map the same species there also, year by year.

In the first place, we confined ourselves to summer migrants—chats, warblers, Tree Pipits, flycatchers, Wrynecks and a few more. As we studied the birds more, we realised that there were other species, such as the buntings, that were as strictly territorial as the summer migrants, and we entered them on our maps. To some extent we limited our work by the exigencies of the scale of our maps. Even so, there were places where Willow Warblers or Whitethroats were so numerous that it was hardly possible to cram them all in, together with all the other species involved. Reed Warblers sometimes have very small territories in their reed-beds. However, the six-inch maps were really adequate for all the species we first of all mapped. But if we had attempted a total bird census, it would have been impossible on anything less than the twenty-five-inch scale. I have an idea that Christopher, before he left Wye for Italy, did acquire one or two of these larger scale maps, and he possibly began to fill in all the commoner species, or at least the territorial ones: Blackbirds, Song and Mistle Thrushes, Robins, Hedge Sparrows, Blue and Great Tits, etc. Colonial breeding-birds, such as Starlings, House Sparrows, Rooks and Jackdaws, would be more difficult. I hardly ever attempted even the common resident territorial birds.

What scientific value, if any, can be found in such work? Even without any attempt at a complete census, it at least provides some indication of the comparative abundance of the species involved, in various types of environment. Moreover, when it is extended over a number of years, it should be possible to make comparisons, indicating increases or decreases. Today (1973), Common Birds Censuses are carried out in many areas as a basis for vital monitoring work on bird populations.

Each six-inch map is eighteen inches long and twelve inches high; so that it covers an area of six square miles. During the years 1907 to 1918, before I left south-east England for the Midlands, Christopher and I had acquired a total of 88 of these maps, which we duly mounted on canvas, for convenient use in the field. On very nearly all of these some birds, suspected of breeding, were entered. To break down this number: 58 were Kentish maps, 20 Sussex, 7 Surrey, and 3 Isle of Wight. The Kent and Sussex maps need to be broken down further: 21 (7 Kent and 14 Sussex) covered the areas round

Tunbridge Wells, extending north to Tonbridge and south-west to all of Ashdown Forest; 18 covered the Wealden country from Hawkhurst and Cranbrook almost to Rye, including the Rother marshes; 6 covered Wye and Ashford (worked by C.J.A. only); 9 more covered the area from Minster to Sandwich, in the extreme east of Kent (again, C.J.A. only: he spent part of one summer at Ash-by-Sandwich); 20 cover the whole of Romney Marsh, including a strip of the hilly country to the north of it, thus practically joining up with the Ashford series at the other end. It extends to Rye and Winchelsea, though I cannot find that I ever entered any birds on the Winchelsea map. Here too the county boundary is crossed, and 5 of the 20 maps of this group are Sussex maps. In the summer of 1911, I spent a week wandering over the north Kent marshes, by the Thames; having furnished myself with three maps, covering the Cooling marshes and the Isle of Grain, I did some fairly intensive mapping there. Finally, I have a map of the Pevensey marshes, on the coast of Sussex, but no birds are entered. My only visit there was in the autumn of 1913, when I was recovering from typhoid. No doubt I got the map so as to find my way across the marshes without too much trouble. The large-scale maps were essential for finding one's way across Romney Marsh, especially the southern part, without getting hopelessly held up by impassable ditches. In Romney Marsh I was able to add some foot-bridges which the maps did not show.

Needless to say, not all of these maps are covered with birds. Only a very few are reasonably well covered. Those immediately round Tunbridge Wells are probably the best; for at some time or other I made special efforts to fill in areas that I had not been able to explore on my usual walks; though there are areas of private woodland or other forbidden areas to be found on almost any six square miles of the south of England. Some of the maps show the results of observations covering several years; others only a single year or season.

In 1914 I prepared a map, based on the six-inch to a mile Ordnance Survey, showing all the birds I had mapped in what I call their breeding areas or territories, for the eight consecutive years 1907-14. This map is reproduced on pages 52 and 53. I should make it clear that it shows all the territories held in any one of those eight years. In the case of the Whinchat, which can be found in the bottom left-hand corner of the map, these three pairs came in a single year, but never returned, although Whinchats were common passage-migrants at the

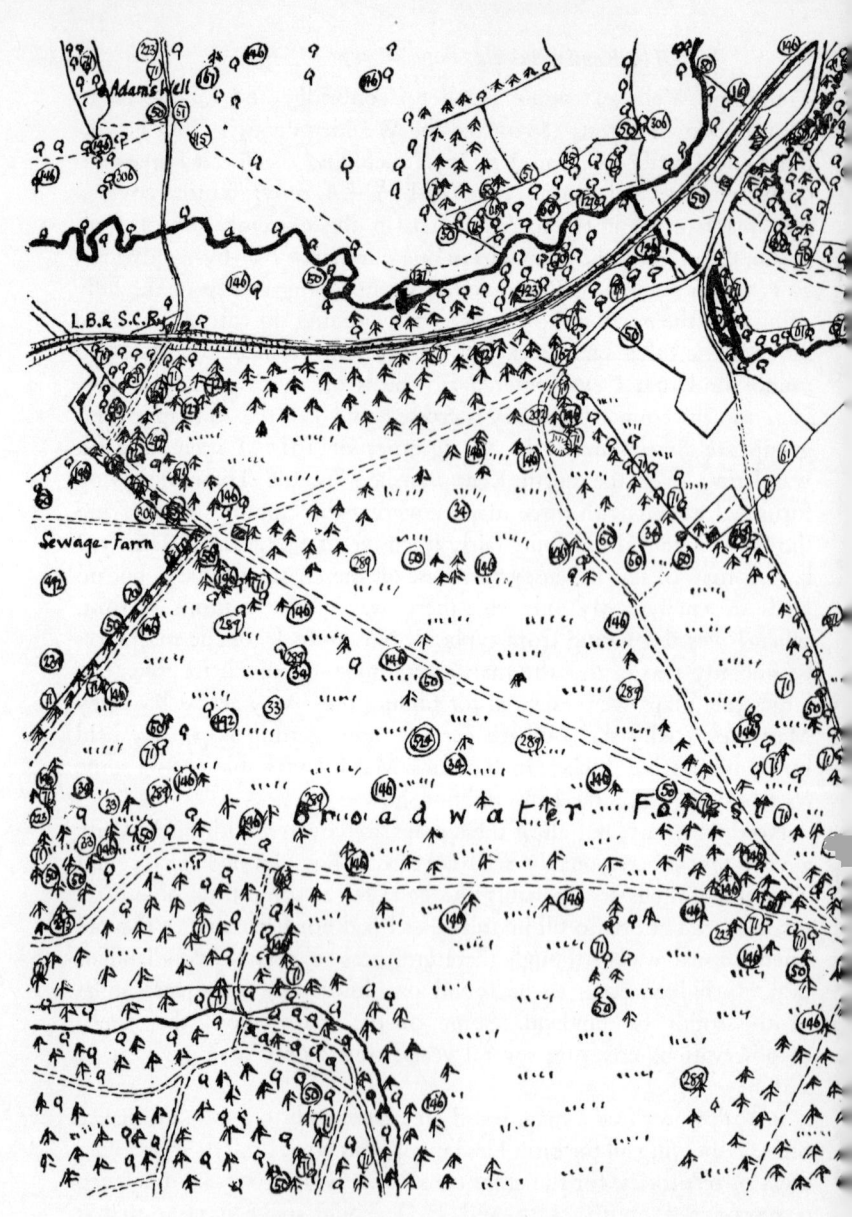

Author's 1914 map: "Section of Country near Tunbridge Wells, showing pairs of Certain Species of Birds in their Nesting Areas. 1907–14. Scale: 6 ins = 1 mile." The numbers, based on Dresser's list (see p. 16) refer to the following species: 33 Whinchat; 34 Stoneschat; 48 Nightingale; 50 Whitethroat; 51 Lesser Whitethroat; 60 Blackcap; 61 Garden Warbler; 70 Chiffchaff; 71 Willow Warbler; 72 Wood Warbler; 115 Marsh Tit; 116 Willow Tit;

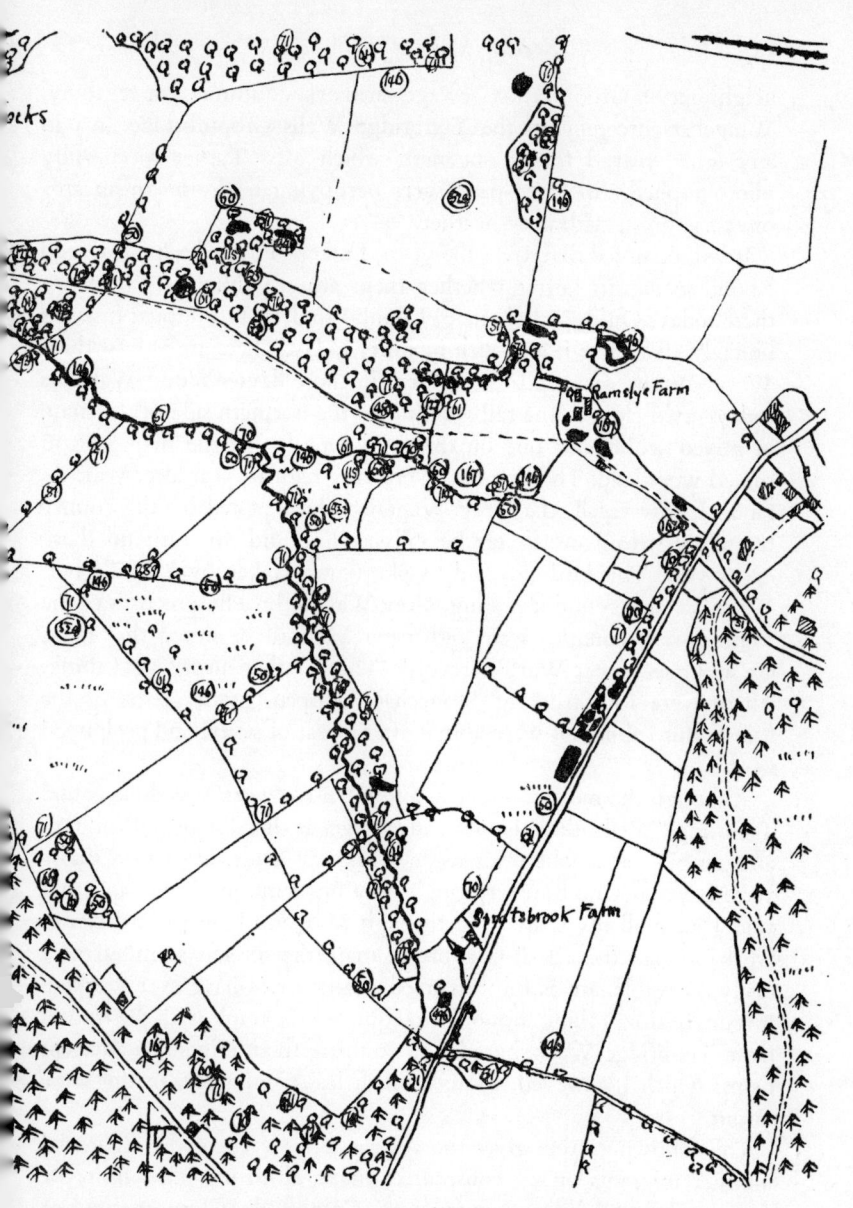

127 Nuthatch; 137 Grey Wagtail; 146 Tree Pipit; 167 Spotted Flycatcher; 202 Lesser Redpoll; 223 Yellowhammer; 234 Reed Bunting; 289 Nightjar; 293 Great Spotted Woodpecker; 299 Lesser Spotted Woodpecker; 306 Wryneck; 307 Kingfisher; 423 Mallard; 492 Corncrake; 496 Moorhen; 524 Lapwing; 533 Snipe.

neighbouring Groombridge sewage-farm every autumn. I never found Whinchats breeding in the Tunbridge Wells–Groombridge area in any other year. I found one nest, which Miss Turner successfully photographed. All three pairs were occupying territories in an area of coarse grass, with little heather.

It will be noted that, over the years, I mapped 9 Nightjars. It would be interesting to know whether there are any Nightjars breeding there today. On the whole map, I think I find 39 Tree Pipits; it seems unlikely that there is any such quantity today. There are at least three Wood Wrens, as we all called them in those days—Wood Warblers today—two close to the railway line on the northern side of the map, in mixed woodland; one on the southern edge of the map, also in mixed woodland. The first two were very regular, year after year. As far as I now recall, the Grey Wagtail, which nested by the county boundary stream, north of the railway line, did not turn up there every year. This bird also had its photograph taken by Miss Turner. When we first found it nesting, Grey Wagtail breeding records in the south-eastern counties were rather rare. It will be noted that there are no Grasshopper Warbler records. This is rather surprising, I think. There were four pairs of Stonechats in open, heathy parts of the forest. But I think all were absent after a year of severe and prolonged frost.

Although the most continuous and intensive work was done round Tunbridge Wells, there is some advantage, at this distance of time, in analysing an area where intensive work was undertaken in a single year. I was at Cranbrook through only one summer, 1916; and that year I gave all my spare time through May and June to bird-census work, so that the actual Cranbrook map, the six square miles most easily accessible, are as fully mapped as any area I have ever worked. It is interesting, I think, not only to compare the result with the figures from Tunbridge Wells, but also to compare the numbers on adjacent maps, which I surveyed, though much less completely, in the same spring.

The following table gives the aggregate for each of the territorial summer migrants on six consecutive maps, all in the hilly, more or less wooded, Wealden country near Cranbrook. Close analysis of each six-square-mile area would no doubt show differences which might help to account for the different proportionate numbers; but this would involve detailed analysis, which it is not easy now to provide. I append some comment after the table.

The Kentish Weald: Population and Territory

	Cran-brook	Cran-brook Common	Hartley	Benen-den	Rolven-den	Chitten-den Woods
Redstart	7	0	0	0	0	2
Nightingale	6	1	0	2	2	4
Whitethroat	54	5	13	5	3	12
Lesser Whitethroat	31	3	7	2	5	7
Blackcap	35	4	5	3	2	2
Garden Warbler	31	14	4	5	3	20
Chiffchaff	29	2	0	12	2	3
Willow Warbler	215	54	33	20	11	103
Wood Warbler	2	1	1	2	0	0
Tree Pipit	9	1	0	4	0	11
Red-backed Shrike	2	0	0	0	0	0
Spotted Flycatcher	28	2	0	5	3	2
Nightjar	14	0	0	0	0	0
Wryneck	9	0	2	2	0	0

Anyone familiar with these species will be able to see for himself some of the factors that lead to such differences of proportionate numbers. Thus, the small numbers on the Rolvenden map, even of Willow Warblers, suggest at once that there is comparatively little woodland. In fact, there are quite extensive woods in the area, but my mapping was simply of birds seen or heard from a bicycle, that is to say from the roads across the map. I did not penetrate into the woods at all. So this is simply an indication of the species likely to be noted from main roads. In the case of the Chittenden Woods map, I covered only about a quarter of the very extensive woodlands. There may well have been 500 Willow Warblers in the whole six square miles. But it is to be noted that there are no Wood Warblers: in other words, the woods I mapped had no areas of high forest. Damp woodland, with plenty of small trees and scrub, seems to favour both Willow Warblers and Garden Warblers.

As I had never found Redstarts breeding near Tunbridge Wells, I was surprised to find a small colony of them in this part of the Weald. The seven Cranbrook pairs were all in Angley Park. Ticehurst (*Birds of Kent*, p. 23) observed that the Redstart was a very local breeding species in Kent, but was sometimes found, almost in colonies, in 'large parks containing old timber'. He mentions Bedgebury Park near Cranbrook, into which I never penetrated. The colony in Angley Park fits his description perfectly. The two pairs I found in the southern part of Chittenden wood were not very near together, but both were in one part of the large wood.

It will be noted that the Tree Pipit only comes as high in the list on one of these five maps as it does at Tunbridge Wells and Wye. On the Cranbrook map it is bracketed ninth out of fourteen species. Only in Chittenden Woods it comes fourth. The 31 Lesser Whitethroats in the Cranbrook map may cause some surprise. I cannot say whether this is unusual for any part of England. It caused me some surprise when I came upon it in my Cranbrook records. But there is no mistake. Each one is separately marked on the map. The absence of Nightjars in all the areas apart from Cranbrook itself probably means no more than that I did not go out exploring for Nightjars on my bicycle late in the evening, but only went into Angley Park and other places quite near to base.

In addition to the five maps here discussed, I entered in the same special book the birds mapped on a six-square-mile map south-east of Rolvenden, which includes the village of Wittersham, but also a great part of the marshy Rother Levels. The result of this mapping is so different from the five Wealden maps that I give the numbers here separately. They are as follows: Nightingale 1, Whitethroat 12, Lesser Whitethroat 11, Blackcap 1, Garden Warbler 2, Chiffchaff 0, Willow Warbler 18, Reed Warbler 20, Sedge Warbler 22, Yellow Wagtail 13, Meadow Pipit 2, Tree Pipit 0, Spotted Flycatcher 1. I entered quite a number of other species on this map (as, indeed, on some of the other maps). These included Reed Buntings, Lapwings, Snipe, Redshank, and, what specially excited me, five drake Shovelers and six drake Garganeys. By the end of the summer I had definite evidence that some of the Garganey had nested. The county boundary follows the river Rother or some of its neighbouring ditches, so it seemed fairly certain that the Garganey had nested in each of the two counties: for Sussex this was at that time something new.

Owing to the fact that I was at Cranbrook throughout the breeding season of 1916, and did more intensive mapping in that year and district than I ever achieved anywhere else, I have given special attention to the results of that effort. But I now return to our earlier efforts at Tunbridge Wells—which is in country very similar geologically and physically, and is only some fifteen miles distant to the west. The main difference is that Tunbridge Wells was in those days well supplied with open heathland, first on Tunbridge Wells common; then, just over the county boundary, in Sussex, several square miles of open heath, with scattered pine trees, called Broadwater Forest; whereas a few miles further south-west, Ashdown Forest covered as large an area of open heath as could be found anywhere in south-east England, until you reached the extensive heaths round Frensham and Haslemere, on the borders of Surrey and Hampshire. Apart from this, the Tunbridge Wells and Cranbrook districts were very similar, with large tracts of woodland, a good deal of meadow-land, little corn cultivation, no river flats apart from the narrow flats by the river Medway at Tonbridge and to the west of it. All this country is undulating, often with fairly steep hills, never rising more than 700 feet above sea-level, and dropping to about 200 feet in the valleys. Apart from patches of clay, the whole subsoil is composed of Wealden sand, occasionally forming a small outcrop, such as the Harrison Rocks near Groombridge and the High Rocks on the Sussex side of Tunbridge Wells. There are also the striking rocks that jut out on both Tunbridge Wells and Rusthall Commons, including the famous Toad Rock.

Such was the background of our earliest efforts at a partial bird census. We rushed into print about this effort, and Witherby published our first article in the March (1909) number of *British Birds* (Vol. II, no. 10): 'On a Plan of Mapping Migratory Birds in their Nesting Areas'. I quote a few sentences that indicate what we had been trying to do.

'After some years' observation of the birds in the neighbourhood of Tunbridge Wells,' we began, 'we came to the conclusion that in many species each pair inhabits a definite area, into which other pairs do not intrude. In the spring of 1907, therefore, we decided to mark in the positions of these pairs on 6 in. Ordnance Survey Maps. In that summer we mapped a considerable area round Tunbridge Wells, while in the summer of 1908 we increased this area, and also began mapping at Wye near Ashford.'

Apart from the title, we provided no explanation of the restriction to summer migrants. Why, in fact, did we in the first place so restrict ourselves? I think almost certainly because it was the time of the B.O.C. Migration Enquiry, and we both busied ourselves throughout April and May in filling in the weekly migrant schedules. Our mapping was, in fact, an effort to be as thorough and exact in our daily

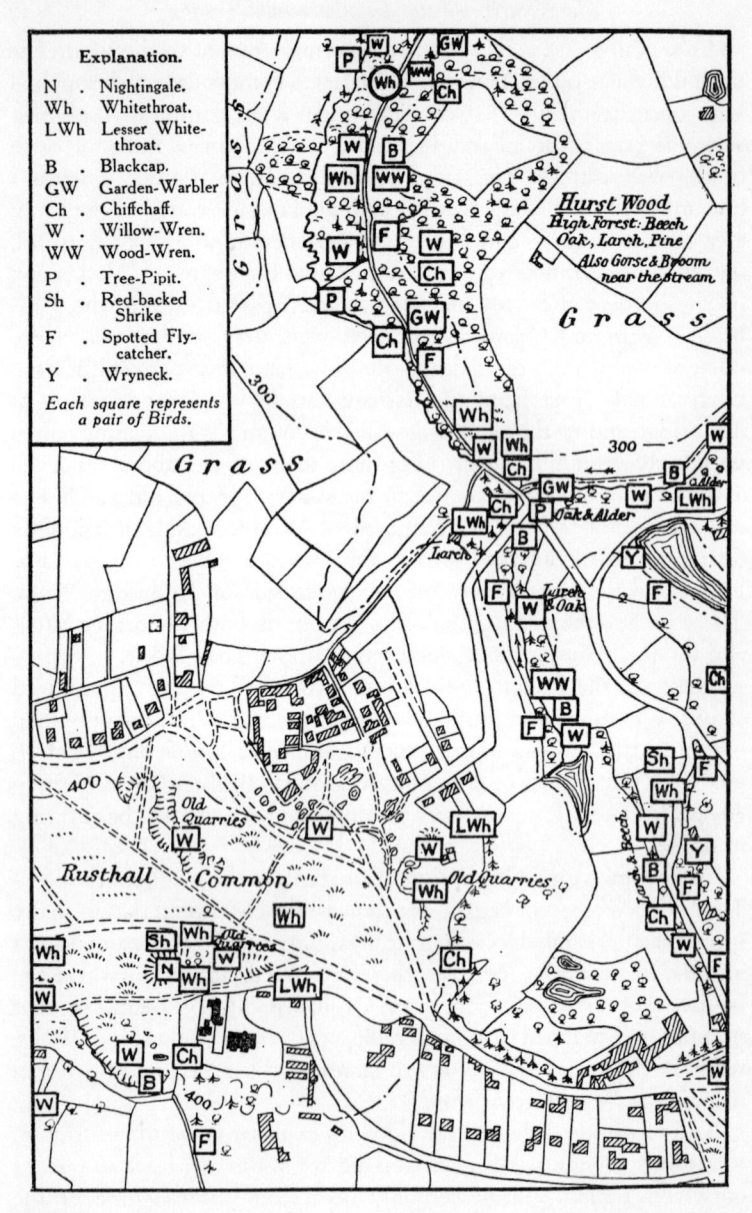

The Map which appeared in *British Birds*, March 1909. The caption read: "Map showing some of the Migrants in the Borough of Tunbridge Wells (Six inches equals one mile)."

migrant watch as possible. It was really an adjunct, a support, to the daily migrant watch. And the whole article sustains this interpretation. The emphasis is on the migratory behaviour, rather than the territorial.

Thus: 'The males inhabiting one small district (such as a wood, or stream valley) often appear to arrive together. In the case of such a district which contained several pairs of a particular species in 1907, but none in 1908, we conclude that the males were travelling together and were overtaken by some calamity.' We assumed that birds that reappeared in the same territory year after year were normally the same individuals; but 'what becomes of young birds we cannot pretend to say. . . . We have occasionally found two males of a species arrived at the same place and singing at one another. Eventually, as with Robins in the autumn, one has disappeared, or else has settled in an unoccupied place nearby.'

In 1911 I wrote a brief supplementary article on the work done in the Tunbridge Wells district in the two intervening years. My chief conclusion was that the numbers of the commoner summer migrants did not vary much year by year. Sometimes all the individuals of a species from a small area might be absent; but if several square miles were covered, as in our work they were, it would be found that the overall totals varied very little. Such an occurrence might well lead a single observer, who, perhaps, noticed the total absence of Chiffchaffs or Blackcaps or Spotted Flycatchers from his own and neighbouring gardens one year to report that these species were greatly reduced in numbers. Such reports should not be trusted, unless confirmed over a wide area—as in the case of the astonishing reduction of Whitethroats all over England in 1969.

I had also by then noted that a territory that was vacant one year might be reoccupied the next year. In other words, some territories are so attractive that they are not likely to remain vacant for long. This would also mean that the individuals found in a territory this year are not necessarily the same that were there last year.

It will be seen that these articles were touching on two important themes without quite coming to terms with either. We did not claim to be undertaking a census, though when some years later E. M. Nicholson, who was, in Britain at least, the pioneer of census work, wrote his article for the *Encyclopedia Britannica* on Bird Populations, he generously quoted some of the figures from our original article, as the first census work undertaken in England.

It might also be claimed that we were to some extent pioneers in the matter of bird territory; but we never used the expression 'territory', preferring the shorter word 'area'; nor did we begin to discuss the significance of territory in bird life. We took it for granted, and demonstrated its existence in the case of a number of summer migrants.

However, when Howard published his classic in 1921, Witherby gave it to me for review, and this appeared in *British Birds*, Vol. XIV. A great deal has been written on territory since the publication of Howard's book; and from time to time the literature on the subject has been fully surveyed, including several of the reviews written in 1921, but my review seems to have been overlooked. When I found it was not referred to, I concluded that it must have been worthless, containing, perhaps, some questionable or misguided criticisms. So I have read it again, more than once, and although I find it rather more critical of Howard than I should have wished, I do not find it inadequate in any other sense. So, I venture here to repeat some of the comments I made when the book was first published.

Howard's thesis, I said, was 'that a great deal of the peculiar behaviour of birds during the breeding-season, commonly supposed to be connected with sexual selection, is in fact due to the necessity for each pair to have its own territory for breeding purposes'. And I went on to summarise his main argument, all of which, from my own close observation, then extending over some fifteen years, I fully endorsed. For instance, he shows why birds require such a territory during the breeding-season. 'At other times the flock can wander at will, and every member has an equal chance when a good feeding-ground is found. But in the breeding-season, not only are suitable nesting-sites required, but, far more important than this for most of the small birds, a plentiful and continuous supply of food must be obtainable at the shortest possible distance from the nest.'

The following criticisms of the book, which I made in my review, still seem to me to be valid. First, Howard does not seem to recognise that the spring-time urge to break away from winter flocking and to establish a territory is not a total break from previous habits, even for a bird of the year. Rather, it is a return to 'home', that is to the territory in which each young bird of the territorial species has been reared. So too, he seems to suggest that the territorial impulse is dominant in the male only; and that females wander more or less aimlessly, until they meet a male in a territory. Rather, my own observations suggested that the female, like the male, tended to return to the ancestral territory, so that often the same pair might be found in the same territory in succeeding years. In a good many species, I suggested, they have spent most of the winter together, even if they have both been members of a flock.

I also took the view, which I would still uphold, that the change of behaviour as between the winter flocking and the spring-time territory is less extreme than Howard suggested. Birds in flocks sometimes break away and form pairs for a few minutes, or become aggressive. In other words, birds are subject to various and often somewhat conflicting impulses at most times of the year—least, of course, during the breeding-season, when 'success in the attainment of reproduction [Howard's phrase] is dominant'.

My next and in some ways my most serious criticism refers to Howard's inclusion of cliff-breeding birds as territorial species, because they insist on keeping others of their species a few feet away on the breeding ledge. He recognises that such birds as Rooks are gregarious by choice even in the breeding-season, choosing to nest in colonies, although clearly they might, like their close relative the Carrion Crow, nest in isolation. But the cliff-breeders, he believes, would be territorial if they could. It is the limited space for breeding that has driven them to place their nests close together; and the fact that they keep one another off the spot used for their nests shows their desire to hold a territory. I do not find this a convincing argument. It may be said that it is all a matter of definition: possibly so; but I think my definition is the more appropriate and useful one—namely that when one speaks of 'territorial birds', one means those that hold not only a tiny nesting territory, but a whole feeding territory to the exclusion of others of the species. Cliff breeders constantly cross one another's paths in collecting food. They do not, to the best of my knowledge, ever drive one another off some special preserve of sea. So I do not think they should be called territorial species.

Then I ventured to question whether fighting is as important a feature of territorial behaviour as Howard makes it. Indeed, most of the illustrations in the book show birds fighting one another. I have seen a great deal of chasing by birds at the edge of their territories, but very little open fighting. This may be partly because Howard did most of his observation in the early hours of the day, at dawn and soon after. That may be, I think, a time when territorial activity is at its height, but it is not a time of day that I know too much about. When I was young I suppose I did sometimes go out for an hour or two before breakfast. It is a marvellous time to be out. Even then, I do not recall often seeing birds fighting. My suspicion is that Howard, like most western post-Darwinians, was so much under the influence of Darwinian ideas of the struggle for survival and 'Nature red in tooth and claw' that he may have extended single incidents into frequent occurrences.

Finally, I raised the question whether the 'territorial imperative' was as strong and widespread among tropical birds, even passerines, as it is in the northern temperate zone. Is its wide prevalence due, in part, to the special circumstances of these zones, where food is not as abundant or even prolific as it is in the tropics?

Some of the matters I raised have been clarified by wider experience in the fifty years since Howard's book was published. Ringing had hardly begun at that time. We can now say in the light of ringing results that some individuals, both of migrants and of resident species, return to the same territories year after year; but some turn up again at some distance from their last year's breeding-site; and this appears to be true of both sexes. Again, some tropical species are territorial in the breeding season, but many of the passerine species are colonial nesters. Rigid territorial behaviour does appear to be more widespread in the temperate zone than in the tropics.

Howard himself wrote a disarming preface: 'Much [of what I have written] is mere speculation; much with fuller knowledge may be found to be wrong. But I venture to hope that a nucleus will remain upon which a more complete territorial system may one day be established." That is surely very much what has happened. One may reasonably disagree with some of his conclusions, but his main thesis stands; and all those who write about territory in bird life rightly recognise him as the pioneer.

Just as we had in a sense anticipated Howard in the matter of territorial studies, so too we seem to have been pioneers in the field of population studies. But, as I have already stated, we did not attempt to make a complete census of all the birds of even a limited area. We confined ourselves to certain species, and tried to cover quite large areas. At the beginning of this chapter I have given in some detail the full particulars of this work as I carried it out in 1916 in the district round Cranbrook, in the Kentish Weald, and between there and the Rother Levels, towards Rye. In a later chapter I give the corresponding figures of territories for the same species in much of Romney Marsh and Dungeness beach. It remains to give figures for other parts of Kent and Sussex from those far away days. I think these

The Kentish Weald: Population and Territory

figures are worth publishing now. For they have, with the exception of the first Tunbridge Wells census, never been published before; and they may be of value for field ornithologists working in the south-east of England fifty or sixty years later. Precise data of this kind are better than general statements.

First, then, let me repeat the data published in *British Birds* for March 1909. The following tables give the totals of each species mapped in approximately eight square miles immediately round Tunbridge Wells (Kent and Sussex) and in about four square miles round Wye (Kent) in 1908:

	Tunbridge Wells	Wye
Wheatear	0	4
Whinchat	3	0
Stonechat	4	0
Nightingale	6	25
Whitethroat	101	30
Lesser Whitethroat	24	15
Blackcap	32	20
Garden Warbler	22	14
Chiffchaff	56	10
Willow Warbler	188	88
Wood Warbler	11	0
Grey Wagtail	2	0
Tree Pipit	55	35
Red-backed Shrike	5	1
Spotted Flycatcher	27	1
Wryneck	13	10
Corncrake	1	1

Before commenting on these first mapping tables, I venture to add some further unpublished material, from the six-square-mile maps of the Ashdown Forest area, which is a few miles south-west of the area included in the 1908 Tunbridge Wells maps. This area is all in Sussex. The following figures do not represent a single year's mapping as the area was surveyed at various times from 1908 to 1916. Thus it does

	Withyham	Friars Gate	Colemans Hatch	Crowborough	Ashdown Forest	Wych Cross	Nutley	Chelwood Gate
Whinchat	0	0	0	1	0	0	0	0
Stonechat	0	3	5	15	31	6	7	7
Redstart	0	1	0	0	0	1	0	0
Nightingale	0	1	2	0	0	1	0	0
Whitethroat	3	5	5	17	29	23	10	6
Lesser Whitethroat	4	3	1	9	3	2	1	0
Blackcap	0	4	1	8	2	7	1	1
Garden Warbler	1	1	0	1	1	4	0	0
Dartford Warbler	0	0	0	2	5	0	0	0
Chiffchaff	5	8	1	14	7	15	8	4
Willow Warbler	49	58	9	48	38	115	33	29
Wood Warbler	0	8	0	2	1	10	0	0
Grasshopper Warbler	0	0	0	2	2	0	0	0
Grey Wagtail	1	0	0	1	1	0	0	0
Tree Pipit	12	15	10	19	18	17	6	6
Red-backed Shrike	1	1	1	3	10	1	4	2
Spotted Flycatcher	4	5	2	6	0	3	0	0
Corn Bunting	0	0	0	0	3	0	8	0
Yellowhammer	5	1	0	12	13	9	4	6
Reed Bunting	5	0	0	3	1	0	1	0
Nightjar	0	1	0	1	0	1	0	1
Wryneck	0	0	0	2	1	0	0	0
Carrion Crow	0	0	0	1	1	1	0	0
Lapwing	3	0	0	0	1	0	2	1
Snipe	1	0	0	0	1	2	2	3

not follow that any one figure represents the birds of a single year, but I do not think this matters much. As it happens, some of the largest totals, as for instance the Willow Warbler totals in one or two of these areas, do all belong to a single season. I doubt if the number is inflated by the sequence of years. It may possibly be so in the case of the Stonechat, a species that was in those days more or less resident throughout the year, though very few remained all through the winter. It is almost certainly true, however, that some of the late arrivals, such as Garden Warblers, are comparatively under-mapped, as a good deal of the work was done in April and early May. Reasons for other low numbers will be discussed later.

The Withyham map does not include any of Ashdown Forest proper. We are still here in lowland country, with the upper reaches of the Medway river flowing across; the rest is undulating, with some parkland, much meadow land, some rather long stretches of copsewood, full of Willow Warblers; two villages with gardens—in fact very similar to the 'biotope' round Tunbridge Wells. I mapped perhaps nearly two square miles in detail, chiefly what was accessible from roads or public paths.

All the other seven maps have some open heath, which is immediately indicated by the presence of Stonechats in every one. Friars Gate has the smallest such area; it also contains the huge Hundred-acre Wood, made famous by A. A. Milne in the Pooh books. I only mapped the edges of this great wood. A complete survey of it would probably have added a good many more Wood Warblers, and perhaps a few more Redstarts. It will be seen that I only found two Redstarts in the whole area. In the Colemans Hatch area, my mapping is very thin. I visited it in three separate years, but hardly penetrated beyond the main road running up to the forest (which here means the open heath).

The Crowborough and Ashdown Forest maps contain the areas that I worked best. On the Crowborough map something like four square miles was covered; on the Ashdown Forest map perhaps five square miles. On both maps I covered almost all the open heath, but large stretches of woodland were unmapped; so, once again, species such as Wood Warbler, possibly Blackcap and Garden Warbler, are no doubt under their actual number, whereas Stonechats and perhaps Tree Pipits are almost fully mapped. I do not claim that the Dartford Warblers were fully mapped. Everyone who knows the species knows how furtive it often is. One day in April I came on the main colony in the Ashdown Forest map, and found at least three males in song. Two or three days later we were there again. In dismal weather we spent an hour in their territory, and apart from one fleeting view of a dark bird disappearing (even that might have been a Wren) we neither saw nor heard one of them.

The Wych Cross map is as well covered as any, or at least the eastern two-thirds of it, covering the open heaths; but again I never attempted a thorough mapping of the extensive woods. The Nutley map is only covered on the open heath in the north-east section—say two square miles. About the same amount of ground is covered on the Chelwood Gate map.

Looking back over more than fifty years, one cannot help noticing that many changes have taken place. Although I have not explored these places for many years, I can say with confidence that some of the species that were then common have disappeared. Shrikes have almost certainly all gone, and Wrynecks certainly have. I do not know when Dartford Warblers were last seen in Ashdown Forest. Possibly there are still a few. My suspicion is that Tree Pipits are greatly reduced. It will be seen that this species was very widely distributed in those days. Every map has a fair number, including also the 1908 surveys for both Tunbridge Wells and Wye. In Ashdown Forest and Broadwater Forest near Tunbridge Wells, they were the commonest species wherever pine trees grew on the open heaths, far outnumbering Meadow Pipits which, unfortunately, I never bothered to map. But they were almost equally common in quite other 'biotopes', as for instance in meadow land near streams if there were any trees to sing from.

Which species have increased? Possibly Grasshopper Warblers. It will be seen that I found very few of them, although some of the country would appear suitable, almost identical with parts of the New Forest where today they are plentiful. In those days I could hear the song without difficulty at a considerable distance. The song is, I think, much more erratic than that of most warblers, so I may well have missed some, but I cannot believe that it was a common species.

I have included the three Carrion Crow nesting places, to emphasise the quite amazing rarity of that species in those days. Ashdown Forest was almost the only place where I saw any regularly in south-east England before the 1920s.

We were amazed when we first found a small colony of Corn Buntings on the slopes of the southern heaths, 600-700 feet above sea-level, and when later we found another small colony. I wonder if there are any today: I expect not. The Nightjar figure is perhaps hardly worth including. Presumably if I had spent evenings in Ashdown Forest I should have found the species in some numbers. There were quite a few in Broadwater Forest, and I do not know why I did not enter them all on the maps. Lapwings are included because I mapped them and they were, as will be seen, quite scarce. Snipe I mapped because it was not a common species in the breeding season in any part of south-east England. It would be interesting to know whether it has increased or decreased.

I entered various other species here and there, including Marsh and Willow Tits, Nuthatch, Tree Creeper, Lesser Spotted Woodpecker and one or two more; but these were not mapped thoroughly, so to give the number actually mapped would be misleading. I also find one, but only one, Lesser Redpoll. My clear memory is that it was a not uncommon breeding species in the birch trees round the heaths. Indeed, in my account of the birds of Tunbridge Wells and District, published in 1916, what I said was: 'Greatly increased as a breeding species in recent years in birchy places near Tunbridge Wells; first record, 1863; remaining from early April to October.' It is unfortunate that I did not map them, so as to give an exact number. I do not know when they decreased, but in recent years it seems that they have increased again.

During my residence in Tunbridge Wells I had no evidence of Woodlarks breeding, though I believe Mr Meade-Waldo, who lived at Edenbridge, and who therefore knew Ashdown Forest well, assured me that they did breed there in the nineteenth century. Some years later, I was spending a day or two at Tunbridge Wells and I took a sandwich lunch to enjoy in my old haunts in Broadwater Forest. The heaths and adjoining woods were rather silent. Suddenly I heard the song of a Woodlark. It came soaring and singing above my head, and the air was full of its wonderful melody for minutes. How long they stayed in the area I do not know, Now, no doubt, they have all gone again.

In addition to the mapping I did in those years in the Wealden areas of Kent and Sussex, I did a lot of mapping in Romney Marsh; and the results are included in the Dungeness chapter, together with a short survey of the north Kent marshes, in the 'Hundred of Hoo', which I visited in the summer of 1912. I now add here two more single-season surveys, one carried out by Christopher in east Kent, in the Ash district, where he spent some weeks spraying fruit-trees in the extensive orchards in the spring of 1910. It will be seen that there are some special features here, especially the astonishing number of Garden Warblers, and the equally astonishing scarcity of Willow Warblers. I do not know the area mapped, but I suspect that there are plenty of tall hedges among the orchards, and almost no woodland. Obviously, we are here faced with an unusual biotope, so unusual that all sorts of comparative numbers are reversed: not a single Tree Pipit, at a time when it seemed that all manner of Wealden country and Downland in south-east England was full of them. More Wrynecks than Blackcaps or Chiffchaffs or Willow Warblers—and so on. Here are the numbers he found: Whinchat 2, Nightingale 5, Whitethroat 33, Lesser Whitethroat 11, Blackcap 3, Garden Warbler 47, Chiffchaff 1, Willow Warbler 2, Reed Warbler 4, Sedge Warbler 4, Spotted Flycatcher 6, Wryneck 5. He also mapped Corn Buntings and found 34. There is no record of either Yellowhammer or Reed Bunting, but I suspect that he did not trouble to enter them.

Finally, in the spring of 1914 I spent a week at Freshwater, Isle of Wight, and did a rather thorough mapping of the area (on two six-inch maps, the first one covering the Needles, with the cliffs for some two miles towards Freshwater, also most of the parish of Totland; more than half of this map is sea; also the map to the east of this, covering Freshwater Bay, Compton Down and some of the country to the north including some of the Yar marshes; again, half of this map is sea only). It will be seen from the figures that follow that I included several species that I had usually omitted in my Wealden mapping. They are as follows: Wheatear 5, Stonechat 5, Whitethroat 10, Lesser Whitethroat 4, Blackcap 2, Garden Warbler 1, Chiffchaff 2, Willow Warbler 9, Reed Warbler 7, Sedge Warbler 1, Coal Tit 2, Tree Creeper 2, Meadow Pipit 10, Rock Pipit 14, Redbacked Shrike 1, Spotted Flycatcher 3, Corn Bunting 1, Yellowhammer 8, Cirl Bunting 2, Raven 1, Wryneck 1, Peregrine 2, Kestrel 1, and Cormorant with seven colonies along the nearly three miles of cliff from Sun Corner to Freshwater Bay. I also noted that the Guillemots, Razorbills and Puffins were spread all along the cliffs from Sun Corner eastwards to near the Tennyson monument, but they did not extend east of that—in other words, all three extended along the cliffs for nearly two miles. Herring Gulls, on the other hand, were nesting all along the cliffs from the Needles to Freshwater Bay and again for about a mile east of the Bay. I did not see any Shag breeding colony.

It may be easier to compare these 1914 figures with figures in the 1970s than it will be to make any comparisons in the inland parts of Kent and Sussex. But I hope some of my Romney Marsh and Dungeness figures may also be of interest to ornithologists now resident in those areas.

Goldcrest Firecrest

CHAPTER V

Firecrests, Willow Tits, Water Pipits

When I wrote to Dr Warde Fowler of Oxford about some birds I had seen in Switzerland, he observed in his reply that Tunbridge Wells was not a good district for birds. It is true that there are no exciting river flats, no large pools of water, no alluring sewage-farms, so the variety of bird life is strictly limited. Yet we soon discovered that even round Tunbridge Wells, careful observation could reveal the presence of some species that are not to be found in every inland district of England. During some ten years of close observation, we found not only such birds of the pine-woods as Crossbills and Nightjars, but Black Redstart, Ring Ouzel, Dartford Warbler, Firecrest, and Siberian Chiffchaff. We begin with the Firecrests.

In the spring of 1906, when I was nearly seventeen, I had to leave school for some weeks with a persistent chest cough, so I was at Tunbridge Wells throughout March of that year. On 3rd March I stumbled upon a Firecrest. The nearest country walk to our home was through Hurst Wood. The wood itself was private and there were fences to prevent people from trespassing, but they were open fences, so that one could see and hear the birds both above and below the path. It was an attractive wood, with a number of old oak trees, and among them newly planted pine and larch. There were open glades, with clumps of broom and bramble. At the end of the wood was a small open meadow sloping steeply to the stream that flowed through the wood. In this field there were also clumps of hawthorn and bramble. As I walked round this field on that March day, a small bird fluttered out from the hedge only a few feet from my face. I registered 'Goldcrest'; but its face looked strange. It was barred with white and dark bands. Surely a Goldcrest did not look like that. Could it be a Firecrest? At that time I had no book of my own that would tell me how to identify a Firecrest. So I wrote a description of my bird to my uncle James Crosfield at Reigate, and to Christopher, who was then at Wye. Both of them confirmed that my bird was indeed a Firecrest. I went to look for it again. There were some Goldcrests also in the area. I soon found it again; indeed, there were two birds, a male and a female. Both J.B.C. and C.J.A. were able to see these two birds through binoculars on 17th March. Meanwhile our neighbour, Miss E. L. Turner, had also come to see them. They remained in the area, sometimes moving a little way into the wood, throughout the month of March. I last saw them on 1st April; Miss Turner saw them on 2nd April, C.J.A. was unable to find them on the 3rd. We had even wondered if by chance they might stay to nest—fifty years before Firecrests were found to be nesting in the New Forest, a hundred miles further west.

At the time, I considered that I had had the good luck to find a really rare bird. When I was able to consult Wilfrid's copy of Howard Saunders' *Manual of British Birds* (1899 edition), which was then the standard book on the status of British birds, I found that he described the Firecrest as 'an irregular visitor to our shores'. He adds: 'between the months of October and April in various years, many genuine examples have been obtained on our southern and eastern coasts, chiefly in Cornwall and the Scilly Islands; more than twenty in Sussex; and some in every littoral county up to Yorkshire'. That was the extent of the knowledge of the status of the Firecrest in Britain at the turn of the century. Unfortunately, when Dr Norman Ticehurst came to publish his *History of the Birds of Kent* (in 1909) he copied our record incorrectly from the *Zoologist*, where I had published it. 'In spring,' he says, 'they are very rare, and the only records I can find is (sic) one of a hen seen by the Earl of Darnley at Dumpton Park, Thanet, in 1887, and another of a pair seen by Mr C. J. Alexander near Tunbridge Wells on 3rd March 1906.' I had no expectation that after a few years we should see Firecrests again in the same spot.

The details of subsequent sightings are worth giving; for they are sufficient to suggest a pattern. In December 1912, a single bird turned up in the exact spot where these two 1906 birds had been. It stayed into January (21st December to 10th January are the extreme dates I have for it), but I was spending term time at Cambridge, so it may have stayed for a longer time. However, Miss Turner and another local observer, Mrs Beecheno, were keeping a look-out in this and subsequent years, and as far as I now recall, they did not extend the stay of this or later birds to any extent. The next winter there was again one. I saw it first on 30th November. Two days earlier, a Siberian Chiffchaff had turned up in the same spot. The Chiffchaff remained till 17th December; the Firecrest till early January 1914. Did they come from the same part of the world? As far as I can tell, their breeding range may overlap somewhere near the Ural Mountains. Perhaps it is enough to suppose that both had arrived by an east-west route. On 15th April 1915, I came upon a Firecrest about half a mile away, in the same valley.

Finally (so far as Tunbridge Wells is concerned) there was one in the 'Firecrest field' in December 1916 and January 1917. It will be noted that the evidence here suggests that at least one Firecrest, in four separate winters (to be more exact, three times in the early winter, once in the spring) stayed for some weeks in the identical spot, whilst another was noticed in the same valley in later spring. Yet during those dozen years when I walked constantly through the woods and lanes and sheltered valleys on the west and south sides of Tunbridge Wells I never suspected a Firecrest anywhere else.

This is not the whole story. During the winters, 1917-18 and 1918-19, I was teaching at the Grammar School at Cranbrook, some fifteen miles east of Tunbridge Wells. I did not find any Firecrest there in the first winter; but in the second I came upon individuals in late autumn and early spring. The spring bird was in a small sheltered valley, not so wooded as the Hurst Wood valley, but with gorse clumps above a little stream. This spring bird stayed throughout most of March, like the 1906 Tunbridge Wells birds. It was not very near to a road, but it was in good song, so I could hear it when I walked along the road.

Thus, so far as the Weald of Kent is concerned, the evidence points to Firecrests staying for some weeks in the same spot both in autumn and in spring, but never remaining throughout the winter. This is, perhaps, rather surprising. We think of migrant birds as having regular breeding places, to which they return year by year, and also often winter quarters, which attract the same species year after year. As far as the intermediate stops are concerned, we incline to think that birds stop over for a day or a few days, in autumn and spring, at good feeding places, but with the idea that they are hurrying on, especially in spring to the breeding grounds, or in autumn to the winter quarters, stopping only long enough to stoke up for the next part of the journey. It is, of course, unusual to find a species that is sufficiently scarce for the observer to be reasonably sure that the bird he sees day after day for some weeks is the same individual. In the case of these Kent Firecrests, it seems fair to assume that they were. So here we have three cases of Firecrests remaining in a spot which was apparently not the final winter quarters in the late autumn or early winter; and, even more remarkable, two cases of birds stopping for some weeks in the spring, before moving on again to their breeding ground somewhere in continental Europe. The two 1906 birds might, indeed, have been in their Hurst Wood territory throughout the winter. But I am satisfied that this was not true of the Cranbrook bird. In those days my ears were so keen that I should have heard its voice from the public road, even before it began to sing.

But I have not quite finished with Firecrests yet. By 1913 I had also made the discovery that Firecrests appear on the autumn and spring migrations in the broom and other scrub on Dungeness beach. I visited Dungeness frequently during the immediate pre-war years, and I also spent some weeks there in the autumn of 1914. In both 1913 and 1914 I saw several Firecrests there: in 1913 the first was on 20th October; in 1914 I saw my first on 16th October. I was again there briefly in the autumn of 1915, and found a Firecrest on 25th October. In subsequent years I found individuals as early as 24th September (1922) and 19th September (1937). Since those days the Dungeness beach has been very closely watched by H. E. Axell and by R. E. Scott. They have confirmed these observations that Firecrests appear on that coast every year in autumn and again, in smaller numbers, in spring. I am not sure, however, whether there are recent records from the Dungeness area in mid-winter. Twice, when I was staying at Dungeness over the New Year, I found a Firecrest: in 1921–2, behind the Romney sandhills; and in 1929–30, at the Lydd edge of the beach.

Do a few individuals occasionally stay through the winter in Kent? As for the main movement, one assumes that it is from east to west in autumn as so much other migration into England at that time appears to be: and presumably it is a return migration, possibly of birds that have wintered in Cornwall or elsewhere in the south-west, that shows up in spring.

During the sixties, our home was in Dorset. There also, the Firecrest is mainly a passage migrant, passing west in September to November, and returning in March and April. But I once saw one on 1st January at Studland. And there were one or two in December and January at Durlston Head, Swanage, at the time the famous Brown Thrasher was there (1966-7). At Portland, where they are seen in some numbers every year, I believe it is thought that most pass on to the continent, rather than to Devon and Cornwall. This may well be. I think there is a good deal of evidence that birds arriving in England on an east-west course in the autumn change course later, and fly south or south-east to winter in the Iberian peninsula or in North Africa.

It remains to note my observations of Firecrests on the Lickey Hills, north Worcestershire, during the twenty years that I lived in South Birmingham. When I left Kent for the west Midlands I assumed that I had gone beyond the range of Firecrests. However, it was not so. The first I found (revealed as usual by its call) was in November 1921. Another appeared in November 1924. In 1930 there was one in the broom scrub on the south side of the Lickey Hills, through much of the autumn, from 24th October at least into December. Ten years later, in 1940-41, there was one among Goldcrests in almost the same spot. This time it remained from 14th November (at least that was when I first found it) till well into January. But here again, it will be seen that I did not prove that any one of these birds stayed right through the winter. Indeed, as far as my experience goes, February is the only month between September and April (inclusive) in which I have never seen a Firecrest in England.

To summarise: my inland observations of Firecrests seem to suggest that some birds may have not merely two territories, but three: the summer or breeding territory, a winter territory and a midway territory. I have seen no evidence that other observers have discovered such a 'third' territory, but it may be that there is such evidence in the voluminous modern literature of ornithological observation. It need not be in England.

When I first began to keep records of the dates of arrival and departure of summer and winter migrants in England, it did not occur to me to include Firecrest in the wintering list. Between 1906 and 1969 I have fifteen arrival dates, or first seen in the autumn; and nine departure dates, or last seen in the spring. Seven of these dates are for Dungeness or Romney Marsh; two for Tunbridge Wells; one for Cranbrook; two for south Birmingham; the remaining twelve are recent dates from Purbeck or Portland. The arrival dates range from 10th September (a Portland date) to 17th November (a Purbeck date); most of them are in October. The spring departure dates range from 16th March (a Portland date) to 24th April (a Purbeck date); most are between 20th March and 15th April.

In the very first number of *British Birds* magazine, which was published in June 1907, Philip Lutley Sclater, one of the surviving founder-members of the British Ornithologists Union, wrote an article called 'Remarks on a supposed New British Tit of the Genus Parus'. He drew attention to the fact that, whereas Howard Saunders, in his 1899 *Manual of British Birds*, had only recognised five species of Parus, Dr Ernst Hartert of Tring, in his German treatise on Palearctic birds, had added a sixth. Hartert was one of the pioneers of the trinomial nomenclature; and so this 'new' British bird was called *Parus atricapillus* (or *P. montanus*) *kleinschmidti*. Sclater did not question the accuracy of Hartert's announcement, but he pleaded that if in fact there was a second species of black-capped tit in England, more should be learnt about it.

In the following number of *British Birds* (July 1907) Walter Rothschild wrote a further article: 'The British Willow Tit (*Parus atricapillus kleinschmidti* Hellm.)'. He explained that Pastor Kleinschmidt and Dr Hartert had found in the British Museum collection of skins of Marsh Tits two skins from Hampstead that were undoubtedly conspecific with the species known widely in Europe as *Parus atricapillus* or *montanus*, but sufficiently distinct to be treated as a distinct race or subspecies. In the very same year the Tring museum received two more specimens from near Finchley. Indeed, by the time when he was writing (1907) the Tring collection had acquired no less than fourteen specimens, including some that were breeding; and eggs had been collected.

Christopher and I read these two articles with great excitement, partly because in both articles specimens from Tunbridge Wells were referred to. Moreover, Witherby, in an editorial note at the end of Rothschild's article, invited further investigation of the status and habits of this 'new' bird. 'It may be found,' he wrote, 'as is already suspected, that the habits and notes of the British Willow Tit differ from those of the British Marsh Tit.'

A further circumstance favoured us. Christopher had spent part of the previous summer at Champéry in Switzerland. In the deciduous woods below Champéry he had seen and heard Marsh Tits; in the pine woods, higher up, he had watched and listened to the species described by Dresser in his *Birds of Europe* as the Northern Marsh Tit, now to be known, species-wise, as the Willow Tit. Even in August, he had more than once heard this bird sing a rich little song of almost Nightingale-like quality. The special song of this species had been noted by other writers, and thus was quoted in 'Dresser', so Christopher had been prepared for it, though hardly for its rich tone.

Now, the questions were: would the British Willow Tit have a comparable song? And how different would its call-notes be from those of the Marsh Tit?

We had not very long to wait. On 20th January 1908, we set off on a rather unusual walk. Taking train to Groombridge, we walked across country to explore parts of Ashdown Forest. We were walking through a wood near Withyham when suddenly Christopher heard what sounded to him just like the Swiss song of *Parus montanus*. Sure enough, the bird was a black-capped tit, and we watched it for some time, and heard it utter a deep-toned 'cha-cha-cha-cha' note, quite distinct from the usual 'typical' Marsh Tit call-note. Our first object was achieved. We had discovered the Willow Tit for ourselves. It remained to work out the language of the two species as thoroughly as possible.

When Norman Ticehurst was preparing his *History of the Birds of Kent* for publication (it was published in 1909) Christopher sent him some notes, which he published, together with his own statement of the visible differences between the two species. This, perhaps, is still worth quoting: 'Firstly, in the Willow Tit the feathers of the crown and forehead are ... of a dull brownish black instead of glossy black; secondly, in the Marsh Tit the tail is almost square, while that of the Willow Tit is distinctly graduated ...; and, lastly, the Willow Tit has wide buff edges to the secondary quill-feathers.' We always found these visible differences hard to discern; or rather, the first two, which in the early discussions were the two that were stressed. Even today, I am bound to say that I think the matter of the head colour is, to say the least, very tricky, and largely dependent on the light. Curiously enough, the third point, the pale edges to the secondaries, I never took to heart till Bernard Tucker showed me how important it was when we were out walking together near Oxford; and this was some ten years later.

Meanwhile, in the October 1910 issue of *British Birds* Christopher published the results of our eighteen months' study of the voices of the two species. This is a full and careful article; but the tits as a family have an astonishing range of language, so it is not surprising that, by the time Bernard Tucker prepared his account of the voice of this species for the Witherby *Handbook* (1938), he had more to add. His account of the various songs, based on the work he himself had done, fortified by E. M. Nicholson and W. H. Thompson, was a considerable elaboration of our pioneer work, though the main items are the same. It is still worth quoting, I think, as recently there have been doubts expressed about the more elaborate songs, presumably due to the fact that it is a very variable matter, and some individuals seem never or very rarely to sing the rich song. So, those who expect to learn all there is to learn by a few brief hours in the woods may well never hear this song. Here is Tucker's summary, which is no doubt as correct today as it ever was:

'Song erratic, some males singing little, if at all, with several variations. Full song, comparatively infrequent, and in some good Willow Tit districts even exceptional (W. H. Thompson), differs from all other tit utterances in including "series of warbling notes of striking richness" (E. M. Nicholson), variously compared to those of Canary and Nightingale; uttered in fairly brief snatches and not audible far. A commoner form (not warbling) is repetition of single note "piu-piu-piu-piu-piu", much like alternative song of Wood Warbler. Other variants with more or less resemblance to notes of Tree Pipit, Goldfinch, etc, are recorded.'

The song-period of the Willow Tit is remarkable. Compare it (as published in the *Handbook*) with the Marsh Tit, and the first thing that strikes you is that the Willow Tit has no time of full, regular song, even in the spring. The second thing is that I had recorded it (over the forty years of my recording) in every month of the year (only once in November). The third singular feature is that in August, when all the other tits are silent, it has been heard singing as much as in any month. The four best months seem to be February, March, April, August. Does song somehow represent something different in the case of the Willow Tit from the song of its closely related cousins? I find this very puzzling, and I have no explanation to propose.

Already, in 1910, Christopher was able to give the following localities in which we had found Willow Tits: 'I have now found the Willow Tit in the following places: Kent: Wye and Tunbridge Wells; Sussex: from Tunbridge Wells to Ashdown Forest; Surrey: Reigate and Leith Hill; Hants.: Ecchinswell, close to the Berks. boundary and the neighbourhood of Selborne; Berks.: Shinfield and Grazely, near Reading; Wilts.: Little Bedwyn; Oxon.: Checkenden in the Chilterns; Herts.: Rothamsted, near Harpenden. My brother has observed it at Capel Curig, North Wales, besides some of the above localities. About Tunbridge Wells the numbers seem to be about one-third or one-quarter those of the Marsh Tit; and near Reading, perhaps about the same. At Wye and other places in East Kent they seem to be rare.'

So much for our early explorations. By 1955, when I began to lose my hearing, I had found Willow Tits in twenty-nine of the forty English counties. I do not happen to have found it in any county in which I have found no Marsh Tit. But there are six counties where I have found Marsh Tits but no Willow. These are: Cornwall, Essex, Cheshire, Westmorland, Durham, and Northumberland. As the Willow Tit is the only one of the black-capped tits that occurs in Scotland, it seems strange that it should be rather scarce in some of the most northerly British counties. Shortly before his death, I had the pleasure of introducing Lord Grey of Fallodon to the Willow Tit in the woods of north Worcestershire. Once he got its characteristic call-notes well into his ear (he was too blind to see any bird except a swan, but his ears were still remarkably keen) he was satisfied that the black-capped tits (dare I say the chickadees?) of Fallodon, Northumberland, were all Marsh, as indeed, he had confidently believed. On the other hand, at a time when I knew some parts of Cumberland quite well, I found only Willow Tits in the low country between the mountains and the sea, but only Marsh Tits in the mountain valleys of the Lake District. This is the opposite of what one might perhaps have expected from the Swiss distribution of the two species.

Willow Tits appear now to be absent from the Isle of Purbeck, where much of the country near Poole Harbour has the kind of birch growth that seemed exactly to fit the species on the Sussex side of

Tunbridge Wells fifty or sixty years ago. During my twenty years' residence in the West Midlands, where both species are fairly common, and often found together, I came to regard the Willow Tit as less restricted to woodland areas than the Marsh. But I have seen no attempt to differentiate the two species by habitat. In many localities they occur side by side. In other localities one occurs but not the other. Why? I do not think there is a simple answer to this question.

In J. F. L. Parslow's very thorough survey, 'Status Changes among (British) Breeding Birds',* published in *British Birds* in 1967/8, based on reports received from all the counties in Britain, he has disappointingly little to say about changes in status of the Willow Tit. His summary is: 'Apparent decrease and contraction of range in Scotland; no marked change elsewhere.' Evidently he considers that there is still some confusion between this species and the Marsh Tit, so that perhaps not all the information received was reliable. However, there are many present-day ornithologists who do know the two species quite well. In the west Midlands, for instance, where I spent most of the twenties and thirties, the species is still quite common, as it was then. A. R. M. Blake, writing in the summer of 1970, says: 'My impression is that it [the Willow Tit] is as abundant as it was when I first came to this area 23 years ago. The recent *Atlas of the Breeding-Birds of the West Midlands* records it as being rather less widespread than the Marsh Tit with probably fewer numbers. This I think is true if you take all three counties (Warwick, Worcester and Stafford) into account, but in Staffordshire and N. Warwicks I'm sure the Willow Tit is the commoner. On the other hand it is certainly scarcer in Worcestershire and S. Warwickshire, being largely absent from south and central Worcestershire.' Is the greater relative abundance of the Willow Tit in the northern parts of the west Midlands due to the comparative absence of woodland? I think it may be so. But that will not account for its scarcity in parts of Worcestershire. I think the Willow Tit, though sometimes occurring away from woodland, likes 'roughage'; so perhaps south Worcestershire is too tidy for it.

The comparatively recent discovery of the Willow Tit in Britain has led British ornithologists, with what is perhaps habitual insularity, to look at the relationship of these two closely related species as something special and abnormal. But if we expand our horizons, and look at the picture of black-capped tits or 'chickadees' from a world point

* Revised and expanded, with 225 distribution maps, and published in book form as *Breeding Birds of Britain and Ireland*, 1973.

of view, we soon realise that here is a group of closely related, but distinct, species that has diverged extensively, though remaining extraordinarily similar in general appearance.

Before turning to other black-capped titmice, let us extend our view of these two species to other parts of western Europe. It was Christopher's experience of the two species about Champéry, Switzerland, that had helped us to differentiate them by voice in the south of England. As it happens, I too had an opportunity of observing both species (Marsh and Willow) at the same place in 1912, when I was on holiday there from 1st to 27th August. As a result I wrote the following:

'Marsh Tit. The birds at Champéry and below it all made the Marsh notes. There were not many of them. The highest I noted was at about 3650 feet elevation.

'Willow Tit. Not uncommon among the firs up to 6000 feet; once seen as low as 3500 feet, but practically the range of the two black-capped tits does not overlap. I should think anyone wanting to know the different notes of the two species would be well advised to go to Champéry and spend alternate days listening to the black-capped tits in the valley and up in the pine woods. If after that he still hardened his heart, I should know that he had no ear for bird-music.' At that time there were still ornithologists in England who professed to disbelieve in the separation of the two species.

We now jump forward to the summer of 1921, when I spent some days at a conference in the pine-woods on the eastern border of Holland, at the village of Barchem, in Gelderland. I had ample opportunities for wandering in the woods, and the result, as far as these two tits are concerned, is as follows:

'Marsh Tit. In the pine-woods at Barchem, fairly common, I think more so than the Willow Tit. I had a very good view of one or two, but could not have distinguished them in appearance from *P. p. dresseri* (*P. p. communis*, which this should be, is described as more buffish-brown), though the notes I think may be slightly different in tone, though obviously characteristic of *P. palustris* as opposed to *P. atricapillus* (now known as *P. montanus*).

'Willow Tit. Several in the pine-woods at Barchem. Here again, the notes, though characteristic of the species, seemed to suggest a sub-specific difference from the English bird (they would be *P. m. rhenanus*, as opposed to *P. m. kleinschmidti* of Britain). It was particularly interesting finding these two species together in pine-woods; for though I have seen Marsh as well as Willow frequently enough in English pine-woods, my continental experience of the two hitherto, in the Alps, has separated Marsh from Willow by the limit between deciduous and pine-wood.'

In 1924 I found both species at Saarbrücken, around Nancy, east France, and in the Vosges mountains. At Nancy, where the woodland is nearly all deciduous, Willow was the commoner species, and I only saw one Marsh; in the Vosges, at rather higher elevations, where there are more pines, it was the opposite: quite a few Marsh and only one Willow. In other words, the reverse of what one might expect from the Alps.

Finally, in 1929, I had opportunities of observing black-capped tits in Norway, first around Hundorp in the Gudbrandsdalen, east Norway, and then on the west coast, including both the Sognefiord and the Hardangerfiord. Here is my comment on the tits:

'Of the tits, I found Willow Tits the most abundant. At Hundorp they were common at all elevations to the top of the woods; and in other parts of the country I noted them frequently, especially in the pine and spruce woods. On 9th August by the bridge over the river at Hundorp, I was struck by the appearance of a black-headed tit, with very white underparts, and dull head, the dark grey extending far onto the nape. There can be no doubt, I think, that it was a Siberian or Lapp Tit (*Parus cinctus*). The next day I saw two in the woods fairly high up, in company with other small birds, including Willow Tits, that appeared to be of this species also; they made a peculiar note, and were similar in plumage. I also thought I saw a rufous tinge on the upper parts, which I had not noticed the day before; but they were above me in spruce trees, so I did not see them very well. It is possible that one of the first black-headed tits I saw, whose extensive black throat I noticed, was also of this species. This is just south of the limit given by Wardlaw-Ramsay, but Scharming, in his *Norges Fuglefauna*, gives records from the Gudbrandsdalen. When I reached the fiords (i.e. the west coast) I found Marsh Tits fairly plentiful; I saw them low down at Laerdal and Fjaerland on the Sognefiord, and at Ulvik in Hardanger. They overlapped the Willow Tits in altitudinal distribution. Whereas in England the Marsh Tit is greyer than the Willow, in Norway the Marsh Tit is the browner bird, nor does the Willow show the whitish secondaries to the same extent; but the dull head I found easier to note than in the British race.' Both are, of course, recognisable races, distinct from those of central Europe and of Britain, namely *P. p. palustris* (Marsh) and *P. m. borealis* (Willow). Both Tucker and Hugh Thompson found some of the language of the Scandinavian Willow Tit distinct from the language of the British race, but in my brief experience in August 1929 I found the language very similar. Both species were readily identifiable by voice.

It is of some interest that in only one of the several countries of Europe where I have observed the two species (there are a few more that do not add to what I have written here) it is only in the Alps that they seem to occupy separate zones. And it will be seen that such partial separation as can be discerned in other parts of their range does not seem to follow any clear pattern.

In the Palearctic region there are at least four distinct species with black or dark caps and generally brownish mantle; all have some black, often on the throat, and the underparts are grey, sometimes with some buff on the flanks. In North America there appear to be no less than seven distinct species all conforming to the above plumage description. It would seem that all these eleven birds might almost be described as a super-species. I am now writing in a part of eastern North America where the Carolina Chickadee (*P. carolinensis*) breeds, and the Black-capped Chickadee (*P. atricapillus*) is a common winter visitor. As I cannot usually hear their voices, I am not always sure which species it is that is coming to our feeders during the winter: both come, no doubt, but they are more difficult to distinguish by plumage even than the two species in England.

It is to be hoped that some day some energetic young ornithologist will attempt a complete survey of the whole chickadee tribe, working out their respective feeding habits, inter-relationships, breeding habits (how many, apart from the Willow Tit, normally make their own nesting holes in stumps of wood?) from Alaska, all across North America and Europe to the eastern limits of the Siberian Tit (*Parus cinctus*).

Before leaving the tits, I yield to the temptation to look at the distribution of the family Paridae more generally; or at least to compare the status of the family in three areas known to me: Western Europe (particularly England), North America, and India with special reference to the Himalayas. The chickadee group need not be considered much further: as we have noted, there are four species in Europe and seven in North America. But it is strange that, whereas the tits are very well represented in the Himalayan region, the only 'chickadee' is a little known race of the Marsh Tit, which is said to occur on a few mountain peaks in the regions between Assam and Burma; none are known from any part of the Himalaya proper. Vaurie (1959) recognises eight distinct races of *P. palustris*. This most south-easterly race, *hypermelas*, he is uncertain about. Should it be treated as a distinct species? The east Asian races of this species appear to be isolated from one another, whereas races of the Willow Tit (*montanus*) and the Siberian Tit (*cinctus*) seem to be very generally distributed in east Asia.

But let us look at the family more generally, especially the large genus, *Parus*. In England we grow up with six common species of tit, five of them belonging to the genus Parus, the other, the charming Long-tailed Tit, now usually assigned to the genus *Aegithalos*. The other five include the Marsh and Willow; also three more gaily coloured birds: Great (*P. major*), Blue (*caeruleus*) and Coal (*ater*). The first two of these three are among the dozen most abundant passerine species in England. The Coal is also a common bird wherever conifers are grown; and this means today that they are common in many parts of the country, though two or three hundred years ago, before conifers were at all widely planted, they may have been scarcer.

On the continent of western Europe, another species, the Crested Tit (*P. cristatus*) is widely distributed. This species, like the Coal Tit, seems to have a preference for pine trees; and in Britain, unlike the Coal Tit, it has failed to adapt itself; it is still strictly confined to the limited range of the native pinewoods (*Pinus scoticus*) in north-east Scotland. For a Britisher, it is surprising to find Crested Tits in France and Germany far away from any pine trees.

In eastern Europe there is another species of Parus, the Azure Tit (*P. cyanus*). This species is tending to spread westward. It is closely related to the Blue Tit and looks like a washed-out version of it.

Outside the genus *Parus* Europe has two species that are placed in separate genera: the Long-tailed Tit, already mentioned; and the very local Penduline Tit (*Remiz*), which is found in marshy country round the Mediterranean and in the Danube valley, and whose elaborate hanging nest is as wonderful a structure as the nest of the Long-tailed Tit. Both of these birds are also found widely across Asia.

What chiefly concerns me is comparison of the main titmouse family in the three chosen areas. So let us next look at India, more especially the Himalayas. In the zone of the so-called hill-stations of the Himalayas, roughly between five and ten thousand feet above sea-level, parties of tits are as common as in European woodland.

They roam through the tree-tops, and sometimes the tree-bottoms too, in the company of small warblers and other woodland species, their twittering call-notes adding to the liveliness of the scene. Several of the commoner species are as brightly coloured as the Great Tit and the Blue Tit of Europe. Two are conspecific with European species: forms of both the Great Tit and the Coal Tit occur, whilst some of their companions in the flocks appear to be very close relatives of these two.

The Indian Great Tit is known, where English is spoken, as the Grey Tit; and it is in fact a washed-out edition of its European counterpart. It has no green on the back, and no yellow on the underparts. It is a very widely distributed species; and I think there is a cline, each race, as you move east, being paler than the birds to the west. It occurs all across the Indian peninsula, and is the only bird of the whole tit family that occurs in Ceylon, where it is found both in the mountains and the plains.

The Coal Tit of the Himalayas has a patchy distribution—but not as patchy as the Marsh. It is easily distinguished from its European relative by a fine top-knot. Several of the Indian tits have crests; it would seem that the genus *Parus*, or even the tit family generally, tends to develop crests. Who has not seen the Blue Tit of England raise his crest in defiance at some intruder who disputes his right to the best place at the bird-feeder? After another thousand years, perhaps all Blue Tits will have permanent crests, so that they can defy the other birds more readily. In the jungles of central India, as also in the Himalayas, you find a bird which at first sight the European is inclined to call a Great Tit. It has the same bright colours, set off against a jet-black cap and breast stripe. It also has a top-knot. It is called the Yellow-cheeked Tit, and that name at once reveals its distinction, for all races of the Great Tit have white cheeks. At one time it was even allowed a genus of its own, *Machlolophus*; but now it is accepted as just one more *Parus*. Then, to confuse things still further, in the tree-top parties of tits in the Himalayas, we find another species, also very similar to the European Great Tit, called the Green-backed Tit. It lives side by side with the Grey Tit. Its distinctive feature is the double white wing-bar.

These are the brightest coloured members of the family in India, but there are several other species to be found in some parts of the Himalayas. Two are very close relatives of the Coal Tit; these are the Crested Black Tit (*P. melanophus*) and the Black Tit or Rufous-bellied Crested Tit (*P. rufiventris* or *P. rufonuchalis*), depending which of the two races of one species you treat as the nominate race. Then, there is a local species, only found in some parts of the Himalayas, which seems to be the counterpart of the Crested Tit of Europe; this is the Brown Crested Tit (*Parus dichrous*). Where it occurs, it is normally in the company of the other tits. Moreover, just as a European party of tits more often than not has a party of Long-tailed Tits at its centre, so in the Himalayas, there is a common and widely distributed species, just as abundant in the mountains of south-west China as in the whole Himalayan range, which belongs to the same genus (or family, if we follow Vaurie), *Aegithalos concinnus*, the Red-headed Tit. This bird has not such a long tail as its northern neighbour, the Long-tailed Tit, but no observer from Europe would be likely to doubt that they are close relatives.

Although several of these birds are of sombre hue, enough of them are bright coloured to give the impression, when you find a good-sized mixed party, of a family of birds that are not only gay in behaviour but also in colour.

India has several tits that do not readily fit into the ordinary tit pattern. These are not members of the genus *Parus*; and as I have no special field-notes about them, they need not detain us. D. W. Snow, in his article on the tits in the B.O.U. *Centenary Dictionary*, refers to them briefly. But I must make one exception. The Sultan Tit, which is the largest of the whole family, and lives all alone in the genus *Melanochlora*, is a bird I have seen once, and it impressed me so much that I did write my impressions of it. It is a very striking bird, black on back and wings and tail, and most of the head and breast. But the rest of the underparts are bright yellow, and it has a brilliant yellow crest. In December 1952, I spent a week in Sikkim with Salim Ali, and one day we met with a party of these astonishing birds. This is what I wrote about them: 'Two or three seen in a party of small birds. Possibly the same birds encountered on our way down the hill an hour or two later. I was amazed at the size of the bird. At first sight it suggested a Golden Oriole, flitting through the trees. Its yellow crest looks as if it had been stuck on artificially. It seems to be much nearer to the North American Tufted Titmice than to any of the Old World Paridae known to me. The calls we heard, which I wrote down at the time but then mislaid, did not suggest a tit to me at all, nor did they seem to fit either of the two notes given by Smythies in the *Birds of Burma*.'

So, if you have travelled through the Himalayas, from west to east, and have ended up in the east with a view of a Sultan Tit, you will tend to think of the tits as birds of bright colours, perhaps the brightest of the small passerines. To American observers, on the contrary, titmice are birds of sombre colour. The bright-coloured groups of the Old World are not represented. Taking North America as a whole, we find two distinct groups, both of them widely distributed, and in many places plentiful. The chickadees we have looked at already. The other is the Tufted Titmouse group. Both are assigned to the genus *Parus*, but they are very distinct from each other. There are four species of Titmouse, all very similar. The Tufted Titmouse (*P. bicolor*) is widespread, covering all the eastern States of the United States from Florida and the Gulf of Mexico northwards, but it has not penetrated to northern New England. As its scientific name implies, it is a bird of sober colour, grey and white, though in fact it has a third colour—its flanks are a fairly bright buff, not unlike the flanks of the British Willow Tit. The other three allied species are all inhabitants of the south-west, and all have quite limited ranges. All have tufted heads, so the name 'Tufted' Titmouse is not distinctive. One is just called the Plain Titmouse—it is in fact just a degree plainer than the rest! The other two have some black on their heads, one simply a black cap and crest, the other quite an elaborate black and white striped face. All are the same size, approximately the size of the Great Tit of the Old World.

The continued use of the word titmouse rather than tit, for the tufted group, is an illustration of the conservatism of America in the matter of language. A hundred years ago, all European or British bird books using the English language called every member of the family titmouse. 'Tit' was just a vulgar contraction, like calling Joseph Joe, not to be tolerated in a scientific work. They were still all titmice in Saunders' *Manual of British Birds* (1899). The change to 'tits' is perhaps the responsibility of H. F. Witherby.

Now what does all this add up to? It seems to amount to a number of contradictions. If we look only at the black-capped tits or chickadees, one might be tempted to see a parallel with the Tree Creepers (Brown Creeper in America) or with the Kinglets (Reguli). These also are birds of poor flight, whose common ancestors seem to have moved round the northern forests of Eurasia and America in the days when the forest was not sundered by a great ocean. Indeed, in the case of the Brown Creeper, this American bird appears to be the same species as the north-west European bird. There are, of course, other species—one in western Europe, several in the Himalayas. But if this leads us to think that the Tree Creepers perhaps originated in the Himalayan massif, that hardly seems to fit the chickadees, unless they have for some reason been pushed out by other species of *Parus*. For the Himalayas are just the area of Eurasia from which the black-capped tits are absent. In most parts of their range they thrive in the company of other tits, so it is strange if they have been pushed out here.

It looks as if the gay-coloured tits may have spread from some central Asian ancestral home; but where has the American tufted titmouse group come from? What is their ancestral home? How do they relate to the rest of the genus? Today they seem to have no counterpart in Eurasia. On the other hand, the gay-coloured tits and also the long-tails and their relatives do not seem to have spread into North America at all.

Thus, we have here a group of closely related birds, from their abundance evidently fitting the present environment well, highly adaptable to man-made conditions in several parts of their range; still apparently breaking up into new forms to fit the changing environment; of which two specialised groups have colonised America. Although they are short-winged birds, mainly sedentary, some do migrate across such comparatively narrow seas as the North Sea of Europe; and they are wanderers. I recall that in the days when I did a little bird-trapping in the 1930s in the west Midlands it was something of a shock not only to me but even to the central ringing office, when one of my Great Tits was recovered a hundred miles east. At the same time the Kenrick brothers had a trapping station more than a mile due west of me. The intervening country was hilly and most of it was heavily built-up. Yet one Great Tit commuted between the two trapping stations.

Since the years when I made most of these observations much has been written about the tits, including prolonged research into their habits at Wytham, Oxford. I have recently re-read some of the main articles published as a result of these researches, especially those by John Gibb and D. W. Snow in *The Ibis*, Vol. 96, No. 4 (1954). Snow's article covers a much wider field than Marley Wood, Oxford. Indeed, it deals with all the Eurasian tits of the genus *Parus*, including a number that form the bands of tits that roam through the Himalayan woods, which have become almost as familiar to me as the species that fill the woods of England with their cheerful twitterings on dark winter days. Moreover, in David Lack's recently published book, *Ecological*

Isolation in Birds (Blackwells, 1971), two extensive chapters are devoted to the tits: 'A Complex Example of Co-existence: The European Species of Tits', and 'A World Survey: Tits (Parus) in Asia, Africa and America'. The chickadees, as I venture to call them, that is, the black-capped, grey and brown tits of the genus *Parus*, are given a convenient (if ugly) common name, sub-genus *Poecile*, by these authors; so when I write of the chickadees let it be understood that I am referring to the sub-genus *Poecile*.

All these discussions are of the greatest interest; and I cannot claim to have undertaken any close, long-term, systematic study in any degree comparable to the work undertaken at Oxford, nor have I ever attempted a careful analysis of the distinctive habits of the several species, in Europe, Asia or America. Nevertheless, some of the observations I have made may be a useful appendix to these more systematic surveys.

Unfortunately there were very few Willow Tits at Marley Wood, so that the full observations were confined to four species: Great, Blue, Marsh and Coal. My impression is that there is still work to be done on the varying relationship of the two *Poecile* or chickadee species in different parts of Europe, including even Britain. Thus it is unexpected to find the two species common, side by side, in the pine-woods of eastern Holland; and to find Willow the commoner in the deciduous woods of eastern France (Nancy), while the Marsh appeared to be the commoner species in the pine woods of the Vosges.

Again, the curious song-period of the Willow Tit, as I recorded it whilst living in good Willow Tit districts (Kent and Sussex border and north Worcestershire) over nearly forty years, does not seem to have been recognised by these authors. It suggests some difference in life-style which perhaps has yet to be elucidated.

Lack quotes Amann's observations on the lowland race of the Willow Tit in Switzerland (a distinct race from the bird found in the pine forest at such places as Champéry), indicating that the feeding habits of the two species are different there. Willow Tits have slenderer beaks than Marsh Tits (yet it is the Willow Tit that has developed the habit of digging out its nest in tree stumps), so they eat more soft seeds of herbaceous vegetation and insects, whereas the Marsh Tit, in Switzerland at least, is much more inclined to hammer hard seeds. When the *Handbook of British Birds*, Vol. I, was published in 1938, Jourdain who was responsible for the paragraphs on food, admitted that the feeding habits of the two species had not been adequately separated; but for both species the emphasis is on insect food. Witherby himself had contributed a note of Willow Tits eating honeysuckle seeds.

My several Continental observations were all made in the late summer when birds move about a good deal; but the tits do not usually go long distances at that season; so I think it is fair to assume that those I saw in the pine-belt of east Holland, for instance, were birds that had nested there.

It may perhaps seem rather ridiculous for an Englishman to publish observations made casually in short periods from countries that are very well supplied with local ornithologists; and no doubt much has been published in Dutch, German and French which has not come to my notice. But the position in regard to these two closely allied species is by no means fully elucidated in England; and I am inclined to think that the relationship of the two species, and their exact habitat, throughout the lowlands of middle Europe, needs further investigation. David Lack, who has surely surveyed the current literature fully, summarises the distribution of *Parus montanus*, the Willow Tit, thus: 'Widespread in northern and central, not southern, Europe; in north especially in birch and mixed forest, in centre in broad-leaved riverine woods or montane conifers.' I doubt if this is adequate for the habitat in the 'centre'. The ecological separation of the two species seems to be very complicated, so that in some areas the situation as between them seems to contradict what is found a hundred miles away.

Lack's summary is, no doubt, largely built on the careful and detailed discussion of the habitats of these two species in Snow's 1954 *Ibis* article. This deserves quotation. He notes that '*P. atricapillus* (we now call it *montanus*) is characteristic of the northern coniferous forests and the more southerly montane forests, and *P. palustris* of temperate broad-leaved woodlands'. Taking the whole distribution of the two species, across Eurasia from Atlantic to Pacific, he finds eight areas from which one or other species is absent, for some unaccountable reason. In some of these the species that is present has occupied the zone appropriate to the second species; in others it has not. 'This suggests that competition still helps to maintain the characteristic ecological separation of the species, and that the different habitat-preferences are still not fully developed specific characters.' I hope this summary does justice to his argument. If, as I think, my observations tend to make the existing picture even more confusing, his final comment seems to be justified, in the sense that the ecological distinctions between the two species are still in a state of flux.

Another aspect of the characteristic habits of the tits seems to me to need some further discussion. Tits are pre-eminently gregarious birds: not only do several or even many of the same species hunt and feed together during the whole year except for the breeding season; but in all parts of the world known to me where tits are found—Europe, the Himalayas and the Indian jungles, and in North America—flocks of tits usually include several different species. Yet this very important aspect of their lives is scarcely referred to, and not at all discussed by the three authors I am here considering. Lack, to be sure, dealt with their behaviour in *Ecological* Isolation *in Birds* (my emphasis). So that the reasons for the flocking of tits would not naturally come within the scope of his discussion. Indeed, the very reason for his examining the tits at length is that, to a superficial observer, it might seem that there is no ecological isolation among the four or five common English species. Lack shows that in fact there is such differentiation. Yet the more important fact about the tits appears to be that they are persistent flockers.

This is, indeed, recognised by Gibb, who writes: 'The several tit species have much in common: their breeding biology and behaviour are similar, and for most of the year they flock together and often eat the same foods. Nevertheless each species has evolved characteristic methods of feeding, with corresponding structural adaptations (especially of the bill ...); this permits it to take certain foods more efficiently than any of the other species. It may be in this way that six members of the Paridae can live together in the same habitat without competing.'

An excellent summary, I should say; but why do they spend so much time in flocks? Surely not merely because they do not seriously compete for the food that is available. There must be some positive reason for their association together. What is the nature of the mutual aid that they provide for one another?

There are, broadly, three types of behaviour that characterise birds during the non-breeding season. Some are as strictly territorial during the winter as they are in the breeding season, driving away all birds of their own species, and any others that appear to be competing for the same food. Others tend to feed in flocks of their own species. Yet others, and the tits are one of the most striking examples, commonly associate with several other species, including, indeed, some species that are not closely related. There must be some positive reasons for this preference. The subject of territory and flocking is a large and very complex subject. I hope to discuss it again in a later chapter.

Robert Gillmor provides a charming picture of the feeding stations of Blue, Marsh and Great Tits in oakwood to illustrate Lack's discussion. Of course it is true that the Great Tit tends to feed in the lower branches and on the ground, the Marsh Tit in the middle branches and the Blue higher up. But if anyone claimed to identify the several tits in a party by the position they were occupying in the tree he would make a good many mis-identifications. They constantly overlap, and mingle with each other. Competition is usually very slight; interspecific fighting is, as far as my experience goes, extremely rare. I find it frankly amazing that, with so much careful study of these birds, none of these four authors seems to think it worth while to discuss the significance of their gregarious habits.

This oversight is possibly connected with the cultural background of the western world, which tends to emphasise competition in nature and also in man, rather than cooperation. By an odd coincidence, just as I was writing these pages, I received from India the June 1971 issue of *Newsletter for Birdwatchers*, with an article by B. D. Rana and A. P. Tyagi on 'Birdwatching around Muzaffarnagar'. They describe the species observed in each of several distinct zones. In the first of these, an orchard association, they noted no fewer than twenty-three species, mostly passerine. The last sentence of the paragraph describing this is: 'We did not witness any interspecific competition in spite of the fact that the bird number was appreciable.' Two further pages give the birds found in other zones of the district; their observations covered a week in May. The final comment is: 'In the avian community of the Muzaffarnagar district, we witnessed such a harmony and peaceful coexistence, that we could only wish that humans could take a lesson from them.' 'Live and let live' is the traditional way of life in India; mutual tolerance, in fact. Normally, I think it is also the way of life of the tits in Europe, in the Himalayas, and in North America, where Tufted Titmice and Chickadees seem to like to hunt together.

In his *Manual of British Birds* (1899 edition) Howard Saunders only admitted six occurrences of the Water Pipit (*Anthus spinoletta spinoletta*) in Britain—four from Sussex, one from Lincolnshire and one from Carnarvonshire. But in 1906, M. J. Nicoll showed that it appeared to be a bird of frequent occurrence on the coast of Kent and Sussex, near Rye, in the autumn and winter. His paper on this was published in the *Zoologist*; *British Birds* had not been started. The first issues of *British Birds*, 1907-8, contained a series of articles by H. F. Witherby and N. F. Ticehurst 'On the More Important Additions to our Knowledge of British Birds since 1899'—that is, since the publication of Saunders' *Manual*. In the case of the Water Pipit they were able to record specimens from the Isle of Wight, Scilly, Oxford, Norfolk, Kent and a number from Sussex as recorded by Nicoll; indeed his total for the years 1900 to 1906 came to over twenty.

Naturally, this stimulated our interest, and we kept a look-out for them along the coast from Rye to Littlestone; but we did not find any that we could call Water Pipits before Christopher left for Rome. The first time I saw a 'Rock Pipit' with distinct white outer tail-feathers on the south coast of England was at Pevensey, Sussex, on 4th October 1913. In June of that year I had been with Christopher in the Roman Apennine, where we found Water Pipits breeding. Although the summer plumage and the winter plumage are very distinct, I was probably more alert for Water Pipits as a result of this Italian experience. In subsequent years I gradually learnt to identify them more readily, so that in 1923, when I found them by Worcestershire reservoirs, I was able to write at some length in *British Birds* (vol. XVII, pp. 304-5). In view of what is now known of their occurrence in England year by year it is surprising to find that in most of the years between 1907 and 1923 there are no records of Water Pipits in England at all. I must confess that I think the pipits are among the most difficult species to identify in the field. As far as the plumage is concerned I should say that most of them are a good deal more difficult than the Leaf Warblers—but not as difficult as some of the *Prinia* warblers of India or some autumn warblers or small flycatchers of North America.

By the time the *Handbook* was published (1938) Witherby was able to say: 'England and Wales. Not often identified but possibly regular winter-visitor in small numbers.' He then refers to my 1923 article in *British Birds*, so let me do the same.

First, I recorded that I had 'several times seen shrill-voiced Pipits, of the general colour of the Rock Pipit (*A. s. petrosus*) but showing some white in the sides of the tail, along the coast near Dungeness between October and March', that is to say in the area where they had been found by Nicoll. Then, at Cambridge sewage-farm, on 10th October 1915, I saw and heard an undoubted *spinoletta* pipit, which was probably Water, but I did not see its tail-feathers. In the winters of 1917-19, when I was teaching at Cranbrook school, within cycling distance of the Rother Levels (still the Kent and Sussex area, but a little further from the sea), I three times saw birds that I suspected to be Water Pipits: on 8th March 1918, 12th February 1919 and 6th April 1919.

Then I moved to the Midlands, and to my astonishment I found *spinoletta* pipits by the Upper Bittell reservoir (North Worcestershire) in November 1919, and again four times in the autumn of 1920—30th September, 13th and 27th October, 24th November. None of these gave me an opportunity to see it at close quarters. They would be feeding inconspicuously on the mud, then up the bird would fly, calling loudly, so that its specific identity was established; but instead of settling again a few yards further on as a Meadow Pipit would normally do it flew right across the reservoir.

At last, on 18th October 1923, at Upper Bittell reservoir, I got close views of three birds of the species and was able to satisfy myself that they were Water Pipits. 'I happened to notice a bird walking by the edge of the water, and as I was nearly hidden by some bushes it did not seem to notice me. Two similar birds were feeding beyond it, and they sometimes came within about fifteen yards of where I was standing. While I was watching them, two Meadow Pipits (*A. pratensis*) most conveniently settled on the mud near them, so that the differences between the two species—the almost uniform dark plumage, dark legs and larger size of the rarer species, as compared with the bright-coloured Meadow Pipits—were very conspicuous. One of the three larger birds had its tail feathers slightly disarranged, and in consequence showed a practically white outer tail feather; otherwise I should not have noticed this feature as they ran about.' After a paragraph on some more Water Pipits observed in January 1924 at Littlestone and Rye (Kent and Sussex coasts again) I concluded: 'My impression is that the note of *A. s. spinoletta* is a trifle less loud and shrill than that of *A. s. petrosus*, but the single note is always quite distinct from that of *A. pratensis*, though the twitter which often follows when the bird rises from the ground is not so easy to distinguish. However, if, as I cannot but believe, the Water Pipit is in reality a fairly common autumn visitor to the reservoirs and sewage-farms of England, I am surprised that other observers do not seem to have noticed it, for anyone familiar with the call-notes of the Rock and Meadow Pipits would assume on hearing it, that he had a bird of the former species under observation, even if he could not determine the subspecies.'

I continued to see birds of the species, most of them apparently Water Pipits, by Upper Bittell reservoir and also, when I came to know it, beside the still larger Belvide reservoir in Staffordshire, through the years that I lived in the Midlands, that is throughout the twenties and thirties. Looking back on it now, I could wish that I had given a rather fuller account of the plumage of those three Bittell birds in October 1923. At that time, I believed that, in their winter plumage, the white outer tail feathers were almost the only reliable field character of the Water Pipit. And so, perhaps, they really are, though Tucker, in his field-notes for the Pipits in the *Handbook of British Birds* (vol. I, p. 204), notes:

'In autumn and winter differs from either race of Rock Pipit in warmer brown upper-parts and whitish under-parts, as well as white outer tail feathers. At that season breast is quite strongly streaked and whole plumage recalls Meadow Pipit, from which it differs in larger size, Rock Pipit-like form and carriage, dark legs, only faintly marked upper-parts, without olivaceous tint, and whiter breast.' Here is a note I made of four birds seen at Belvide reservoir, Staffordshire, on 9th October 1943. 'Under-parts, especially on sides, almost as strongly marked as in Meadow Pipits, but throat conspicuously white. Upper-parts fairly uniform olive-brown, some variety in colour, three being rather greener, the fourth browner. Eye-stripe not strongly marked in any. Legs dark. All seen running about on mud at distance of

15-20 feet.' I recorded these quite confidently as Water Pipits. Years after, when I came on the record, I began to wonder. I did not see the white outer tail feathers, apparently. But the strongly marked underparts, and the white throat, surely rule out Rock Pipit; and if Witherby and Tucker are right in claiming that the Scandinavian Rock Pipit is indistinguishable in winter plumage, that too is ruled out.

My 1923 note in *British Birds* brought me correspondence two years later from F. L. Blathwayt, of Dorset and Somerset fame. He had found a bird on Lodmoor, Weymouth, which obviously was a Water Pipit in full spring plumage. In 1929 I was spending some days in mid-April in Somerset, and I was able to spend two days with Blathwayt, who introduced me to Weymouth, Portland and Abbotsbury. A Golden Oriole coming in from the sea at Abbotsbury was the great event of those two days, but he had also shown me one of his spring plumage pipits on Lodmoor. It was the first time I had seen one in that plumage in England. As we watched it, I commented: 'When you see it at rest on the ground it looks quite like a female Wheatear.' 'I am so glad to hear you say that,' replied Blathwayt; 'for I said just that in my note to *British Birds*, when I first saw one here in 1925; but Witherby said it was absurd and cut it out.'

Blathwayt found at least one spring plumage Water Pipit on Lodmoor each year from 1925 to 1929 inclusive. Yet, from 1956 to 1969, when I lived at Swanage, and frequently visited Lodmoor, I never saw a Water Pipit there, in any plumage; nor, as far as I know, have there been any satisfactory reports by the many observers who now keep a close watch on Weymouth birds. They are found in other places, such as Dorset cress beds. Why have they forsaken Lodmoor and why do they now so rarely visit the Midland reservoirs?

One more spring-plumage observation needs to be recorded. In the spring of 1934, from late March to early April, I was staying at Cambridge, and on my first visit to the sewage-farm I found a strange wader. Miss Turner accompanied me the next day, and we concluded that it was a Lesser Yellowlegs (*Tringa flavipes*) from America. At the same time we found a Water Pipit in beautiful spring plumage. I rang up my brother, W.B.A., at Oxford, and a day or two later he came over with a car full of Oxford undergraduates to see the Yellowlegs, which duly performed for them all. As Wilfrid's car was full, Bernard Tucker chartered a taxi for the day, and he came too. They also saw the spring-plumage Water Pipit, and I think B.W.T. was about as excited at this as he was with the Yellowlegs.

As to pipits seen at the Cambridge sewage-farm, I had some correspondence with David Lack, when he was preparing his book on the *Birds of Cambridgeshire*, and his letter on the subject, written on 13th November 1932, is worth quoting at length, as an illustration of the care taken over these difficult identifications in those days:

'The birds I have seen throughout the last two winters at the Camb. Sewage Farm differed from Rock Pipits in call and white outer tail feathers—but only (really appreciably) in these two characters. None had a more conspicuous eye-stripe than that of the Rock Pipit.

'But one bird seen in mid-March last year had white eye-stripe and pinkish underparts—clearly a Water Pipit in summer plumage. It was associating with one of the other pipits, which seemed identical save for eye-stripe and pink (I think the calls were the same). I therefore assume the other birds to be Water Pipits in winter plumage.

'Against these birds being Water Pipits is that, if one was in spring plumage in mid-March, the other should have shown at least traces. Further, as you say, there is no conspicuous eye-stripe (But in the winter specimens in the B.M. there seems also no prominent eye-stripe, so I *think* this may be all right.) Thirdly, the summer distribution of the Water (Alpine) Pipit makes it curious it should winter regularly in Britain.

'The only other possibility is the Scandinavian Rock Pipit. But this is said to have grey outer tail feathers (the Cambridge birds have definite white). It is also said to have v. little streaking on the breast (? referring to winter plumage). In the Cambridge birds the streaking is well marked, though stopping abruptly on the lower chest, and the chin is also white. I have seen two Cambridge birds streaked all over the under-parts, like some Rock Pipits. I assume these were birds in first winter or juvenile. (Seen early October.) One Water Pipit in the B.M. shows such streaking all over. But the breeding quarters of the Scandinavian Rock Pipit makes it a likely winter visitor.'

This letter of Lack's demonstrates, I hope, that identification of these difficult pipits in the thirties was not a matter of rash, ill-considered conclusions. The full field notes of the *Handbook* were still in the future; indeed, I suppose we were gradually accumulating the evidence on which Tucker built his remarkable work. It was two years later that, as already noted, Tucker himself saw one of the spring plumage Water Pipits at Cambridge. I think it was his first in that plumage. What Lack has written here about the differences between the plumages of Water and Scandinavian Rock Pipits seems adequate.

It is extraordinary that Water Pipits come to England at all. Their breeding range is in the high mountains of central and south Europe, including the Alps, south Germany, and Galicia; none of these countries is as far north as England. So presumably those birds that come to England for the winter must migrate in a north-westerly direction. Recently it has been shown that they visit cress beds in the south of England in small numbers every winter, and I. G. Johnson has given a full account of this (*Bird Study*, vol. 17, pp. 297-319). I have identified several at cress beds in Dorset.

In the days when I was free to move about England a good deal, and when my ears helped me even more than my eyes, I recorded Water Pipits in no fewer than eleven English counties, namely Kent, Sussex, Dorset, Berkshire, Suffolk, Norfolk, Cambridgeshire, Warwickshire, Worcestershire, Staffordshire, and Cheshire. I believe that in every case the identification included clear views of the white outer tail feathers as well as the sound of the very distinct *spinoletta* call-note. I was particularly pleased that, soon after I had told A. W. Boyd of the Water Pipit I had seen in his county (Cheshire) on the Dee marshes, he found one.

In 1966 Kenneth Williamson published a very exhaustive article on the taxonomy of the European *spinoletta* pipits (*British Birds*, Vol. LVIII pp. 491-503). I am puzzled by one or two features that do not seem to be resolved. As I understand this article, Williamson seems to suggest that both the Alpine Pipit and the Scandinavian Rock Pipit (*A. s. littoralis*) occur fairly frequently on the south coast of England and are very difficult to distinguish in the field, even in spring plumage. Can he really mean this? Witherby in the *Handbook*, and Tucker in his field notes, make *littoralis* indistinguishable from ordinary Rock Pipits (*A. s. petrosus*) in winter, but not from Water Pipits. Moreover, a year later, Williamson himself was accompanying I. G. Johnson in identifying Water Pipits at cress beds in the south of England. A *spinoletta* pipit with white, truly white, outer tail feathers must surely be a Water Pipit, especially if it is also seen to have brown, not blackish, legs, and a very conspicuous pale superciliary stripe. And if it is in that remarkable 'female Wheatear' spring plumage, it is unlike any other race of the species known to me.

I think it is fair to say that the Water Pipits observed by M. J. Nicoll on the Sussex coast, and by several competent observers of my generation in the 1920s, including F. L. Blathwayt, A. W. Boyd and B. W. Tucker, were just as well identified as the birds recently recorded at cress beds in southern England. Whether the species has for some reason changed its habitat in the past forty years is uncertain but possible.

In India I have observed the so-called Chinese Water Pipit (*A. s. blakistoni*) and in China the Japanese race, so-called. *Blakistoni* turned up from time to time near Delhi, where the members of the Delhi Bird Club recorded eight species of pipit. Indeed, I believe I myself identified all these species, and I made some careful notes on some of them, which I quote here. Just like the European Water Pipit, in the days when I used to find them by Midland reservoirs, these birds (*blakistoni*) were addicted to the margins of jheels (the Indian name for a reservoir) and they would fly up suddenly uttering their single *scree* note, and then fly down again a hundred yards further on, where they would be invisible in the long grass. However, the Dasna jheel, some eighteen miles east of Delhi, was surrounded by shorter grass, so on 8th January 1951 I managed to get quite near to several. 'On today's observations I would say: the upper parts are grey-brown, not very dark, but with darker streaks on the mantle; the closed wing, as in *A. rufulus* (the so-called Indian Pipit), looks rather pale as seen from behind. The under-parts are smoky grey (especially on the breast) streaked with small dark streaks, thickly on the sides. Bill dark, legs yellowish or horn. A clear, but narrow and rather short, whitish eye-streak above and behind the eye, much less pronounced than in *A. roseatus* (Hodgson's Pipit). Smythies, *Birds of Burma*, calls this species *A. palopus*. Ripley, *Synopsis of the Birds of India and Pakistan*, calls it *A. penopus*. It is very similar to *spinoletta*, and I found the two species in just the same habitat, in the grass round jheels, so that they were not easy to separate. (I return to it in a moment.) The general colour of the black looks greyer and lighter than in either *A. trivialis* (Tree Pipit) or *A. hodgsoni* (which is *not* "Hodgson's Pipit", but is known to British ornithologists as the Greenish Pipit since it occurred as a vagrant to Britain) and the sides are less boldly streaked.'

On Hodgson's Pipit I noted that it was a very dark bird, the upperparts warmer brown than the Chinese Water Pipit, and the under-parts thickly streaked with black. Colour of the legs, pink or buff, rather pale. The call-note is almost identical, though rather fainter, less shrill. After one observation, I noted that 'I find the note indistinguishable' from the Chinese Water Pipit.

An observation of the Greenish Pipit may also be worth quoting. Three or four were under observation by the irrigation canal, Dasna.

Chinese Water Pipits and Indian Pipits (*A. rufulus*) were watched the same day (8th January 1951). 'The mantle is olive-brown, heavily streaked with black. Wing-feathers also sharply contrasted—pale and dark. Throat whitish; under-parts light buff (paler than in *A. spinoletta blakistoni*), heavily barred and streaked on the sides with black.'

CHAPTER VI

Migration

PART I

In the first chapter, 'Beginnings', I have explained how I began to keep records of the arrival of summer migrants in the south of England—just as, I am sure, most other field ornithologists have done. But perhaps not many can boast that they began to keep such records before their eighth birthday, and have continued to their eightieth. I have also told how Christopher and I bought specially made books for entering our annual records. Although Wilfrid did not contribute many of the early dates, after he returned to England to live, following his fifteen years in Australia, he let me have his dates for many years; and we had friendly competition as to which could get the first dates of the spring migrants, just as Christopher and I had in the early years of the century.

When I lost my *Naturalist's Diary* in the stolen suitcase in 1946, I also lost my migrant record book. This was a severe blow. On my return from India in 1948 I turned up Christopher's copy, which had all the earlier records from 1897 to 1912; then I went through all my old note-books, and rescued all my migrant dates from 1913 onwards. Wilfrid also nobly went through his diaries and was able to send me all the dates he had for arriving and departing migrants, from the year of his return from Australia (1926), so I do not think any essential dates have been lost with the book.

The astonishing thing is that, in spite of our family tendency to go abroad for long periods—Christopher to Rome in 1911, Wilfrid to Australia in 1912 for nearly fifteen years, I myself to India for a good many years in the 1940s and '50s—there is only one year when no one of us was on the watch for some of the returning migrants in the south of England. Down to 1968 we have 68 records for the following species: Whitethroat, Sedge Warbler, Swallow, Swift and Cuckoo. There were a few years when both Wilfrid and I were out of England in the early part of the season, so both Chiffchaff and Willow Warbler have only 66 dates. So have Blackcap, Garden Warbler and House Martin. Whinchat, Lesser Whitethroat, Tree Pipit, Sand Martin and Turtle Dove also have at least 60 dates. Wheatear, Redstart, Nightingale, Wood Warbler, Yellow Wagtail, and Spotted Flycatcher are well up in the fifties.

The arrival of the spring migrants in our gardens and woods from the first Chiffchaff in mid or late March to the first Spotted Flycatcher in the first or second week of May, and perhaps a churring Nightjar on the heath a few evenings later, is such a feature of the year for every bird lover in England, that one tends to speak of 'migrant dates' as if this only meant the arrival of the spring birds. But of course there is much more to it than this. I think it is somewhere in Warde Fowler's *Year with the Birds* that he wrote some such words as these: 'We all look and listen for the returning migrants each spring and welcome them as they arrive, but when do they leave? They slip away so silently that we hardly notice when they go.' This question stimulated our observation. In the year of our first active partnership, Christopher and I watched carefully on our walks round Tunbridge Wells to see how late we could find a Whitethroat, a Tree Pipit, a Spotted Flycatcher, and all the rest. This was in 1905. But our migrant record book has quite a few autumn departure dates before that year. There are none for 1897. But in 1898 we had all seen a Redstart in the Isle of Wight on 22nd August, probably a bird of passage (possibly my first Redstart ever, for they were scarce birds at Tunbridge Wells and

Reigate); and on 26th September of that same year I had heard a Chiffchaff singing at Tunbridge Wells; so there were two departure dates for that year. In 1899, five dates, and remarkably, Wilfrid and Christopher saw a Nightingale as late as 23rd August.

In 1900 we had five departure dates, and in 1901 twelve, but in 1902 only two and in 1903 only four. In 1904 the number rose to thirteen; perhaps I had read Warde Fowler already. But in 1905 the real effort began, resulting in twenty dates. This was Christopher's first year at Wye, where his daily walks by the river Stour gave him remarkably late dates for all the swallow tribe: Sand Martin to 24th October (a date he repeated two years later—still the latest dates we have ever recorded for the species); House Martin to 10th November, Swallow to 7th November.

Over the past seventy years, there have been more gaps in our autumn records than in the spring ones. However, we have 62 records for a last date for both Swallow and House Martin, and 60 for Chiffchaff; over 50 for Wheatear, Whinchat, Redstart, Whitethroat, Lesser Whitethroat, Willow Warbler, Yellow Wagtail, Tree Pipit, Sand Martin, Swift, Turtle Dove and Common Sandpiper. It is curious that Blackcap comes here quite low in the list (only 45 records) and Garden Warbler even lower (38) just above Wood Warbler. For some reason, Blackcaps do not seem to show up as much as some other warblers in the autumn, even on the coast. It is inland records that are scarce for Garden Warblers. When I lived at Tunbridge Wells, and later, in the twenties and thirties, when Wilfrid was mostly at Oxford and I was at Birmingham, these two species did not seem inclined to show themselves on their autumn passage. On the other hand, for some reason, Lesser Whitethroats are apt to be conspicuous on their autumn passage, inland as well as by the coast.

Some of our early records naturally implant themselves in the mind most vividly. Thus, in the autumn of 1907, Christopher and I were both at Tunbridge Wells in late September and early October. Very few summer birds remained by the end of September, though we saw a late passing Redstart on the 28th. But some of the local Flycatchers were very late that year. One was to be seen on a house roof day after day right into October. Day by day we looked for it; day by day it still remained. Its last date was 7th October. In recent years, on the Dorset coast, I have seen one or two later in the month than that, birds which might well be passage migrants from north or central Europe; but this is, I think, a quite unusually late date for a Spotted Flycatcher to remain at its English breeding place.

In those days, before the first world war, we often spent a few days in the autumn in Romney Marsh and at Rye and Dungeness. Our means of transport were foot-slogging or going by train. We quite often used the train, especially at the end of a day. Two species might often be spotted from the train on the fences or wires by the Romney Marsh railway tracks in those days that must be very rare there now: Wrynecks and Red-backed Shrikes. Four of the seven late dates for Red-backed Shrikes in the years before 1914 were seen in Romney Marsh; three out of seven Wryneck dates. Memory suggests to me that in late August or early September one might spot three Wrynecks and two Shrikes, or thereabouts, in the few miles between Lydd and Appledore. Both were plentiful breeding species all over south-east England in those days.

Still, we are only thinking of the summer migrants. What about arrivals and departures of winter visitors to England from the north? In the past dozen years, I have been living on the Dorset coast, where some twenty species of seabird and waterfowl are regular winter visitors. In an inland district, such as Tunbridge Wells, Reigate, Wye and other such places the situation was very different. Our original list consisted of six species: Redwing, Fieldfare, Grey Wagtail, Siskin, Brambling and Hooded Crow. Then, in 1907, finding that the Tree

Sparrow was a purely winter migrant at Tunbridge Wells and Wye, we added that; and by 1914 we had six arrival dates for it, in late September or early October.

This list did not last long. Already, by 1914, I had begun to get arrival dates for two other small passerines: Firecrest and Black Redstart. The latter had not yet, as far as was known, begun to breed in England; the New Forest nesting of Firecrests was still far away. Then in 1914 I got early arrival dates for the south of England of both Merlin and Snow Bunting; but I dropped Tree Sparrow and Grey Wagtail. Tree Sparrows nested in Romney Marsh; a pair of Grey Wagtails nested by the county boundary stream that I walked along every week at Tunbridge Wells. Then also I began to see some inland waterbirds that were winter migrants, especially Jack Snipe and Green Sandpiper. For both of these I had early dates in the Romney Marsh area in 1914: a Green Sandpiper on 22nd July, and a Jack Snipe on 27th October. Both of these were species I was able to observe regularly when I moved to the Midlands in 1919, and during my Midland years I got dates, some regular, some more occasional, for such wintering waterfowl as Wigeon, Goldeneye, Goosander and Smew.

Later, Wilfrid supplied occasional dates for two other passerine winter migrants: Lapland Bunting and Shore Lark. It is only in recent years—the sixties—while I have lived on the Dorset coast, that I have entered a few dates for arrival in autumn and departure in spring of such birds as Red-throated and Great Northern Divers and Black-necked and Slavonian Grebes, and at least one more duck—Red-breasted Merganser, which might well be the most reliable of all winter migrants for the resident of Purbeck, as indeed, of other coastal places in south Britain that have a ready access to estuaries or muddy harbours.

It will be seen that the list of winter migrants to southern England depends very much on the locality you happen to live in. To the autumn of 1967 inclusive, I have 56 records for both Redwing and Fieldfare; and no less than 44 for Brambling, a bird I could by no means rely on in the past few years at Swanage. It is of interest now to note that we accumulated as many as 23 autumn records of Hooded Crow before this species (or race) became a rare visitor to southern England. We achieved 36 autumn dates for Green Sandpiper, and 35 for Wigeon; 29 for Goldeneye, 23 for Goosander and 22 for Jack Snipe. Seventeen for Firecrest seems to me rather a triumph.

The spring departure tables of wintering birds are similar to the arrival tables. From 1915 to 1948 there are a good number of records in each year; but for various reasons, in the past twenty years, there have been many gaps. The last year with a fairly full list (eleven species) is 1955-6. Here too, Redwing, Fieldfare, Brambling, Wigeon, Goldeneye, Goosander and Green Sandpiper are much the most regular during the inter-war and both earlier and later years.

We have 51 spring (departure) dates for Redwing, 49 for Fieldfare. Just as Redwings tend to arrive before Fieldfares in the autumn, so they usually depart earlier. The Redwing average for those 51 years is 8th April, the Fieldfare 18th April. The latest Redwing date was one seen by Wilfrid on 1st May 1938; the latest Fieldfare date is 13th May 1917. As it happens, both these are Midland records; the Redwing in Northamptonshire, the Fieldfare near Warwick—at the end of a severe and prolonged winter. But this is probably no more than a coincidence. Christopher had seen Redwings as late as 28th April 1908 at Wye, Kent; in the same year he saw Fieldfares two days later. Over the years we saw Fieldfares in May in seven different years; although all of these were in some part of the Midlands (near Birmingham, or in Oxfordshire, Berkshire and Cambridgeshire) I recently saw a good-sized flock at Spettisbury, Dorset, as late as 21st April, and I think they occur on passage at Portland late in April or even in May. Several of these late Fieldfare dates have involved fair-sized flocks, in open country. I can readily believe that some farmers see them every year in May.

We have had fewer spring departure dates for Firecrests than autumn dates. As it happens, three of these dates are in mid or even late April, one at Tunbridge Wells, the other two in Dorset.

It is harder to decide what dates can be treated as genuine 'departure dates' for some of these wintering birds than for the summer migrants. A party of Siskins feeds in some alder trees during January and February. They then disappear, and I see no more that spring. Is the late February date a 'good' departure date or not? Jack Snipe are to be found in swampy ground beside a reservoir during an open winter. Then comes a late frost and the ground freezes up. They do not reappear after the frost. (Of course, sometimes they do show up again on the spring migration north.) In the case of the wintering finches, I discovered long ago at Tunbridge Wells that in late spring, in April, finches of many kinds, including both Brambling and Siskin, turned up in the pine-belts of the Sussex borders—but not every year. Later, I occasionally found exactly the same phenomenon on the

Lickey Hills to the south of Birmingham. In areas where you would never find a Siskin or even a Brambling in mid-winter, they would appear just before their departure for Scandinavia. It would seem that commercial planting of pine-trees, which is now widespread over England, has provided a habitat, and presumably also a food supply, similar to the habitat of their breeding grounds, which attracts them, and possibly even delays their migration for a few days, at about the time when they are due to fly north.

It may be said that there is no special value in the migration records of one family that is not better served by the mass observation of numbers of different observers. If we had always lived in one locality for the seventy years of our observations, there might have been some special interest in such a prolonged effort, but of course this is very far from the truth. Although I accept the criticism to some extent, the main value attaching to these observations is that, every season, we did keep up a persistent watch on the coming and going of all these birds. But inevitably such long-continued efforts teach you things which the mass observation technique does not reveal. Thus, some of the observations that gain acceptance in the local reports seem to me frankly incredible. For instance, neither of us ever found a Garden Warbler before 18th April. It is only in unusually early seasons, indeed, that you can expect to find a Garden Warbler in any part of southern England until the very end of the month. Near Oxford, year after year, early Garden Warblers were reported from one special locality—but Wilfrid never found one there. Our average date for sixty-six years is 1st May; and I regard even that as a surprisingly early average.

Our April dates for Garden Warblers are as follows: once on the 18th (W.B.A. at Oxford in 1949); twice on the 22nd (Oxon and Dorset); twice on the 23rd (both Dorset); five times on the 24th (Kent, Cambs, Hants, and twice Dorset); once on the 25th (Dorset); three times on the 26th (Kent, north Worcs, Dorset); three times on the 27th (all Worcs); twice on the 28th (Cambs and north Worcs); once on the 29th (north Worcs); twice on the 30th (Worcs and Berks). Apart from two dates (10th May 1942 and 11th May 1950), all our other dates are in the first week of May. My impression is that Garden Warblers are more regular in their arrival dates than many of the migrants. The first seem nearly always to arrive in southern England between 24th April and 7th May, but no doubt the odd bird will arrive out of its normal time. I recall, for instance, that about 1912 I was staying at Dungeness in early April. Another ornithologist was staying at Lydd at the time, and one day he found a Garden Warbler in a ditch near the sea, on or about 5th April. Probably he identified it correctly. In the course of fifty years or more, one may note these abnormal occurrences in almost any species. A single Redstart on 1st April by a reservoir in the Midlands; a single House Martin, also at the same Midland reservoir, with a few Swallows and Sand Martins, also on 1st April but in another year; a Yellow Wagtail at another Midland reservoir on 25th March; a Whinchat on 28th March in Purbeck, also one on 10th April by yet another Midland reservoir; such dates, and a few more that I could quote, are, I do not doubt, instances of individual birds that have somehow got carried north a week or two before the regular migration time of the species. If you rely on a host of observers, a good many of these eccentric birds are likely to get recorded, whereas the chances are that a single observer, especially if he spends most of his time in normal country rather than at points of exceptional concentration on the coast, will get these abnormal stragglers so rarely that his average dates are likely to reflect the real norm better than the mass observation data.

It is of some interest to give average dates in 1970 for certain species that are no longer common in the south of England. Four species belong to this category, namely Red-backed Shrike, Wryneck, Corncrake and Kentish Plover. Our arrival and departure dates for these four species are as follows:

Red-backed Shrike—Spring average, 12th May (the average of 41 years' dates); the earliest being 29th April 1915, at Reigate, Surrey—Autumn average, 7th September (27 years); the latest 23rd September 1946, Purbeck; also 21st September 1922 and 1925, both in Romney Marsh.

Wryneck—Spring average, 8th April (30 records); the earliest 25th March 1905, Wye, Kent—Autumn average, 8th September (18 records); the latest, 27th September 1922, Dungeness.

Corncrake—Spring average, 8th May (24 records); earliest, 21st April 1922, south Birmingham—Autumn average, 22nd September (8 records); latest 9th October 1922, Dungeness.

Kentish Plover—Spring average, 12th April (17 records); earliest, 29th March 1920, Dungeness—Autumn average, 19th September (13 records); latest, 10th October 1907, Dungeness.

These Kentish Plover dates are not, of course, exact evidence of arrival dates. Rather, they simply indicate how many times we (usually H.G.A. alone) visited Dungeness in the early spring (late

March or early April) and autumn (September or October) during the years when Kentish Plovers were still breeding there. The earliest and the latest dates do, no doubt, give approximate dates of first arrival or late departure. If the records kept year by year through the years before 1935 by Fred Austen and Jack Tart are still available in the archives of the R.S.P.B., they would of course give very accurate dates for the period. Anyhow, I know that the first Kentish Plovers were usually seen in the last week of March or the first week of April, and they left about the end of September.

Of other summer migrants that do not come into the regular lists let me simply note in passing that in the course of years we had three good spring Hoopoe dates and two Golden Oriole dates; on the other hand, we only had one real arrival date for Little Ringed Plover, now one of the regular summer migrants to England. Doubtless, if Wilfrid had remained in Oxford for another ten years, or if I had stayed in Birmingham, we should have begun to record them. Kentish Plovers must do instead.

I append tables of the average dates of those remaining species that we were in a position to record with some regularity, together with the earliest or latest dates, and localities, from my diaries.

Arrival of Summer Migrants in England, 1897 to 1968

Species	Average Date	No. of Records	Earliest Date and Place
Chiffchaff	24th March	66	26th Feb 1957 (Purbeck)
Wheatear	26th March	57	12th March 1926 (Birmingham) 1938 (Staffordshire)
Garganey	3rd April	32	27th Feb 1927 (Purbeck)
Willow Warbler	5th April	66	20th March 1947 (Thanet)
White Wagtail	5th April	31	16th March 1940 (Birmingham)
Sand Martin	6th April	62	17th March 1967 (Weymouth)
Sandwich Tern	7th April	31	11th March 1969 (Purbeck)
Swallow	9th April	68	23rd March 1957 (Purbeck)
Yellow Wagtail	10th April	59	25th March 1926 (Birmingham)
Blackcap	11th April	66	9th March 1967 (Purbeck)
Tree Pipit	12th April	63	28th March 1927 (Surrey) 1969 (Middlesex)
Redstart	15th April	58	1st April 1929 (Staffordshire)

Migration

Species	Average Date	No. of Records	Earliest Date and Place		
Cuckoo	18th April	68	10th April	1911	(Kent)
House Martin	19th April	66	1st April	1944	(Staffordshire)
Nightingale	21st April	54	3rd April	1959	(Purbeck)
Whitethroat	21st April	68	5th April	1926	(Surrey)
Common Sandpiper	21st April	49	8th April	1911	(Romney Marsh)
Grasshopper Warbler	22nd April	31	14th April	1957	(Purbeck)
				1966	(Purbeck)
Sedge Warbler	23rd April	68	4th April	1936	(Romney Marsh)
Whimbrel	24th April	33	3rd April	1923	(Norfolk)
Common Tern	25th April	42	5th April	1925	(Dungeness)
Whinchat	26th April	63	28th March	1964	(Purbeck)
Lesser Whitethroat	26th April	63	14th April	1916	(Kent)
Wood Warbler	27th April	55	14th April	1905	(Kent)
Swift	30th April	68	18th April	1922	(Somerset)
				1947	(Weymouth)
Garden Warbler	1st May	61	22nd April	1945	(Oxfordshire)
				1947	(Portland)
Little Tern	1st May	28	12th April	1926	(Dungeness)
Turtle Dove	2nd May	60	19th April	1909	(Kent)
				1944	(Oxfordshire)
Reed Warbler	3rd May	45	20th April	1929	(Weymouth)
Hobby	8th May	28	26th April	1966	(Purbeck)
Spotted Flycatcher	9th May	59	27th April	1961	(Purbeck)

Departure of Summer Migrants from England, 1897 to 1968

Species	Average Date	No. of Records	Latest Date and Place		
Wood Warbler	13th Aug	34	25th Aug	1909	(Kent)
				1916	(Kent)
Cuckoo	19th Aug	48	22nd Sept	1922	(Romney Marsh)
Nightingale	27th Aug	16	12th Sept	1908	(Kent)
Nightjar	28th Aug	18	26th Sept	1922	(Dungeness)
Grasshopper Warbler	5th Sept	7	26th Sept	1965	(Portland)

Species	Average Date	No. of Records	Latest Date and Place	
Swift	6th Sept	56	21st Oct	1918 (Kent)
Little Tern	6th Sept	30	29th Sept	1914 (Thanet)
Reed Warbler	14th Sept	38	2nd Nov	1914 (Dungeness)
Whimbrel	14th Sept	31	25th Oct	1956 (Norfolk)
Pied Flycatcher	16th Sept	32	6th Oct	1967 (Purbeck)
Sedge Warbler	18th Sept	47	3rd Oct	1934 (Isle of May)
Hobby	18th Sept	12	24th Oct	1922 (Birmingham)
Garganey	18th Sept	16	17th Oct	1948 (Norfolk)
Turtle Dove	18th Sept	56	20th Oct	1961 (Purbeck)
Lesser Whitethroat	19th Sept	51	12th Oct	1947 (Isle of May)
Garden Warbler	19th Sept	38	10th Oct	1957 (Purbeck)
Redstart	20th Sept	53	12th Oct	1959 (Dungeness)
Tree Pipit	20th Sept	54	14th Oct	1908 (Kent)
Whitethroat	22nd Sept	52	27th Oct	1961 (Purbeck)
Common Sandpiper	22nd Sept	54	14th Nov	1940 (Birmingham)
Willow Warbler	23rd Sept	54	9th Oct	1912 (Romney Marsh)
Spotted Flycatcher	24th Sept	57	13th Oct	1967 (Portland)
Black Tern	24th Sept	25	16th Oct	1933 (Hertfordshire)
Yellow Wagtail	25th Sept	58	16th Oct	1961 (Purbeck)
Sandwich Tern	25th Sept	42	29th Oct	1961 (Purbeck)
Whinchat	26th Sept	58	19th Oct	1930 (Berkshire)
Arctic Tern	28th Sept	29	14th Nov	1936 (Birmingham)
Blackcap	29th Sept	45	30th Nov	1962 (Purbeck)
Sand Martin	29th Sept	57	24th Oct	1905 (Kent) 1907 (Kent)
White Wagtail	2nd Oct	23	22nd Oct	1933 (Berkshire)
Wheatear	3rd Oct	54	28th Oct	1914 (Dungeness)
Common Tern	5th Oct	34	9th Nov	1959 (Purbeck)
Chiffchaff	8th Oct	60	7th Nov	1957 (Staffordshire)
Ring Ouzel	10th Oct	29	13th Nov	1938 (Birmingham)
House Martin	24th Oct	62	4th Dec	1956 (Purbeck) 1957 (Purbeck)
Swallow	25th Oct	62	21st Nov	1961 (Purbeck)

Migration

Arrival of Winter Migrants in England, 1897 to 1968

Species	Average Date	No. of Records	Earliest Date and Place	
Green Sandpiper	7th Aug	36	30th June	1948 (Birmingham)
Wigeon	20th Sept	35	10th Aug	1946 (Cambridge)
Merlin	29th Sept	19	13th Sept	1917 (Romney Marsh)
Redwing	7th Oct	56	28th Sept	1922 (Kent)
Jack Snipe	9th Oct	22	16th Sept	1926 (Birmingham)
Snow Bunting	12th Oct	14	15th Sept	1952 (Suffolk)
Brambling	17th Oct	44	22nd Sept	1954 (Fair Isle)
Firecrest	19th Oct	17	10th Sept	1961 (Portland)
Black Redstart	20th Oct	15	24th Sept	1922 (Dungeness)
Fieldfare	25th Oct	56	24th Sept	1932 (Holy Isle)
Hooded Crow	26th Oct	23	9th Oct	1914 (Kent)
Siskin	27th Oct	28	1st Oct	1913 (Sussex)
Goldeneye	27th Oct	29	9th Oct	1954 (Staffordshire)
Goosander	3rd Dec	23	27th Oct	1956 (Leicestershire)
Smew	13th Dec	13	16th Nov	1941 (Hertfordshire)

Departure of Winter Migrants from England, 1897 to 1968

Species	Average Date	No. of Records	Latest Date and Place	
Smew	5th March	16	21st April	1952 (Suffolk)
Goosander	25th March	24	16th May	1928 (Birmingham)
Jack Snipe	27th March	18	27th April	1918 (Dungeness)
Hooded Crow	29th March	29	18th April	1933 (Suffolk)
Siskin	30th March	31	29th April	1916 (Birmingham)
Firecrest	4th April	8	24th April	1967 (Purbeck)
Black Redstart	5th April	18	23rd April	1968 (Purbeck)
Merlin	5th April	21	24th April	1917 (Romney Marsh)
Redwing	8th April	51	1st May	1938 (Northamptonshire)
Brambling	8th April	40	25th April	1929 (Birmingham)
Goldeneye	9th April	36	4th May	1941 (Staffordshire)
Green Sandpiper	14th April	23	26th May	1923 (Romney Marsh)
Wigeon	15th April	43	21st March	1928 (Birmingham)
Fieldfare	18th April	49	18th May	1917 (Warwick)

It will be seen that I have not followed a consistent principle in selecting the species in the foregoing tables. As I have just said, in the case of the arriving spring migrants, I have only included those birds that one or other of us brothers could be fairly sure to find within a few days of the actual first arrival date—first arrival, that is, of more than a single erratic forerunner.

I have not been so exacting in the other tables—for a variety of reasons. The most important is the fact that these other seasonal movements tend to be much less regular, and more spread out over the season, than the return of migrants to their breeding areas. Moreover, there are some species that show themselves much more regularly on passage in the south of England in the autumn than in the spring. Thus, both Pied Flycatcher and Ring Ouzel can be found, the former often in large numbers, on any part of the south coast in the autumn; the spring passage is a good deal more uncertain. Some of the departure dates vary greatly from one area to another. The hirundines are a striking example here. If all my recording had been done in the west Midlands, and away from any river flats, the average date for both Swallow and House Martin would have been early in October, not late in the month. On the other hand, if my whole life had been spent on the Dorset coast, both would show an average last appearance well into November. The actual average shows the effect of the change of habitat of the observer. Rather to my surprise, Wilfrid rarely saw a late Swallow or House Martin during his twenty years at Oxford. As it happens, my student days at Cambridge did provide November dates for both species. Similarly, it may well cause surprise that the Swift departure average is in September. Most of the breeding population of Swifts in English towns has gone for good by mid-August. But birds from northern Europe pass through England, chiefly near the east coast, all through September. So our average reflects the fact that one or other of us was often on the east coast during September.

I am not sure that the winter tables are worth publishing, except for the long continued observations on Redwing and Fieldfare; perhaps also the Siskin and Brambling records—though even with these species, they are so uncertain in Dorset that recent records are few and erratic. The Hooded Crow records are perhaps of some slight historical interest. And it is intriguing to realise that, whereas Green Sandpipers regularly return to some of their sewage-farm or other haunts in July and August, the immigrant Goosanders and Smews do not usually reach their south of England or Midland reservoirs till early December.

The author and his brother, W. B. Alexander, (*first and second left*), with companions at Blakeney Point, Norfolk. Date unknown but probably 1949.

Above, A. W. Boyd.
Right, Bernard Tucker. Photo C. A. Norris.

Or so it seemed to be before 1960. They may have changed their habits since then.

PART II

My study of migration began with that March Chiffchaff at Reigate in 1897. And for some years, 'migration' meant to me the coming and going of species that moved in and out of southern England—I am tempted to restrict it still more, and say *inland* south-east England—in the course of the year. To all intents and purposes, this meant migration into England (with a few species departing for the north at the same time) in late March, April and early May, let us say for two months and no more in the spring; and in September and October, with some slight extension, in the autumn, when the summer birds were leaving and the winter birds returning. Now, seventy years later, I can record that I have watched the coming and going, not to say the passage, of migrating birds in three continents and in every month of the year.

Christopher and I soon learnt that the times of the year during which genuine migratory movements could be observed, even in south-east England, needed to be extended far beyond the brief weeks that our early observations and our study of the available books had suggested. It must have been about 1907 or 1908 that Christopher heard a Common Sandpiper flying over at night during the first week of July at Wye, Kent. By 1912, when he left England to work in the International Institute of Agriculture at Rome, we had discovered for ourselves that quite a number of waders from the far north (shore-birds as they are called in America) had already returned to the shores of Kent before the end of July: Knots, Godwits, Turnstones, Whimbrels, northern Dunlins, Sanderlings and others. But I think we still put the end of the spring passage to the north in the last days of May. It was not till I began visiting Midland reservoirs in the 1920s that I discovered small parties of these birds, especially northern Dunlins and Ringed Plovers (both of them species that breed in Britain, but both have races with far northern breeding ranges) still passing through, probably on their way to the far north, in the first week of June.

It astonished me, a good many years later, to come upon a Red-necked Phalarope in the first week of June at a jheel just north of Delhi. Delhi is not quite in the tropics; even so, from north India that

Phalarope had a very long journey still to make before it could reach its northern breeding grounds in arctic Siberia. How long would it take? Possibly not more than ten days. In that case it would be on the breeding grounds by mid-June, when the winter snows have barely melted, so perhaps it would be reasonable to expect far more of these birds to stay at least in the temperate zone till early June.

As I write this, I have just had an experience which underlines the same extraordinary nature of the spring journey of these 'globe-spanners', as the old British ornithologist Abel Chapman called them. I am in Pennsylvania, in mid-June 1971. We have just spent three days on the New Jersey coast, latitude about 39 degrees north, the days being 14th, 15th and 16th June. I assumed that we should be too late for any northern shore-birds (waders) apart from the odd first-year or non-breeding bird that might spend the summer here, without attempting the long journey to the Arctic. Each day we passed an area of muddy pools that are very attractive to waders, especially at high tide; and each day, high tide or low tide, several species of waders were there. On our last visit, at 5 p.m. on the 16th, I counted eighteen Semi-palmated Sandpipers by one small pool to the north of the road; there were several more on neighbouring pools, say thirty in all. The south-west side of the road, which had proved to be the more productive, was exactly in the glare of the sun, so we did not try to find out what was there. Earlier on that day, as on each of the other two days, there had been parties of both Least and Semi-palmated Sandpipers on the south-west pools, and one or more of the following species: Grey Plover, Ringed Plover (*Charadrius semipalmatus*), Dunlin, Dowitcher, and a probable Knot. Moreover, on the seashore, both at Avalon and four miles further south at Stone-Harbor, there were still plenty of Sanderlings, all in spring plumage—perhaps fifty in the two places together. It is reasonable to assume that there were other Sanderlings on other parts of that long sandy beach; and other Least and Semi-palmated Sandpipers, to say nothing of other 'globe-spanners', in other parts of the long New Jersey mud-flats. Let us say some hundreds if not thousands in all, still a thousand miles and more from their arctic breeding grounds. It is possible that 1971 was for some reason a year of unusually late northwards passage (in North America it was a late season for the warbler migration to the north, but the shore-birds are not usually affected by the same factors that affect the small passerines); for, strangely, a few days later came a letter from Tony Blake, telling of the spring passage at the Midland reservoirs that I knew well in the twenties and thirties, with the final comment (referring more particularly to Cannock reservoir): 'Yesterday, Sunday 13th June, there were still a few migrant waders there, astonishingly late.'

Here is another report from 1971. In the last week of July, a neighbour rang me up to tell me of the occurrence of both European godwits, Bar-tailed and Black-tailed, on the New Jersey coast at the remarkable reserve, Brigantine, close to Atlantic City. But the appearance of these two rarities was less remarkable than the numbers of other waders already present. I was able to visit the sanctuary on 30th July, nearly a week after the first observations had been made. On that date we found literally thousands of Dowitchers, and large numbers of other waders, especially Semi-palmated Sandpipers, perhaps twenty Stilt Sandpipers (a species that is never common on this coast) and so on. What is the explanation? Even if we recognise that arctic breeding species that are still in the latitudes of the forties or even further south in the second week of June may reach their breeding grounds in time to breed there during the short but late arctic summer, what of these birds that have travelled over a thousand miles south already by the middle or the second half of July? I cannot think that they have bred successfully. If this kind of thing happened only once in every ten years, one might suppose that some area in the arctic had been exposed to catastrophic summer weather, so that a large proportion of the breeding birds had failed in their efforts and had already come south after their failures. But many come south in July every year. They are, of course, all adult birds, or at least birds in adult, not in first-year, plumage. Are they, possibly, second-year birds, which have made the journey north to the breeding grounds, but are not in fact mature enough to breed? It seems to me possible; though in that case one would expect them to stay nearer to their winter quarters, rather than undertaking two immense journeys. Indeed, when I see the odd Grey Plover, Sanderling, or whatever it may be, on the English or North American coast in late June or early July (as one often does) I think: 'Presumably a non-breeding bird.' It is difficult to account for these large flocks that appear so far from the breeding grounds, year by year, in the second half of July. If some other observer has discussed the subject and offered a solution I have not seen it.*

* When I wrote that sentence, I had forgotten the excellent book on *The Shorebirds of North America*, with illustrations by Robert Verity Clem and text by

Let us look at the return migration especially its early start. In 1970 we visited a pool on the Audubon sanctuary near Eastham, Cape Cod, Massachusetts, on 16th July. One of the advantages of such a place, which is never disturbed, is that the birds are remarkably tame, so it is not difficult to identify them and to count them. While we were there I noted about a hundred Dowitchers, some twenty Greater Yellowlegs, a few Lesser Yellowlegs, some thirty or so Least Sandpipers, a smaller number of Semi-palmated Sandpipers, several Ringed (Semi-palmated) Plovers, and a probable Pectoral Sandpiper. We were told that both Whimbrel and Stilt Sandpipers had been there earlier in the day. The latitude is a little south of 42° north. Of course, in these days, there are many ornithologists who are keeping daily watches on these and other sanctuaries, and who could supply daily particulars of the early and late migrations. The situation has changed radically since those far-off 1910s and 1920s when there were very few field observers so that almost every observation involved a new discovery. But it seems useful to emphasise from one man's personal observations how short is the period between the last northward flight in June and the first southward flight in July.

What then of the other end of the year? How long, if any, is the winter gap between the last southern flight and the first northern? I began by assuming that the autumn migration in the north temperate zone ended about the end of November, and the northern flight began

---

Peter Matthiesen; both the pictures and the text are among the outstanding recent contributions to ornithology. If it had been published in 1908, and I had read it then, I should not have forgotten it. But as it was only published in 1968, of course I had forgotten it. Such are the tricks that memory plays in old age.

Yet, even Matthiesen does not seem to me to tackle my problem. He tells us that at his famous Sagaponack Pool on Long Island: 'the least sandpipers appeared first, on 6th July, followed within the week by semipalmated sandpipers, lesser yellowlegs, whimbrel, a pectoral sandpiper, and dowitchers, in that order'; nothing surprising in this. It fits my own observations. But his following sentence, on page 109, is, to my mind, startling and slightly unexpected: 'Preparations for long-distance flight demand a great part of the wind-bird's year [Matthiesen's 'wind-bird' is Abel Chapman's 'globe-spanner'], and birds nesting on Alaska's northern coasts begin to form migration flocks as early as late June.' But when do they begin to breed in northern Alaska? Surely not before early June. So how can the breeding-birds be ready to collect into flocks before the end of that month? Matthiesen confirms my impression that after the July migration wave there is usually a gap of several weeks before the main mass of wader migration from the north sets in. Does not this later migration include not only the birds of the year but also all those that have bred successfully?

in late February or early March. But I soon began to see things that undermined this view.

I first made the discovery that normal southward migration may continue into the early days of January in the winter of 1920–21; and I published a note about it in *British Birds* (vol. XIV, pp. 232–3) which I think is still worth transcribing, on the principle that an ounce of fact is worth a ton of general statement; and also because, from what I have or have not seen in the subsequent fifty years, I think these observations were slightly unusual. It will be seen that at least five species were involved.

'I was at Dungeness from 30th December, 1920, to 3rd January, 1921. 31st December was wet and stormy; 1st January less windy but very wet after 10 a.m.; 2nd January wet and stormy; and 3rd January sunny with hardly any wind. The temperature was well above the average all the time, and 3rd January would have done credit to the south of Italy. I believe similar conditions prevailed generally over our islands and the neighbouring parts of Europe. The shingle bushes, in which there are often a few Pipits and Linnets, as well as Larks, in mid-winter, were exceptionally empty. I saw nothing but Larks in them.

'At dawn on 1st January I rather thought I heard a Brambling's note but as I did not hear it again I inferred that I had imagined it. Before sunrise on 3rd January a Meadow Pipit came flying south along the shingle towards the point, and during the following hour or more (8–9 a.m.) small parties of Linnets and a few Greenfinches were frequently passing, flying in directions between south and west. A few of these seemed to have come in from the east, but they may only have been flying parallel to the coast a little way out, and come in at the point. Most of the morning I was on Littlestone sands, where I saw two Skylarks flying in from the east, but I could not be sure they had not been feeding nearer the sea.

'About 11.15 I saw a party of about fifteen Linnets flying steadily south over Littlestone sandhills. On my return to the point I specially crossed the ground on which finches commonly settle, but I found none that had alighted. About 1.15 I heard a Goldfinch flying (apparently) west or south-west; and a moment later two or three Linnets going in the same direction. Apparently this was about the end of the day's migration. In fact, the whole thing was just like a rather poor migration day in October or early November.'

When we began to keep our family migrant records, Christopher rejected an early December House Martin that Wilfrid had seen, on the ground that it was probably a bird that had failed to migrate and would stay in England and die. Later observations have led me to doubt this view. At Dungeness or Portland Bill, the two south coast stations best known to me, you may see passerine birds, such as Skylarks, Starlings or finches arriving from east or south-east across the English Channel at any time in December, or even in early January. In another chapter I have given evidence that suggests that Firecrests may spend some weeks at a late autumn station, and then move on again, presumably further south or west, in late December or January.

After heavy snowfalls or severe frost, there may be extensive weather movements of ground-feeding birds, Lapwings, thrushes, Skylarks and others, at any time in the winter. These should not be regarded as normal migratory movements, even though they may carry the birds for some hundreds of miles. Often a return movement will follow when the weather ameliorates.

Even apart from this, strange things can occur at almost any time during the winter. On a mild January day about 1907, we were starting out for a morning's walk from our home at Tunbridge Wells when a small flock of Linnets flew past us at the top of Tunbridge Wells common going rapidly north. They seemed to be following the ridge, and so would have several miles of built-up town before finding any open country to feed in. Now, Linnets are scarce birds in winter about Tunbridge Wells; the country does not (or at least in those days apparently did not) seem to suit their winter feeding habits. Many of the English breeding Linnets are known to be migrants that cross the Channel and spend the winter in continental Europe. A single observation of this sort does not by itself prove anything; but it suggested to us then, as it still does to me, that those birds were shifting their winter quarters in a manner that was, to say the least, akin to a regular spring migration. On 14th January 1909, while we were watching Dartford Warblers on the top of the main ridge of Ashdown Forest, Sussex, some twelve miles from Tunbridge Wells, a Linnet flew over going north. Here too, it is far from any likely feeding ground for Linnets in winter. In the diary I then kept, in which I recorded this, I added: 'I think a line of flight of these birds [Linnets] must pass over the top of Ashdown Forest about here.' In other words, I had seen them fly north (? and south) in that area before.

Here is another record, from the same month of the same year. On

22nd January I left Southampton by ship for Marseilles. On the 23rd, while we were still off the north coast of Brittany, about midday 'a flock of about fifty Skylarks flew over the boat, going northwards; it was pleasant thus to have a proof of migration as early as this across the Channel to England'. I have more recent evidence, from observations in Dorset, that Lapwings also migrate north across the Channel in January, indeed, as early as 1st January. These northward movements, as far as my observation goes, seem to follow not long after weather movements have driven birds south from what is perhaps their 'preferred' winter quarters. But I confess I find it odd. Do birds really have a 'preferred' area for winter quarters? And is this preference so strongly built into their systems that, after a few days of mild winter weather, they will take a long flight, including a hundred-mile sea crossing, in order to return to the preferred area? How, indeed, do birds 'know'? or even do they know, when their territories, in winter or in summer, are ready for them? I recall that, one spring, whilst he was in central Italy, Christopher noted that the Alpine Pipits that winter along the coast of Latium, and breed in the high mountains, had stayed later by the coast than in other years. And, he added, it was also true that the mountains had remained snow-covered later. 'Do they,' he wrote playfully, 'fly up into the air and look to see whether the snow has gone?' Presumably not; but what *does* tell them?

Reverting to the topic of January migration, here is an observation I once made in south Asia, quite near to the Equator. On 12th January 1928, when the ship was approaching Penang from Colombo (we reached Penang on the 13th), a thrush of some sort flew round the boat for some time and then disappeared southwards, presumably to reach Sumatra. Now, what should a thrush be doing at that time of the year migrating across the Indian Ocean? No 'weather movement', at least. Therefore I can assume that this was as genuine a migratory flight as if it had been the middle of October. This is another way of saying that the urge to migrate long distances, not to escape some sudden acute food shortage, but because of some intense inner compulsion, can carry a bird far further than apparent necessity demands, in January no less than in earlier months from July to November. Or, let us say, there is no time of year when the migratory impulse may not dominate the action of some bird of the northern hemisphere.

PART III

In recent years some new terms have come into vogue among migration experts, as in so many other fields. When first I read about 'visible migration', I could make no sense of it. To be sure, plenty of bird migration takes place at night, when it cannot be seen by man; and much migration goes on at heights above the earth that are beyond the range of ordinary vision. 'Visible migration' is not the whole of migration.

Many of the researches carried out by British ornithologists in the nineteenth and early twentieth centuries were concerned with invisible migration. The British Association conducted an enquiry into migration as it can be observed at lighthouses round the coast; but hardly any of this is visible migration in the strict sense. Birds that rest or flit around lighthouses are not migrating; they are interrupting their migrations. The lighthouse observer may record the days when many birds appear, and other days with few or none; but this really tells us very little about the migration pattern. It does not tell us where the birds have come from or where they are going.

In the early years of this century, from 1905 to 1914, the British Ornithologists' Club conducted a similar enquiry; and I enthusiastically participated in this, year by year. This time, ordinary field observers were encouraged to note the times of arrival of migrant species all over the country, including the numbers present from day to day. But, once again, it was not visible migration in action that we were invited to record, but only the fluctuating numbers of birds to be found, day by day. It was still assumed, I think, that the process of migration was almost entirely nocturnal, and therefore was almost wholly invisible.

Yet anyone who walks about the countryside, especially if he lives near the coast, will soon discern, if he keeps his eyes open, that birds can be seen migrating. Much more migration takes place by day than was formerly recognised, and not all of it is too high above the earth to be visible to the naked eye. But it is not always easy to say whether the birds one sees flying over are migrating or not. Something, of course, depends on one's definition of 'migration'. Were those Linnets that we saw flying rapidly north over Tunbridge Wells common one day in January migrating? It is impossible to say. Or the Skylarks already flying north over the English Channel in late January? Many years later I happened to see Meadow Pipits flying south-west, parallel to the English coast, but out of sight of land, in the Straits of Dover, as late as 1st November. I had no hesitation in calling this 'migration'. Why? Because the birds were flying in the appropriate direction, at the right time of the year, and showing no inclination to find the first resting place.

Much migration follows coast-lines, where coast-lines exist; so, if you watch at such places as Dungeness Point or Portland Bill, to name two of the best vantage points for observation on the south coast of England, you can soon see massive migration movements. The first time I was able to witness this kind of large-scale visible migration was in October 1914, when I spent three weeks at Dungeness, and watched the migratory movements every day. Whatever the weather (and it was often stormy) almost every morning large numbers of small passerine birds, chiefly finches, came flying south along the beach from the direction of Littlestone; and it was interesting to watch their actions when they found the right-angle turn of the shore. Having watched the Dungeness migration many times since, I can summarise by saying that some continue out over the sea, some rest for a time on the shingle near the Point before continuing their journey, and some round the Point and continue to fly along the coast westward. But the 'visible migration' at Dungeness is much more complex than this, and it deserves a fuller treatment.

Most of my watching was done on the Point of Dungeness or just north of it. This position gave one the opportunity to observe three main autumn movements and their points of convergence: birds that came in on an east to west route, off the sea, mainly Starlings and larks in October; those that came south along the coast from the direction of Littlestone, most of them finches; and smaller numbers from the north-west, coming across the beach. Those that came in from the east mostly continued their journey, west or north-west (in *British Birds* it is printed 'east or north-east'—how I came to pass that in the proofs I cannot imagine), whilst the other two streams tended to get confused on reaching the Point. Some continued across the sea, but usually the flocks began to fly round and round, and either settled for a time or continued to follow the coast to the west. Earlier in the season I had seen Swallows flying south over the marsh, but changing course, to fly west or south-west before they even reached the coast. Other Swallows would come in from the Continent on an east–west route and would then change course to fly south-west along the coast or parallel to it.

Even this summary is a simplification. The visible movement varies a great deal with the wind—and with the season. In both spring and autumn one may see birds migrating in almost any direction at Dungeness Point. Visible migration, which means inevitably migration close to the ground, can be very misleading. Birds that are in the main streams of full long-distance migration high overhead may be following a steady course in their 'preferred direction', while birds of the same species, which for one reason or another are flying close to the ground, may be deflected into all kinds of apparently perverse and illogical movements by the air currents near the earth. Such birds, for instance, for some reason very often fly for long distances into the wind, though this must increase the amount of flying they need to reach their destination. Such movements, though they probably do not represent a very large proportion of the actual migration, must nevertheless represent something and should not be ignored. Dungeness is a very good place for observing the extraordinary complexity of migrational flight.

CHAPTER VII

Dungeness and Romney Marsh

Look at the map of England, and you see a sharp corner pointing towards the coast of France. One would naturally expect to find high cliffs there, but in fact there are no cliffs. Dungeness Point is composed of a vast accumulation of shingle which has been thrown up over many centuries by the tides working up Channel from the chalk cliffs of Beachy Head, and down Channel from the chalk cliffs round Dover. Between this great shingle beach and the 'true' English coast a great marsh slowly developed. All this is now drained—overdrained in recent years, but not when I used to walk all day across the marsh fifty years ago—so that if you stand on one of the higher ridges of Dungeness beach and look north and west you see the English hills rising out of the marsh fifteen or twenty miles away.

'They do say this is the fifth quarter of the globe, whatever that may mean,' said a local inhabitant to me one day long ago, as we sat talking in the Woolpack Inn. The Woolpack is as remote as any inn in the South of England, or it was before the invention of the motor car; it is not in any village; in the days when I knew it, it was nearly surrounded by deep marsh ditches. In all directions there stretched away acres of green grass, the feeding ground of thousands of Romney Marsh sheep. Two winding marshland roads met near the inn; on one corner there was a gate with a cart track leading through it. If you went through this gate, and if you carried with you a set of six-inch-to-the-mile maps to show you where small bridges crossed the ditches, you could walk across the marsh for five or six miles, passing several badly drained sections, the haunt of water-birds, and in the end you came to the dirt road near Jury Gap, the point where, seven miles west of Dungeness Point, the shingle ended and the marsh began: called Jury Gap because it was the place where the sea was most likely to break through. Today, you can still follow that same route to what is still called the 'bird sanctuary'; but the marsh has been so effectively drained that instead of 'fleets' that attract rare ducks and waders, you will find dry ground producing crops of beans, cereals or potatoes.

Dungeness beach itself is not so easily transformed by human ingenuity. Many years ago, as I sat in the train that used to run from Lydd to the Dungeness lighthouse, a fellow traveller commented, as the train came over the first shingle banks: 'This is the last place God made, and he forgot to finish it.' Which really does give some idea of the strange nature of Dungeness beach. No wonder there are odd plants and moths and frogs on Dungeness beach. It can, indeed, look very beautiful at certain seasons; as, for instance, when the grassy strips among the shingle come to life with splendid groves of fox-gloves in full flower, or when the soft blue of the Sheepsbit, *Jasione montana*, clothes these ridges. Some sections are bright with the gold of gorse or of broom in their seasons. Even when there are no gay flowers, the great shingle banks are not necessarily gloomy to the human eye. Many of the stones are a warm brown colour; not all are grey. As you walk across the beach, you find some ridges composed of larger stones, many of them grey and flinty; others are composed of much smaller stones, mostly brown; and in the main it is these smaller stones that have become partly grass and plant covered. No doubt small particles of sand and other material, in which plants can grow, settle more easily among the small stones. But it is amazing how many plants manage to root themselves and flourish even among the stones close to Dungeness Point, where they may have had only fifty years to begin their colonisation, since the stones were thrown up from the sea. Here, at midsummer, the bright yellow Horn Poppy flourishes, together with intense blue Viper's Bugloss, Sea Holly, and a few plants of the rare Sea Pea, *Lathyrus japonicus*.

My first visit to Dungeness was at the beginning of August 1905. We were staying at Rye for a few days, and we decided to go by train to Dungeness and spend the day there. This then meant taking the Ashford train from Rye to Appledore (the next station) and changing; then came the train down from Ashford, and when it had left Appledore a special train took passengers across the marsh to Lydd, where again we changed, to wait while our train went to New Romney and back; then it made its separate journey to Dungeness lighthouse! It sounds complicated and tedious, but apart from the necessity of climbing in and out of trains three times it was not as bad as it sounds. The trains were arranged to connect, and as far as I recall, the whole journey took little more than an hour. Even today, when there is a road from Lydd to Dungeness (there was none in 1905) the journey by car from Rye to Dungeness would normally take half an hour or more, with so many right-angle turns along the marsh roads.

Unfortunately, that day in August 1905 was wet. It rained steadily all day. My parents sat in the small shed at Dungeness station and read or wrote. But when we had had our lunch I ventured out to look for some of the rare birds that were reputed to visit Dungeness. I found some Common Terns near the sea. That was quite enough for a sixteen year old. They were the first terns of any kind I had ever seen. The day before I had identified a Kentish Plover on the shore at Rye. A few pairs of this bird, now no longer a regular breeding species in England, then nested on the shingle banks near the mouth of the Rother at Rye (in Sussex, not Kent) in addition to the fair-sized colony that still bred every year on the beach between Dungeness and New Romney.

Three years later, on 1st July 1908, I was introduced to Dungeness more appropriately by Fred Austen, who had been appointed official watcher of the Dungeness breeding birds by the Royal Society for the Protection of Birds. At that time he still lived in Lydd, with his wife and daughter. He spent a great part of each summer's day walking out onto the pathless beach to keep a watch on the nests of Kentish Plovers and Stone Curlews. He showed us (Christopher and myself) Stone Curlews' nests that day, and he found the young birds crouching on the ground beside the low broom bushes where they were only to be detected by a practised eye.

A year or two later, the Austens moved into a bungalow close to Dungeness Point, north of the foghorn, where you could watch all the Channel shipping and the passing seabirds from the front window. Over the years I spent very many hours at those windows or on the beach just outside. From here Austen was in a much better position to control the Kentish Plovers, although even so he had a couple of miles to walk over open beach before he was really on their territory. Under such circumstances it was obviously impossible for him to guarantee these birds' safety from a really determined egg collector, of whom, alas, England had a plentiful supply. The Austens' bungalow remained as a refuge for birdwatchers right through the first world war, when it was once bombed, till the second world war, when it was taken over by the military and finally demolished. Fred Austen had died before the second world war, but his wife had to leave the old bungalow, and she and her daughter were unable to return to it.

I have known five generations of that family. Austen's father-in-law, Mr Mills, kept the Hope and Anchor Inn, nearly two miles west of Dungeness Point, where a rough road reaches the sea. Once or twice, when we stayed at the Austens' before the first war, I slept at the Hope and Anchor and walked across the beach before breakfast and after supper, as we could not all be accommodated by Mrs Austen. Mr Mills was over eighty then. A year or two later he died in his chair, and Mrs Mills went to live for her last few years with the Austens. Then their daughter, who had become Mrs Nelson Freathy (the Freathys are an old local family) gave birth to a son; so, when the house was bombed in October 1916, four generations were living there. Happily, nobody was hurt; the room where I had often slept was the only one that was badly damaged. The one room that was quite undamaged was the kitchen, where the adults were all sitting that evening.

Jack Tart, member of another old Lydd or Dungeness family, was appointed R.S.P.B. watcher a year or two after Austen. His territory consisted of the whole of the beach to the west of Dungeness Point. For many years he had a large ternery to protect. He was a younger man than Austen, and I went long walks with him over the beach at all times of the year, in all weathers. We were sometimes soaked to the skin.

In those days all the local people wore wooden slats under their boots with a leather strap over the toe, to help them in walking over the shingle, and to protect their shoe leather. These slats were called 'backstays'. It was an art to keep them from slipping off the shoe, an art I never mastered. You could hear people going cloppety-clop a long way off. If the footsteps came nearer and nearer, a caller could be expected. No one could arrive unannounced. Mrs Austen's brother, who was the Dungeness postman for some forty years, must have walked more miles on backstays than any other man. For some reason which I never understood, he and his wife lived quite alone, miles from any other human beings, four miles north of Dungeness, not far from the sand dunes of Greatstone. So, every morning throughout the year, except Sundays, he had first to walk three or more miles to the post office to collect the mail, which had been brought by a horse-drawn cart across the beach from Lydd. Next he would walk all round the beach, perhaps a total distance of four or five miles, to deliver the mail; finally he had to walk home again. I believe he often did the walk between his house and Dungeness Point twice in the day, so presumably he walked twelve miles or more every day. When he finally retired, his nephew, Austen's son-in-law, Nelson Freathy, became postman. By then, no doubt, the number of Dungeness residents had increased, so the amount of walking over the beach within a mile of the Point was greater. But at least he did not have those long walks to and from the Greatstone end of the beach to traverse early and late. Before he died, there were some roads to mitigate the shingle walking, but I believe he used backstays to the end. Today I think they are extinct.

Fred Austen and Jack Tart were men of very different temperament. Austen had been a wildfowler when he was young, with a typical countryman's nature lore. He knew some birds well, but others not at all. He was proud of a stuffed Ruddy Shelduck in a case, and he liked to tell of the long chase over the pools to the west of Dungeness before he could get near enough to shoot this very wild duck. Another of his chases over the Holmstone, perhaps in the 1880s, before they became the Lydd ranges, was in pursuit of a great eagle, presumably a Sea Eagle, but in that case the bird got away. Once, when I was out on the marshes, Austen, bait digging at low tide on the Littlestone sands, saw two tired Spoonbills come in over the sea and settle on the sands. There they rested for some time, but when the tide came up they flew right away again, and no one else saw them. One very stormy day (16th March 1914) I was watching from the front window at the Austens' bungalow as quantities of gulls congregated on the top of the beach, just above high water. They were barely fifty yards away. Suddenly a fine adult Iceland Gull appeared among them. I knew that Austen was having his afternoon nap in the back room, but I thought he should not miss such an exciting bird. So I went through and roused him. When he had looked at the Iceland Gull his only comment was: 'Oh yes, I often see them on the beach.'

Jack Tart, as far as I know, never carried a gun in his life. He was a 'learner', always wanting to know something more about birds. The R.S.P.B. had given him a copy of Saunders' *Manual of British Birds*, at that time much the best small book available. This book he constantly used. It helped him to identify several rare birds that he found on the beach, including a male Rock Thrush and the corpse of the first British Bridled Tern. At that time, as an R.S.P.B. watcher, with the famous Mrs Lemon at headquarters in London, he knew that he had no business to be associated with any dead bird! Awkward questions might be asked. So the bird was recorded by the Dover taxidermist, Mannering (to whom Tart had got it as quickly as possible—it was almost too far gone to preserve) as if he had himself found the corpse on the beach. I corresponded with Witherby about the record after it had been published in *British Birds*, as I already knew the story from Jack Tart. Witherby found that the facts were as I thought.

For some twenty years I corresponded with Jack Tart between my visits, and I shall be quoting from his letters; they help to give a picture of what was happening at Dungeness in the twenties and thirties. Jack Tart was only fifty-eight when he died, a victim of cancer.

When we first began to know Dungeness, its main attraction was its breeding birds: Terns, Common and Little, Kentish and Ringed Plovers, Stone Curlews and a few others. The colony of Common Gulls, the only known breeding place for them south of the Scottish border, was not founded until 1919. In the 1941 edition of Witherby's *Handbook*, it is claimed that the number of pairs had then grown to more than thirty. I remember how excited Norman Ticehurst was when the first breeding occurred. Today the number is, I believe, very much reduced, if, indeed, any still breed on the beach.

I have said that Fred Austen and Jack Tart were employed by the R.S.P.B. to guard the rare breeding birds. Something more needs to be said about this; and first we must look at it from the London end. When I first joined the R.S.P.B., about 1914, it was still a fairly new organisation though already it had been granted the right to call itself 'Royal'. It is, I think, not unfair to say that at that time and for many years it was dominated by the personality of Mrs Frank Lemon of Redhill. Her husband, who was a lawyer, was the Honorary

The Alexander brothers at Dungeness, c.1951. W. B. Alexander is examining a bird taken in a nearby trap.

Above, from a colour snapshot of the author and his wife between Bert and Joan Axell, Swanage 1965. *Below*, Salim Ali with the author near Bombay, 1971.

Secretary; and Mrs Lemon's only official position was Hon. Sec. of the Watchers Committee, but she was in the office most days of the week. She knew exactly what she wanted the R.S.P.B. to do, and she usually got her way. Her colleague, Miss Linda Gardiner, who edited the Society's journal, *Bird Notes and News*, used to refer to the Council, on which I served for over twenty years, as 'the rubber stamp'. This was not an unfair description. There was no point in fighting Mrs Lemon. She would defeat you sooner or later. I decided quite early on that the best plan was to go along with her, and try to be sure that the birds did not suffer.

The R.S.P.B. was not very well off. In those days, the idea of supporting a man all through the year to protect birds was regarded as impossibly expensive and quite unpractical. After all, it was argued, the birds only needed to be protected through the breeding season, and you could not support a man in idleness for eight months in order to protect the breeding birds for four months. So the plan was to find some local man, a fisherman if it was a bit of the coast that needed watching, and pay him for a part-time watch during the breeding season. It was understood that this must not interfere with his earning his livelihood. It will be seen at once that this was an unsatisfactory arrangement. The would-be egg-snatcher had only to find out when the watcher was off fishing or bait-digging (that meant several hours of low-tide at Dungeness) and he could be sure of several hours in which he would be free to find and take the eggs. To be sure, at Dungeness, anyone wandering at large over the beach could be seen for miles. And there really was nothing to induce anyone to wander about on the beach except egg-collecting, or, conceivably, some more innocent form of nature study.

Under the circumstances, it is remarkable that the protection was as effective as it was. In the twenties and thirties, we did in fact provide the two men who were the senior watchers with an adequate living wage for the summer months; and they also had a retaining fee for the rest of the year. Undoubtedly, they did give the whole day to their work, day after day, in May and June—all through the longest days—and by that time they both had assistants. Austen, in particular, was getting old.

There is always plenty of 'politics', unhappily, in bird preservation, as in most other human activities in this world. For some years, about 1930, I think, the Mayor of New Romney became interested in the protection of the local birds. He wanted to have a finger in the pie.

That made quite a lot of sense. But it was not Mrs Lemon's way. She was determined to keep the control of the Watchers in her own hands and I have no doubt that was their preference too.

Then rumours began to spread that the beach between Littlestone and Dungeness, the northern area, where the postman did his daily walk and where the Kentish Plovers were nesting, was going to be developed. Faced by this threat, an elderly member of the Watchers Committee from Lancashire, R. B. Burrows, heroically decided to put most of his life-savings into buying the threatened part of the beach. Soon after, he retired from business, bought a small house in Lydd, where I stayed with him once or twice, and remained there till he died. He lived to see the ruin of most of his hopes. The sea-front of the northern beach had been reserved; and soon a road was built, and the bungalows began creeping along it. Today, summer bungalows are strung most of the way from the Greatstone sandhills to Dungeness Point.

The only regular colony of Kentish Plovers in England had for a good many years nested on this beach, north of Dungeness. In the middle of the nineteenth century, the species nested plentifully on the beach both north and west of Dungeness. A Lydd doctor, Plomley by name, discovered them and spent many happy hours watching them. Unfortunately, he gave the information to Yarrell, the author of what was to be for many years the standard book on British birds, and Yarrell published the locality in his first edition (1837–43).

Later in life, Dr Plomley wrote some notes, which were made available to Dr Norman Ticehurst when he published his *Birds of Kent*. 'I believe,' wrote Plomley, 'I was the first to make known of this bird being a regular visitant to this country, and much more numerous than was formerly thought; so rare was it supposed to be before the publication of the first edition of Yarrell's *Birds* that, with one or two exceptions, no British-killed specimens could be found in public or private collections. Since then the demand for them has been so great that persons from London and the north of England have been regular annual visitants to Dungeness shingle for the express purpose of obtaining specimens, and to my great regret hundreds have thus been destroyed.'

Let Ticehurst continue the story up to 1909:

'Since Plomley wrote Dungeness has been almost the only locality in the British Isles whence specimens have been obtained for public and private collections, and not a year has passed until quite recently without the birds being constantly harassed and shot to satisfy a demand which is ever greater than the supply.... The eggs, we know, were constantly taken both by collectors from a distance and by the local people to supply the ever-ready markets of the dealers, but the birds are naturally persistent, and will go on laying even up till the beginning of August, so that there was always a good chance of a number of pairs rearing their young. The chief cause to my mind of the almost successful extermination of the species was the shooting of the old birds during the breeding season, which went on more or less every year until the appointment of an authorised watcher. As recently as 1902 I received information of twenty-one being killed, of which at least six pairs were old birds shot during the breeding season. Another factor that has been detrimental to their increase has been the shooting in August. At this time young and old are to be found in flocks on the sands and, being very tame, large numbers not only fell to the gun of the "pot hunter", but I have it on good authority that professional collectors were in the habit of firing into the flocks and picking up the adult birds only, leaving the dead and dying on the sands to fall a prey to the rooks and gulls.' It is to be noted that, according to the law of the time, the Kentish Plover was a strictly protected species in England throughout the year; but several of the species with which they consorted on the sands in August and September, Dunlins, Ringed Plovers and the rest, were not protected. So the gunner could always claim that he was shooting at the non-protected birds.

Yet when Ticehurst wrote, after a few years of protection, he was able to give an encouraging account. The shooting on the breeding grounds had ceased entirely (I must say that I never heard of this in the period after 1907 when I came to know Dungeness well). Between 1870 and 1900 the number of pairs still nesting on the beach was reduced to about fifteen. In 1902 there was an increase, but some were shot, and 1903 was a bad year.

However, in 1905, the first year of protection, Austen knew of twenty-one pairs that reared young; in 1906 about forty-four pairs were found, and in 1907 and 1908 between thirty and forty. This is as far as Ticehurst takes us. What happened after that?

In the *Handbook of British Birds* (vol. IV, pp. 361–2) Witherby gives the last breeding date for Dungeness as 1931. Why did the remnant disappear? I do not think there is any very clear answer. Shooting had stopped, unless an occasional bird was shot on the sands in August and

September, but egg-collecting had not, and the rarer a species became the more determined became the craze of the collectors ('craze' is the only adequate word) to obtain a genuine British egg. Eggs from the Mediterranean or other parts of the breeding range of this widely distributed species were presumably identical in appearance; so the only proof that a particular egg had been taken in England was the label attached to it. But, so it was; and I do not think it was possible for the watchers to prevent an expert collector from raiding the Kentish Plover ground in the early hours of the long June days. So the egg-collectors must remain under suspicion, although I do not think there is any proof that they were responsible. The bungalow-building along the beach from Greatstone to within a mile of Dungeness Point came after the Kentish Plovers had disappeared. Possibly this would have driven them off a few years later, but not necessarily. I believe quite a number of Ringed Plovers still breed on that desolate waste behind the line of bungalows, bringing food for their young across from the sands and the tide-line.

It has also been suggested that Ringed Plovers have increased, displacing the Kentish Plovers. I am not sure that there is clear proof either of such an increase, or that they tended to drive the smaller species off their chosen breeding grounds.

I was intimate with Jack Tart from the time of the first world war, or even earlier, until his death. He often wrote letters to me. From 1922 onwards most of these letters are still in my possession. Beyond his reports to the R.S.P.B. office and letters to Mrs Lemon, and also his daily diary, these letters probably give as good a picture of what was happening at Dungeness in the twenties and thirties as anything now available. Although the Kentish Plovers nested on the ground controlled by Austen and George Tart, not by Jack, he made a point of telling me what he could about the Kentish Plover situation, year by year. So I quote his letters here. It will be noted that in the years between 1908 and 1924 the number is already slightly reduced. The first reference to the breeding of the 'Kentish' is in a letter dated 21st May 1924, as follows:

'There are about eight pairs of Kentish on the beach and I should say about thirty running about on the sands. The weather here is now very fine and warm which ought to bring them all on to the nesting grounds.' Unfortunately, the reports in his letters for the next few years are defective; either I visited Dungeness during the breeding season, or some of his letters are lost. Thus, on 3rd June 1926 he was only able to say: 'I cannot say really how many Kentish there are on the Littlestone Beach. I have had no time to go there yet. I dont see much of Austen it being so late before we finish. I must see George Tart as to how many Kentish have hatched off.' But there is no record in my letters beyond this for that year. For 1927 and 1928 there is no reference to Kentish in any of the few letters I have; in 1929 he writes on 8th May: 'I hear the Kentish Plovers have not arrived in good numbers yet. Perhaps the cold weather has checked them a bit.' And the next letter is dated September. In 1930 the letters are more complete again, but the picture is not good. On 7th May he wrote: 'George Tart tells me he has a Kentish with three eggs hard sitting and ought to hatch out in a few days and there are three other pairs he knows of round about.' Then, on 10th July: 'I am writing to say we had a very successful season with the Birds although the Kentish were not so plentiful as we should like but we knew of five lots hatched which means fifteen chicks and other Kentish were seen about the beach so I should think there were about eight pairs.'

On 30th July 1931 he wrote: 'Stone Curlew are still increasing and the Kentish about the same as last year.' 1932 seems to have been the year of the crash. Writing on 3rd August Jack Tart said: 'There was not a single nest of Kentish found on the Littlestone beach but four birds were seen from time to time. I have reason to believe that Kentish nested on the west side about a mile from Galloways near the South Brooks.' Again in 1933: 'Kentish Plover very poor. I don't think any nests were found again this season, but four birds were seen by the Watchers.' However, by the next summer he had heard of one pair succeeding in 1933, as the following letter shows: 'June 18th, '34 ... There was a pair of Kentish near the water tower. George Tart saw them and I have heard them since. I remember Kentish nesting there many years ago quite regularly ... one Kentish nest was found last season near the butts on the military grounds, she had three eggs and from what I heard got away with it.' So to 1935. Writing on 19th July, Jack Tart says: 'George Tart says only one Kentish have they seen at Great Stones and that went off somewhere else.' His last letter to me about Kentish Plovers is written on 10th July 1936. He wrote: 'By what I can gather three Kentish Plovers were seen on the sands at Great Stone but where they went seems a mystery as no nest was found, I really think they still nest in some isolated spot in Dungeness just two or three pairs would not be noticed. In time they may increase.' But, alas, they did not.

Jack Tart's own territory, to the west of Dungeness Point, covered an area west of the Hope and Anchor Inn, where there was a large ternery, which he fostered and saw grow and expand during his twenty years of daily activity. Naturally, his letters to me report much more fully about this ternery than about Austen's Kentish Plovers. His most important discovery was the regular breeding of Arctic Terns, whose presence so far to the south of their normal breeding range was regarded with considerable scepticism. So, even today, the evidence may be worth publishing at some length. The ternery was destroyed during the second world war when the Lydd firing ranges were extended. Fortunately, Jack Tart did not live to see that catastrophe.

His first letter on the subject of the Arctic Terns was written on 15th June 1923. He had written to me on 15th May, so another letter so soon was unexpected. The Arctic Terns were, of course, the reason:

'I am writing to inform you we have the Arctic Tern nesting among the Common. I found one nest with two young yesterday 14th. I spent about two hours watching the parent birds feeding the young and there is no doubt they are Arctic. I had a good view really close to the nest which was on a small shingle patch very much like the Ringed Plover use and the nest was made of small white stones. The parent birds' beaks are blood red right out to the point and I noticed the forked tail was much longer than the Common and the call note is much different; I cannot give it here will tell you just how they go on when I see you again: I'm sure you will be glad to hear of this.' Later he continues: 'There are still Sandwich Tern about along the shore and sometimes on the nesting grounds of the Common Tern. I cannot really make out why they don't nest.'

He wrote again a month later, 16th July: 'Everything is going well with the birds thanks to the fine weather which has helped the Terns wonderfully; there were three pairs of Arctic and all had young. I have no doubt the Arctic were here in previous seasons but I was not able to detect them from the Common they are so much alike; now I know them well I hope to find their eggs next season. The Sandwich I could not find on the protected area of Dungeness but I firmly believe there must be a colony not many miles from Dungeness as I have seen the parent birds with fish in their beaks flying westwards towards Rye.'

On 5th June 1924 he wrote: 'I am writing to tell you the two Arctic Tern have nested and will soon be hatching.' Here is his report for 1925: 'June 10th.... The birds are doing exceedingly well this beautiful fine weather. The Thicknee [Stone Curlew] are all hatched and practically all the Kentish [Plovers]. The Common and Lesser Tern are hatching out fast and I am pleased to say the Arctic are there again this season. Mr Rudge Harding [a member of the R.S.P.B. Watchers Committee] was down at Dungeness on Sat. last 6th. I took him to see the Arctic which had then one chick and one egg. I also had the pleasure of pointing out the Sandwich Terns which happened to be passing. Unfortunately I cannot find their nests.... There have been several Black Terns going east since last I wrote you surely this is late for migration.' In 1926 he only recorded one Arctic Tern's nest. In 1927 he wrote (7th June): 'This season I really think the Terns are more plentiful than ever. The Arctic are nesting [but he does not say how many] and there is one Roseate amongst the Common; has been there for about a fortnight. I cannot yet see its mate.'

In a letter dated 21st July 1927 he records seeing 'a very strange Tern at first I could not make it out on closer examination I found it to be a Whiskered Tern. I spent all the morning of June 10th watching it to make sure.' Unfortunately that is all. Probably it was a Whiskered Tern; but under modern scrutiny the lack of any adequate description means that it cannot be acceptable as a valid record.

Letters for the breeding seasons of 1929 and 1930 are missing; but in 1930 he wrote (10th July): 'The Terns were about the same or perhaps rather more with several Arctic as last season: the Sandwich I'm sorry to say did not nest.' In 1931 he wrote (30th July): 'The Terns were more numerous than ever and we had two pairs of Roseate there for about six weeks and I really believe one pair nested only the Common kept driving her off her nest.' 1932: 'Several Arctic and one Roseate.' 1933: 'Common and Arctic Tern about the same as last season.' 1934 (18th June): 'Several Arctic have hatched along the seaweed near the shore. They are much bolder than the Common.' In the same letter: 'I have seen two pairs of Roseate Tern on the western end of the ternery I am wondering what is going to happen in the way of nesting'; but my letters do not relate what did happen.

A letter of 20th May 1935 at last records the nesting of Sandwich Terns: 'I am writing to say the Sandwich Tern have at last nested on the western beach near the Ternery. I found one nest with one egg and saw the bird go down to it.... There is two pairs of Roseate Tern to be seen hanging about the Ternery. I have great hopes of them nesting too. I saw four Black Terns feeding along the shore they of course were just on passage to the north, what beautiful birds they are.'

Later that season a Sooty Tern spent a day at the ternery. Jack Tart wrote on 19th July: 'I saw on June 29th one Sooty Tern on the Ternery; it remained there for that day but was gone the next.' I wrote and asked him for fuller details, and he replied (29th July): 'About that Sooty Tern: I am quite sure it must have been Sooty it had the white frontal band like the Lesser Tern underparts pure white upperparts or back sooty black, rather larger than the Common Tern.' I was at Dungeness later that summer, and wrote the following points on the side of his first letter, following a talk with him about it: 'Sooty Tern seen with Mr Baker [whom I cannot now identify] from watcher's hut. From N. over the ternery, mobbed by the other terns; then went over the sea and disappeared. Half an hour later it came back along the coast, moving up to the east and fishing. Very dark on back and light below, slower wing-beat than the Common, and larger. Shorter in tail. J.R.T. has seen one many years ago.'

After this we begin to find his health giving way and he has a time in hospital at Folkestone; but he was able to continue his work during the season of 1936, though his nephew George Tart, who for many years had assisted Fred Austen in looking after the northern beach, now undertook the regular watching on the ternery. He had already reported the arrival of a Roseate Tern by the end of April. But this year neither that nor Sandwich nested.

My last letter from Jack was written on 15th June 1937. He died in November. This is the relevant part: 'First of all the Roseate has nested on the Ternery near by that old iron tank practically in the same place as in 1934. George Tart tells me she goes on to the nest quite easily so there cannot be any mistake.... Then there is a Sandwich Tern or rather a pair on the west end of the Ternery. G.T. says by the action they too have a nest.'

There are two further documents to quote on the matter of the Arctic Terns breeding at Dungeness. Sometimes I copied Jack Tart's diaries, or extracts from them, before they were deposited at the R.S.P.B. office. Thus, in 1933 I copied the following summary of breeding birds on the beach, under date 5th July:

'Common Gull 5 pairs, Lesser B-b Gull 5 pairs, Lesser Tern c. 40 pairs on west side. Common Tern c. 1000 pairs on west side. Arctic Tern c. 40 pairs on west side, B-h Gull c. 500, Herring Gull c. 400,

Stone Curlew 16–18 pairs over the whole area. Kentish Plover 4 birds seen, no nests.'

The total of about 40 pairs for Arctic seems so much above anything in the letters I have quoted that I might almost suppose I had copied it wrongly and had repeated the Lesser Tern number by mistake. But I find in my Dungeness file a letter from Phyllis Barclay-Smith, written on 23rd June 1932. She had just spent a weekend at Dungeness and was chiefly concerned to see if any Kentish Plovers were still on the beach; she saw none. But this is her paragraph about the Terns: 'The Terns seem to be flourishing and I saw a good number of Arctic among the Common. I saw only one pair of Sandwich.' So perhaps in the thirties the Arctic colony had grown to a good size. The wording of the very brief references to Arctic Terns in the letters Jack Tart wrote me in 1932 and '33, as quoted already, would fit these larger numbers, so I believe they are correct.

Probably the Dungeness beach is becoming less and less attractive for breeding birds. Human activity is encroaching from all sides. When I was there in 1969 I learnt that Stone Curlews were no longer breeding on the beach. That was something of a shock. There are still areas that should suit them well enough, far from any road. Again, it may well be that the reasons for their disappearance are obscure and not related to human interference.

Our discovery of Dungeness as a place for watching birds in winter began with an experience that Christopher had in February 1909. He wrote to me on 22nd February; I was at Hyères, on the Riviera, hence the full account of the weather. As this is relevant to the observations he made at Dungeness, it is worth quoting.

'Since I last wrote (Thursday evening, 18th) I have not seen a cloud; there has been an anticyclone over western Europe, gradually moving towards (or increasing over) our country, so that yesterday it was reported as centred over Denmark and the Netherlands; we have had the wind moving from S.S.E. gradually to E.N.E., but very slight, particularly since Friday (19th). The thermometer charts for the last three weeks are very different: in the first week of the month the curve moved in broad sweeps, practically independent of night and day; in the second week it was mostly a straight line along 30° with a slight rise in the middle of each day. This last week it has been very regular curves for night and day, becoming more and more marked, so that yesterday was the highest maximum ($43\frac{1}{2}°$) and last night the lowest minimum (18°); it is highest at 2 p.m. . . .

'On Saturday (20th) I went down to Littlestone (by bicycle). I left before ten and got there soon after twelve. . . . Arrived on the shore (the tide had only just turned) I as usual looked at the Scoters in the bay; I noticed that some of them seemed to show some pale below at times, and also seemed to have white beaks or foreheads; presently one stood on end and flapped its wings, showing broad bands of white; and another flew along a bit and showed the white: so I had no doubt they were Scaup, and I have confirmed this from descriptions.' These were, I think, the first Scaup that either of us had

identified. Further on, he had close views of 'one of the "other" grebes', and he copied for me the drawing he had done of it. As it had a distinct, tufted head, he concluded from the very inadequate books then available that it was Slavonian, not Eared; the plumage description: 'Black on the head and the rest practically black and white'; 'the beak was very pale grey or pale straw colour, shining in the sun, the feet dark'—all seems to support his identification. This too was what now we call (if we are under American influence) a 'Lifer'.

We must get on with his walk along the four-mile beach to Dungeness. 'In walking on I fairly soon got to where I had to go onto the shingle [it is only at dead low tide that you can walk along wet sand almost to the point of Dungeness]. Before doing so, I saw a Diver asleep on the water with its head in its back, no doubt Red-throated. . . . At last I reached the point and hastened to sit down and eat an apple to slake my thirst; I soon saw a Guillemot and several Divers flying westwards as usual; after I had seen about a dozen go by I began to count them; I soon caught sight of a Great Crested Grebe, but it very soon disappeared; however I found it again later and it stayed up a good while; there were plenty of Herring Gulls flying about. I stayed there about a quarter of an hour, and was walking back for half an hour before I got to where the tide had left the shingle; in that time I had got to 114 Divers flying past; from 65 to 80 and from 96 to 111 were practically in a body: I did not reckon very distant ones that I saw with my glasses while I was counting the nearer ones; so I probably saw close on 150!'

During the next thirty years, I frequently watched seabirds flying past Dungeness Point, at various times of year, though never in February. I never saw 150 Red-throated Divers within the space of an hour or two. Presumably this large movement was the result of the weather; such an anti-cyclone at such a time of year suggests severe cold to the north-east, which drove these birds further west and south. During my many later visits, the birds most often seen in some numbers passing the Point included Scoters, both Common and Velvet, auks, meaning Razorbills and Guillemots, Kittiwakes and other gulls, terns, divers, nearly all Red-throated, Great Crested Grebes, Gannets, various ducks, especially Red-breasted Mergansers, Brent Geese, and a few others. In those days Cormorants were scarce.

I kept full notes of all that I saw. There would often be quite strong movements for an hour or half an hour, then very little for some hours. Sometimes the main movement was down Channel, at other times it was up. Try as I would, I was never able to correlate these movements with changes of tide or wind, with rough seas or smooth, with the hour of the day or with any other special meteorological phenomenon. Presumably all these factors might enter in. It would be reasonable to suppose that some of the movements seen were (or are) quite local, only carrying the birds a few miles, and these might well be influenced chiefly by the tides and the winds. If birds are carried too far from their main feeding grounds by the tides, they will presumably ultimately fly back again to the feeding ground (or water). But at a place like Dungeness, or any other special coastal viewpoint, it is difficult to separate these daily or tidal movements from stronger migratory movements. Occasionally, I had the luck to see a big migratory movement of seabirds. Once it came just as I was obliged to leave on the train. As I stood on the little station platform, close to the lighthouse, I could see flock after flock of Brent Geese and ducks coming up from the south-west, passing near the Point. They were still passing when my train took me away.

Jack Tart kept a daily diary of birds seen for many years. He sent me these diaries at the end of each year, and I then forwarded them to the R.S.P.B., who for a few years sent me typed copies, which I still possess. The original diaries seem to have been lost. He saw the odd skua in almost every month of the year; all, as far as he could tell, were Arctic (*Stercorarius parasiticus*). He may have seen a very occasional petrel, but I believe he only once saw a shearwater. Writing to me on 7th November 1923 he said: 'There has been an occasional Skua off the point and one Shearwater which I saw on the 26th of October. I could not say for certain which kind. It was too far out at sea.'

Here is my own strange experience of shearwaters. On 20th October 1913, I had just arrived at Dungeness with my uncle, Albert Crosfield. We arrived on the midday train and decided to spend half an hour on the beach, looking out to sea, before going in to the lunch that Mrs Austen was preparing for us. As we came over the top of the beach, a party of shearwaters appeared, quite close in, flying down Channel. They were in sight long enough for me to count them: thirteen. In 1914, I was at Dungeness all through the last half of October, and spent hours on the watch from the Point every day. I did not see any shearwaters. But in 1915 the experience of 1913 was repeated. I was able to spend two or three days at Dungeness in late September. On the 23rd I saw a flock of fourteen fly past the point, south-west. These shearwaters looked almost entirely dark; so in my ignorance, at that time shared, I think, by every field ornithologist in Britain, I unhesitatingly recorded them as Sooty Shearwaters; and they appear so in *British Birds*. To the best of my recollection, Witherby did not suggest that they might have been Balearic Shearwaters. W. J. Clarke had recorded the occurrence of Balearic Shearwaters off the Yorkshire coast in autumn in *British Birds* several years before this; and Christopher and I had duly noted this; but we had no idea that this race of *Puffinus puffinus* was so sharply distinct in appearance from the common Manx Shearwater as in fact it is. An almost wholly dark shearwater in British waters in those days was assigned to *P. griseus*; it could be nothing else; especially quite a number together. Now, looking back on it, all that I recall of the observation leads me to conclude that both were flocks of Balearic (*P. p. mauretanicus*). The wing shape was right for this species, wrong for Sooty; the closely packed flock suggests Balearic; they were dark, not blackish. I do not seem to have recorded anywhere what was the visible colour of the under-parts; but as to this, an observation in the Straits of Dover in August 1912 is relevant. Returning from a holiday in Switzerland, on 28th August 1912, we were crossing from Calais to Dover on a very calm day when my cousin Redford Harris and I spotted a shearwater flying quite close to the boat. I had an excellent view of it and duly recorded its colours in my diary. This includes the tell-tale observation that it was dull white on the under-side. It was clearly not a Manx Shearwater, so this too I recorded in my note-books unhesitatingly as a Sooty Shearwater. But obviously it must have been a Balearic. I can only suppose that at that time, at least from 1912 to 1915, probably in other years before and after, Balearic Shearwaters were frequenting the Straits of Dover much more than they have done in recent years. What, after all, has happened to the Yorkshire birds that W. J. Clarke found year after year? Or is it that actual off-shore watching is still a very rare event? Surely not.

In recent years I have come to know the Balearic Shearwater quite well, from observations at Portland and Swanage; once also quantities off Gibraltar. Sooty Shearwaters I have watched from ships in the north Atlantic, but I believe my first British observation of a true Sooty Shearwater was a bird seen at Fifeness on 2nd October 1951. It had the authentic long-winged appearance, which these old Kentish birds lacked; and it looked dark, or nearly as dark, when it turned to show the underside as when its back was facing me.

A few of Jack Tart's rare birds, which he saw and reported, are worth rescuing. First, for instance, was the Bridled Tern (*Sterna anaethetus*) which he picked up dead (19th November 1931). This I have already noted. Then there are two records of Mediterranean Gulls, both of them interesting to read in the 1970s when this species has begun to breed in Britain.

On 28th April 1930 he wrote: 'Near the Ternery I saw a strange pair of Gulls in summer plumage they were a little larger than our Brown-headed Gull. Their heads were jet black with white eyestripe and yellowish feet and legs their call note was much lower than our Brown-headed Gull: I looked them up in the book and I find they were the Mediterranean Black-headed Gull very seldom seen in this country.' He wrote again on 7th May: 'I fear the Mediterranean Black-headed Gulls have gone again. I last saw them on Sunday 4th at the Hoppen Pits with the crowd of Gulls that assemble there.'

On 13th May 1932 he wrote: 'I saw a few days ago one pair of

Mediterranean Black-headed Gulls on the Hoppen Pits. I believe I told you of the pair I saw a season or so ago.' This is the sole reference to this pair. Apparently they only stayed one day. It should be noted that there was at that time a large colony of Black-headed Gulls breeding at the Hoppen Pits.

The only rare passerine bird that Jack Tart successfully identified in all his years of watching was a male Rock Thrush (*Monticola saxatilia*). On 3rd July 1933 he wrote: 'I saw on Friday June 23rd between my house and the old revetments a real male Rock Thrush. I had a good view of it for an hour. It was so very tame. Its head throat and neck was bluish grey: upper back bluish black, lower back white patch; tail rich chestnut: white patch and tail very conspicuous in flight. Perhaps you have seen one abroad, but I have never seen one before, but of course no one with me to confirm it.' When I sent this to Witherby to record in *British Birds* he was not quite happy about it at first as there was no reference to the chestnut underside. This did not surprise me for, of course, at Dungeness every bird that is seen is seen from above; there are no trees or tall bushes for a bird to perch in, so that the colour of the underparts would not be conspicuous. It also tended to show that the report was a genuine account of field observation, not a write-up after looking at the description in a book. However, I wrote to Jack for fuller particulars, if he could remember them; and so I received the following: 'Jan. 23rd 1934.... The Rock Thrush I saw in June last year near my house was very tame, in my opinion quite tired out as though it had travelled a great distance. It just flitted from bush to bush resting on the leeward side. It did not go into the bushes nor settle on the bushes. It did not attempt to feed but just really wanted to rest. I had good views of it from all quarters back front and sideways; I got within thirty yards and spent about an hour watching this beautiful creature. In my opinion it was not quite so large as our common Song Thrush, but more sturdy and plump. The white patch being very conspicuous when flitting from bush to bush also the chestnut tail.' To satisfy Witherby completely, I asked for a complete description, which he sent. Most of this was repetition of what he had told me already, but 'wings dark brown' and 'under plumage bright chestnut' were added; and I do not doubt that he had noted these colours at the time; but to my mind the earlier accounts are more than adequate.

In one of his earliest letters to me, he sent a very clear account of a Red Kite (*Milvus milvus*). Writing on 3rd November 1922 he said:

'Since my last letter I have seen the Tawny Owl [at the time I do not think he knew the owls well: this may have been a Short-eared Owl; Tawny Owls rarely if ever occurred on the beach], Hooded Crow, Cormorant, Kestrel, Sparrow Hawk and Red Kite. The last named beautiful bird I saw near the Hoppen Pits Nov. 2nd. Its gliding flight, at times remaining motionless in the air; its forked tail, long narrow wings, with dark patches on the under wing, very conspicuous in flight; undoubtedly this was the Red Kite. I had a good view of it for some minutes it did not seem to be at all frightened it just kept gliding on and on until it passed over the water going in the direction of the French coast.'

I always knew that he would write me a letter each year in late March when the first Wheatear arrived. Once or twice a Chiffchaff put in an appearance before the first Wheatear; but in some years the early Chiffchaffs passed through without stopping. The Wheatears, on the other hand, were quite reliable. More than once, the first Wheatear was accompanied by a male Black Redstart, a species that only appeared at Dungeness in those days as a passage migrant. In recent years, in Dorset, we have several records of early Wheatears and Black Redstarts arriving together. It seems that they travel together; but have they come from the same winter quarters? Surely not. So where do they join up? In Iberia, North-west Africa or where?

Bluethroats were among the birds Jack Tart saw round his house or by the lighthouse in the spring in certain years. Here is a remarkable record, taken from a letter written on 7th November 1923. 'I saw Mr Bertram Lloyd on Oct. 15th and went with him to the Hoppen Pits. We saw no less than six Bluethroats which was very interesting being the first I had ever seen. We also saw one Nightingale which was somewhat late in migrating I think.' It would be easy to keep on quoting from these letters. Unfortunately they only give a partial account of one man's life work among birds. And they need to be related to his daily diaries, which he kept most methodically for about twenty years. Most of these seem to be lost. I have copies of about two years, no more.

Although Jack Tart was a good field ornithologist, careful and accurate in his observations, his knowledge was necessarily limited, and I am not sure that every record in his note-books and letters is acceptable without qualification. Among the winter birds on the sea he would often report both Red- and Black-throated Divers, but I am not sure that he knew how to distinguish them in winter plumage. So too with Eared (Black-necked) and Slavonian (Horned) Grebes. I must have discussed these matters with him during my frequent winter visits to Dungeness, but nearly all my own records for those years are of Red-throated Divers. I identified a very few Great Northern and Black-throated, but we were only beginning to learn how to distinguish them by bill shape. Occasionally, one would appear with enough summer plumage for adequate identification. The present generation of British field observers can have very little idea of the amount of time and effort and argument that went into these identifications. One winter in the 1920s a diver on Staines reservoir, which was alternatively identified as a Black-throat and a Great Northern, nearly caused a bloody war. I forget which it really was. But it was a great relief when, a year or two later, one of each appeared there, as if to invite comparison.

So too with the smaller grebes. The event that helped this was the great freeze of 1925, when many of the main inland waters of England were covered with grebes; and Dr Carmichael Low triumphantly saw all five species in one day, although he had a job to find a Dabchick. Now we really learnt about the shape of the bill and outline of the bird. Travelling to London from Birmingham one day during this freeze, I saw a grebe on the pool (in those days there was only one pool, now there are two) as we rushed through Bletchley. From its silhouette I judged it to be a Slavonian. I accordingly told Wilfrid in Oxford, and asked him to go to Bletchley to make sure. This he did, and I was right. So both of us were able to add the species to our county list. Did Jack Tart know about their beak-shape? I am not sure. Then, too, he several times recorded seeing a Raven. Were they really Ravens or only Carrion Crows? This may seem an odd question, for today there are plenty of Carrion Crows on Dungeness beach. But in the twenties and thirties there were not. Hooded Crows were common in the winter, but Carrion Crows were almost unknown. As I have said, I remember Jack Tart once telling me that the first time he saw a Carrion Crow he mistook it for a Raven. This should mean that his later Raven records are reliable, but I am not quite sure. There are, I think, very few genuine Raven records for Kent in this century.

Those who know Dungeness today may wonder what the 'old revetments' were, which Tart mentions in his first letter about the Rock Thrush. When I first knew Dungeness, some three-quarters of a mile west of the Point, just at the top of the tide mark, there were still quite extensive remains of the old 'containing walls' (the dictionary definition of a revetment) dating from the time in the middle of the nineteenth century when there was firing practice at Dungeness. Gradually the tide at that side has encroached, as the shingle banks have pushed further and further out to sea to the east, so that now not a trace of the 'revetments' remains. For some years they were only banks of shingle; before that the old walls were still visible. These walls provided convenient shelter for incoming migrants, and I have found warblers and other small birds sheltering and feeding on insects for a few minutes before moving across the beach to a better feeding ground. Also, as it happens, my one really rare bird was on the beach just to the north of these revetments.

On 9th September 1916, in the late afternoon, I went a long walk over the beach and returned by way of the revetments. It was a beautiful afternoon; but there were no unusual birds around; just the usual Wheatears and Skylarks. I do not think I saw much at the Hoppen Pits. Suddenly I came on a bird which was so distinctive as to be immediately recognisable: a Cream-coloured Courser. It was quite tame. I watched it for some time; then it flew a short distance and settled again. So I left it and went to look for Jack Tart. It was a bare half mile to his home. When I got there the front door was open; but no one answered my knock. I knocked again; still no answer. I thought he must have gone for a short walk; but I could not find him. 'Well,' I thought, 'the bird will surely be there again tomorrow morning.' But it wasn't. Jack and I were out on the western beach between 9 and 10 o'clock, and we spent a long time looking around for the Courser, but all that we found in that area was a single Golden Plover—in fact that too was unexpected. The weather was still warm and summery. The Courser had moved on.

It is not easy to recapture the atmosphere of those remote years. Some of the western beach is hardly changed, as little crossed by human foot as it ever was; indeed, if anything probably fewer people walk across it today. A Courser might spend a week on that most bleak part of the beach without ever being seen. But the great Nuclear Power Station dominates the scenery; even the new, tall and narrow lighthouse looks wrong and foreign to the eyes of an old man. The glory of Dungeness has not departed, but it has undergone a strange and subtle transformation.

In the past twenty years I have revisited Dungeness several times, mostly during the autumn migration: that, of course, can mean any time between July and November. During the years of Bert Axell's reign the beach seemed to be very much as I had known it. The Nuclear Power Station was only a dim threat. Someone who had been paying occasional visits to Dungeness during the late 1940s told me he had never seen a Firecrest there. That seemed odd, and I wondered if they had changed their migratory habits. So, on my return from India, it was reassuring to learn from Wilfrid that when the Observatories Committee met at Dungeness, at the beginning of October 1954, they found several Firecrests near Dungeness Point. In early November 1955 I visited Bert Axell and found that he had seen several that year. As we walked across the beach towards the coast, just north of the Point, he heard one calling. A few moments later it came up from a patch of broom, caught an insect in the air, and returned to cover: no doubt a bird that had come in over the sea a few hours earlier, a late east to west migrant on its way, perhaps, to winter in Dorset or further west. For me, it was like a greeting from an old friend I had not seen for many years.

Other things I connect with those Axell visits, if I may so describe them, are an occasion when we sat on the Point and saw birds taking off to sea over our heads. There were one or two mysterious little birds that we could not at first identify. They proved to be Great Tits. A Great Tit migration south across the English Channel was unexpected.

But the day of days was 1st September 1956. I had motored from Swanage; and 31st August, the day of my journey, was a nasty day with rain from the north-east. During the night the wind changed to the south-east, and all the birds that were migrating south along the French coast were drifted onto the English coast. One of Bert's volunteer assistants in trapping and ringing that morning boasted that they had ringed a hundred birds before breakfast—which meant, in part, that he and his colleagues had been much too busy trapping and ringing to stop for breakfast till about noon. There were swarms of Garden Warblers, Redstarts and Pied Flycatchers, plenty of Wrynecks, three Ortolans, one Icterine Warbler, a Hoopoe (which refused to enter a trap) and vast numbers of the commoner warblers, Whinchats, and so on.

In 1959 I put Dungeness to its severest test. It was called on to show its best face to my best beloved, recently arrived from America. We could not get away from Swanage till the second week of October. It had been a wonderful summer but it was hardly reasonable to hope that the sunny weather would endure to the middle of October. We moved from Dorset to Kent by stages, calling on various friends along the route. One of our days was a day of miserable drizzle. The weather was breaking down, no doubt. But no: next morning was fine again, and so it remained for most of our Dungeness week.

Our first exploration of the Dungeness bushes was perfect. The lighthouse gardens were full of ridiculously tame Goldcrests; no Firecrest this time, but what can be more attractive than a dozen tiny Goldcrests flitting about almost at arm's reach? Round the coastguard station we were still able to find late Blackcaps and a Redstart, to say nothing of Ring Ouzels. Beside the Vicarage Lane at Lydd, always one of my favourite resorts when I have stayed, as we did this time, at the George Hotel, some Redpolls were feeding on the willowherb seeds. As we walked along that pleasant lane the air was full of the cooing of Collared Doves. Could anyone have conceived of such a possibility fifty years before? Only two years earlier, in 1957, Bert Axell had taken me to a secret place, somewhere on the Downs between Canterbury and Dover, where a pair of Collared Doves were nesting close to a farmhouse, and we gazed up at the bird's tail protruding from the nest: one of the earliest of the Collared Dove invasion (though I had in fact seen the Norfolk birds a year or two earlier still). Now, here they were, in 1959, already so numerous in Lydd that the local inhabitants were finding them a nuisance. Wrynecks and Shrikes had disappeared, Collared Doves had arrived. What causes these drastic changes of population?

One day we penetrated to the old Hope and Anchor outflow and found Twites in the bushes—an unusually early date for this species on the Kent coast, I think. The sunshine was so balmy that we sat on the beach one day, opposite the pathetic shell of what had been the Austens' bungalow, and gazed across towards Cap Grisnez. A Red Admiral butterfly came flying past us and went out over the water, flying steadily east towards the invisible French coast. Then another and another and another, twelve or thirteen in the course of half an hour. I had told Rebecca that we might see some birds actually migrating in or out of England. I had not reckoned on butterflies.

My latest visit to Dungeness was in July 1969 with Trev Haysom. I cannot pretend that I admire the great Nuclear Power Station, but not all its effects are negative. In particular, it has caused the extraordinary turbulence of the water above the outflow of the warm water, west of the Point, which brings an astonishing concourse of birds to feed there, as fully described by the present Dungeness ornithologist, R. E. Scott, in a recent *British Birds* article.

Among the swarms of Common Terns, Kittiwakes and other species flying round and round over the water or resting on the shingle near, we were able to find one or two Mediterranean Gulls, a species I had never seen in Kent in the old days; also Roseate and Black Terns. Perversely, even when we used the telescope at its 30 magnification, working through the crowd of Common Terns on the beach, we could find no certain Arctic Tern among them. The bill colour was most variable. Yet, some twelve years earlier, Bert Axell and I had found undoubted Arctic Terns on Dungeness Point in July. In the fifties I also found Arctic Terns in some numbers in July on the Suffolk coast at Benacre, thus confirming observations made more than fifty years earlier by Rev. Julian Tuck, which had been regarded with some scepticism. So too, in Dorset, in late July, especially on the Chesil Beach near Weymouth. This July movement of Arctic Terns seems to be an annual event, though the numbers occurring year by year probably vary considerably. Arctic Terns start their migration when the young are still being regularly fed by the parents, thereby giving the false impression that they have nested in the locality. Common and Sandwich Terns also do this, so probably it is true of most of the sea-terns.

Although Jack Tart's great ternery has not been re-established on the western beach, the creation of large new ballast pits, one near Lydd, the other at Camber, on the Sussex side, have provided the Common Terns with new nesting grounds. The new diggings on the R.S.P.B. land must bode well for the future. Both new colonies seem likely to be well protected. We watched the Camber colony for some time one July day in 1969. An adult Common Tern brought a fish in its bill, and held on to it, not offering it to any of the several young birds that were still on the nesting ground waiting to be fed. Nor did the old bird swallow the fish itself. Once or twice it flew round with the fish and then settled again. Strange behaviour.

Not much migration of small land-birds was visible in July; but as we crossed the ground near the old railway, where the willow bushes are much taller than they were fifty years ago, we put up some eight or nine Cuckoos. 'In August go he must,' says the old jingle. For 'August' read 'July'.

In the early years of our explorations of Romney Marsh and Dungeness, we did quite a lot of mapping of breeding birds on six-inch-to-the-mile maps, just as we had done in the Weald and round Wye; indeed, I note that some of the birds marked on the Rye map

Dungeness and Romney Marsh

have the year 1906 attached to them. But the more intense mapping was begun in 1908. I continued to map the breeding species, chiefly summer migrants, after Christopher left England; some of the individuals have years noted beside them right on to the 1920s; but after 1918 I was rarely in this area at the right time of year to do any mapping of birds in their breeding areas.

I append some of the results of this work. I have divided the whole area into three: first, the parts of Romney Marsh proper that were fairly well mapped (three maps); secondly, Dungeness beach (four maps); thirdly, the Sussex end (three maps), including Rye town and two maps immediately east of it, covering Camber and Rye Harbour and extending to Broomhill and Jury Gap.

(1)	Snargate and Fairfield	Brookland and Woolpack	Cheyne Court etc
Wheatear	0	0	4
Whitethroat	4	4	0
Lesser Whitethroat	1	0	0
Willow Warbler	4	0	0
Reed Warbler	49	36	5
Sedge Warbler	17	28	1
Spotted Flycatcher	0	1	1
Tree Sparrow	2	4	1
Corn Bunting	0	1	0
Yellowhammer	1	4	0
Reed Bunting	15	11	11
Magpie	1	2	5
Carrion Crow	0	0	1
Wryneck	2	0	0

It will be seen that Reed Buntings are the only one of these species that were generally distributed over the marsh. Reed Warblers depend on reed-beds, of which there were none in the Cheyne Court area; Sedge Warblers on bushes or scrub, usually to be found along roads above a ditch—of which again there were none on the almost trackless drained marshland of the third map. The track we used in crossing from the fleets (the local name for an undrained or badly drained swampy area, where ducks and waders were often to be found) to the sea-coast at Jury Gap, passed through a derelict pile of buildings known as Rabbiting Farm. This provided accommodation for the one

Flycatcher found on this map, also for a pair of Pied Wagtails, a Wren or two, a pair of Tree Sparrows, a Little Owl, a pair of Magpies and what at that time was the only Carrion Crow, or pair of Crows, that I knew on the whole area of the marsh. I noted it in both 1915 and 1916.

It will be seen that I did not map Yellow Wagtails. This I regret: but the explanation is simple. Instead of staying in one spot and singing, as most of the passerine summer migrants do, they tend to undertake long flights; so when you are crossing the marshes on a ten- or fifteen-mile walk you cannot stop long enough to check the actual number of pairs. Yellow Wagtails have always been common birds in Romney Marsh, and no doubt still are. Their numbers would almost certainly be above the number of Reed Buntings. But in parts of the marsh that are dry with only narrow ditches separating the fields they are by no means common. In the next table, two Blue-headed Wagtails appear. Another widely distributed species that I did not map is the Skylark. Meadow Pipits, which also I did not usually map, are not found on most of the marsh, but they are plentiful in some areas near the sea.

(2)

	Dungeness	Holmestone	North Dungeness	Lydd
Wheatear	73	19	37	12
Stonechat	0	0	1	2
Whitethroat	0	0	1	6
Lesser Whitethroat	0	0	0	1
Blackcap	0	0	0	1
Willow Warbler	0	0	0	3
Reed Warbler	4	4	8	9
Blue-headed Wagtail	0	0	2	0
Red-backed Shrike	0	0	0	2
Spotted Flycatcher	0	0	0	2
Tree Sparrow	0	0	0	8
Corn Bunting	1	4	8	9
Yellowhammer	4	2	4	11
Reed Bunting	15	2	8	6
Wryneck	0	0	0	1
Nightjar	0	0	2	6
Stone Curlew	10	0	5	0
Common Gull	8	0	1	0

Dungeness and Romney Marsh 151

Much of this mapping was done in 1908 and immediately succeeding years; and so far as Dungeness beach proper is concerned, I covered almost all of it at one time or another. But in some ways these figures, covering a number of years, are less satisfactory than those that reflect a single year. Thus the Wheatear total covers a number of seasons; whether there would ever be seventy-three pairs on the six square miles of the Dungeness map in any one year I cannot be sure. These represent occupied territories in various years.

Several comments seem to be called for here. The Stonechats in the Lydd map were two pairs that were in the long gorse patch to the west of Lydd Camp in both 1914 and 1915. The other pair, on the north of Dungeness map, was close to the junction of the railways to New Romney and to Dungeness (New Romney Junction, it was then called), also in 1914. Although Stonechats are common winter visitors to the Kent coast. these are the only breeding pairs I have known in the Dungeness area. The gardens and hedges round the town of Lydd provide the environment needed for several species rarely found on the open marsh, such as Lesser Whitethroat, Blackcap, Willow Warbler and Spotted Flycatcher. There is also a rookery in Lydd, and there are Green Woodpeckers, Tree Creepers, Marsh Tits (which I might well have 'mapped'), and other woodland species.

The single pair of Nightjars nested on the beach in 1915. I think Jack Tart showed me the nest. The Stone Curlews I mapped in various years, from 1914 on; the Common Gulls chiefly in the 1920s, including one pair well to the north of the railway line (most of them to the south and east of the railway) as late as 1932.

I marked the general areas of colonies of most of the breeding seabirds on my maps. In view of the restricted areas in which Common and Little Terns nest today, it may be of interest to say that in the 1920s there were colonies of both species to the north of Lade. Indeed, I have two circles for 565 (Common Tern) well north of Lade, the more northerly quite near the Greatstone end of the beach, in 1932. There was also a colony of Little Terns there at that time and a second colony south of Lade. Two more colonies existed between this and the Point of Dungeness, all of them close to the sea. The Common Tern colonies, all small compared with the large colony west of the Hope and Anchor, were further inland, but all on the open beach. There were also some Ringed Plovers nesting to the north of Lade: a colony slightly to the south of the main stronghold of the last Kentish Plovers, and in 1932 I noted a single pair to the north of the main Kentish

Plover ground. I entered three colonies of Ringed Plovers to the west of the Point: one a mile from the sea, north of Lloyds Signal Station; the other two close to the sea, more or less between or near three colonies of Little Terns. South of the Hoppen Pits, but east of the Hope and Anchor, there were two small colonies of Common Terns.

Finally, we come to the birds on the Sussex side, including the neighbourhood of Rye itself. First, the table:

(3)	Rye	Camber, etc	Broomhill
Wheatear	4	30	26
Whinchat	1	0	0
Nightingale	2	0	0
Whitethroat	6	1	0
Lesser Whitethroat	11	1	0
Blackcap	2	0	0
Garden Warbler	4	0	0
Chiffchaff	2	0	0
Willow Warbler	5	0	0
Reed Warbler	8	10	1
Sedge Warbler	9	2	0
Red-backed Shrike	2	0	0
Spotted Flycatcher	1	0	0
Corn Bunting	2	2	1
Yellowhammer	1	0	0
Cirl Bunting	3	0	0
Reed Bunting	5	6	11
Wryneck	2	0	0
Kentish Plover	0	1	0

Quite an interesting list, which demands some comment. The single pair of Whinchats was well out on the marsh, on the railway embankment, north of East Guldeford. A pair was present there in both 1906 and 1909. These are the only Whinchats I ever suspected of nesting on any part of Romney Marsh; but the species is very common all over the marsh during the autumn migration. The strip of low cliff, where the marsh meets the dry land, north of Rye, well wooded and largely covered in scrub, was at that time full of birds that do not occur at all on the marsh, hardly even in the well wooded gardens round Lydd. Here were the two Whitethroats, Blackcaps, Garden Warblers, Shrikes and Flycatchers, also the three pairs of Cirl Buntings and the Wrynecks. It is unusual to find the four species of English resident buntings in one area; Wilfrid was proud of having them all in the parish of Benson, near Oxford, when he lived there in the 1930s and '40s. Here, north of Rye, they must have been all within sound of each other's voices.

Cirl Buntings have now (1971) become so scarce in the south-east of England that it may be worth recording here that, in the days when I first knew this part of the country, they occurred in small numbers all round the edges of Romney Marsh, to the north as well as the west. This is a species recorded on some of the maps I am not reporting in any detail here. Reed Buntings, it will be again clear, are the species most widely distributed all over the marsh. Wherever there is water and some cover they seem to occur.

As an appendix to this chapter, I add some mapping statistics from the north Kent marshes. In the summer of 1911, when all the breeding birds were busy in their territories, I spent a few days tramping across those marshes, and entered the birds I found on three six-inch maps all in the Hundred of Hoo (wonderful name!). I tried to cover all the areas that looked from the details on the maps as if they should be attractive to birds; so the area covered is, I think, approximately six square miles, nearly all marshland, except for a small area of agricultural land, both arable and grass, in the parishes of St Mary's and All-Hallows. Here are the figures: Wheatear 1; Whitethroat 2; Reed Warbler 70; Sedge Warbler 1; Corn Bunting 5; Yellowhammer 9; Reed Bunting 16.

The low numbers of Sedge Warbler and even Reed Bunting indicate that, compared with Romney Marsh, there are very few bushes along the north Kent ditches. I do not now recall whether there were many Yellow Wagtails or whether there were Meadow Pipits along the seawall area. Skylarks I am sure there were. It is a pity that I did not try to include them. I did enter quite a number of non-passerine birds, as follows: Sheldrake 7; Mallard, several colonies; Teal, one colony, quite small; Coot 12; Ringed Plover 8; Redshank, several colonies; Little Tern 12; Dabchick 2. The only one of these species that was not at that time also present in the breeding season in the Dungeness area is Sheldrake. All those I came upon appeared to be nesting in or beside the Thames wall.

CHAPTER VIII

West Midland Reservoirs

The years between the two great wars might be described as the years of reservoirs and sewage-farms, so far as British field ornithology is concerned. If anyone ever undertakes a serious research into the development of field studies among British birdwatchers, they may push the discovery of both reservoirs and sewage-farms further back. The Cheshire meres were famous for their birds far beyond the bounds of Cheshire; the Frensham ponds, in south-west Surrey, were visited by my Crosfield uncles before this century began; and we were taken there as soon as we were old enough for such long walks. I have an idea that Julian Huxley also visited them when he was a boy. Not all the modern reservoirs have such good herbage to provide cover, but those that feed canals, dating back to the early nineteenth century, had mostly developed reed-beds or other good cover at their shallow ends by the beginning of this century, or even a good deal earlier. Presumably they only began to attract birdwatchers when the telescope and the binocular began to replace the gun, and this means the end of the nineteenth century or the beginning of the twentieth.

The attractiveness of the old-fashioned sewage-farm with its extensive muddy settling beds for migrating waders came later. Probably Norman Joy of Reading first made this discovery, when he began to report the remarkable waders (including four Stilts), hitherto only known as birds of coastal marshes and mudflats, that he had found on an unnamed 'marsh' near Reading. Later in the same year (1923) he revealed that this was Reading sewage-farm. The most attractive sewage-farms, such as Northampton and Nottingham, and some of those near London, were only discovered in the late twenties or early thirties. But why did we regularly visit Tunbridge Wells sewage-farm in 1910 and even earlier? It had no alluring settling tanks; but it was a good place for birds if one was content with the commoner species. In my first two years at Cambridge I did not know that the sewage-farm there was worth visiting, even though I walked round the adjacent Chesterton ballast-pits sometimes. Then someone told me that a Grey Phalarope had been seen on the sewage-farm, so I began to go there, and found that Norman Ticehurst had known it and visited it from time to time in his day, ten or fifteen years earlier. But the fact is that the larger sewage-fields, which attracted waders at a later date, only came into being after my time. Lack, in his *Birds of Cambridgeshire* (1934), hardly gives any sewage-farm records before 1927. By 1934 he was able to record that 152 species had been recorded at the sewage-farm and adjacent ballast-pits; this he compares with 132 at Reading sewage-farm in the ten years from 1922 to 1932. No other sewage-farm is mentioned.

My first visit to Upper Bittell reservoir, north Worcestershire, was in early October 1906. The reservoir was already known to local birdwatchers, but when I came to compile a list for the two Bittell reservoirs in the late twenties (1929) I was only able to get a small number of specific records for the earlier years. Most of what I published was based on my own observations, which were systematic (or at least frequent) from 1919.

One day in the late twenties I had my first day in the field with T. A. Coward. I took him round Upper Bittell reservoir. While we were there he asked me if I had ever explored some large reservoirs in Staffordshire, near Watling Street. He had heard of them recently from his friend and neighbour, Arnold Boyd; but Coward thought they must be nearer to me than they were to Boyd in north Cheshire.

Sections from two of the author's 6-inch Ordnance Survey maps showing species recorded. Above, the Upper Bittell Reservoir area in 1930. Opposite, the area south of Grantchester, Cambridge. Circled numbers are the author's version of Dresser's list (see p. 16): 33 Whinchat; 36 Redstart; 48 Nightingale; 50 Whitethroat; 51 Lesser Whitethroat; 60 Blackcap; 61 Garden Warbler; 65 Goldcrest; 70 Chiffchaff; 71 Willow Warbler; 72 Wood Warbler; 87 Reed Warbler; 92 Sedge Warbler; 94 Grasshopper Warbler; 115 Marsh Tit;

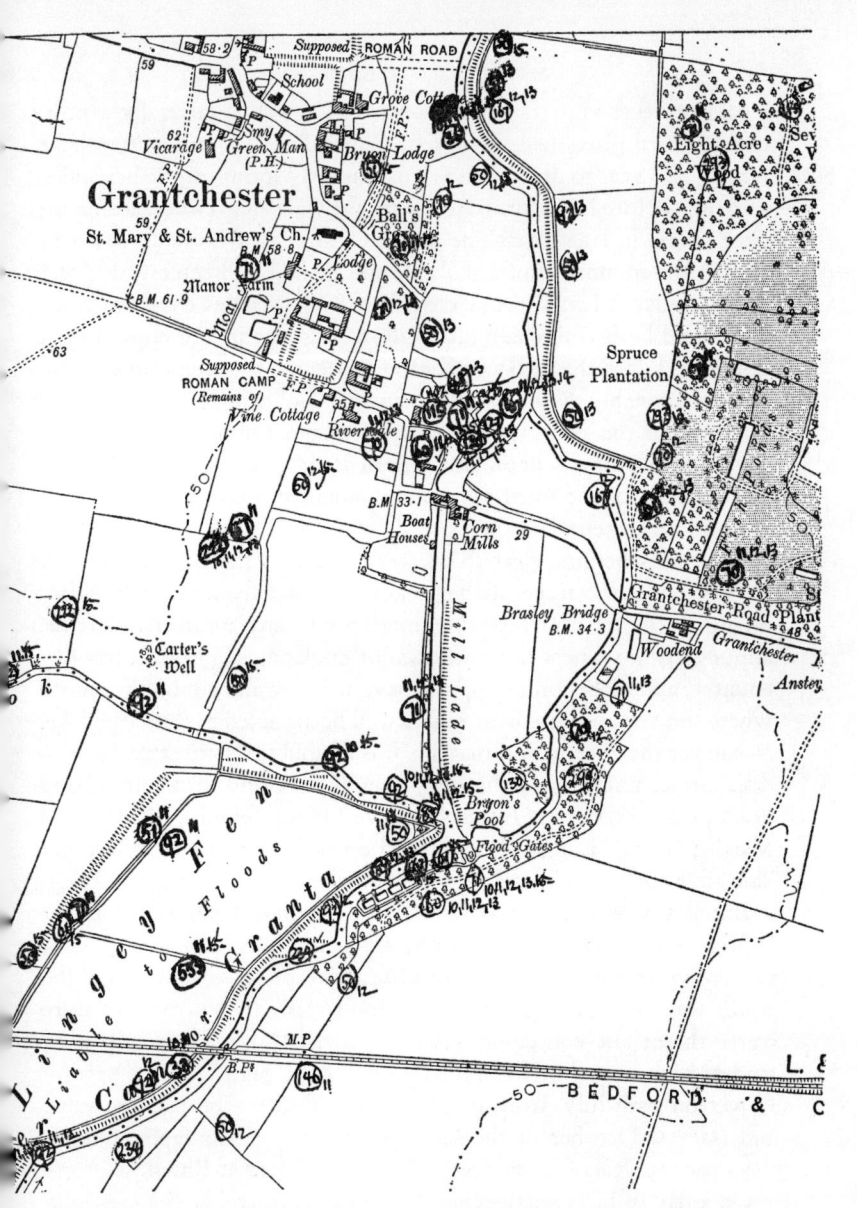

116 Willow Tit; 127 Nuthatch; 130 Tree Creeper; 137 Grey Wagtail; 141 Yellow Wagtail; 146 Tree Pipit; 161 Red-backed Shrike; 167 Spotted Flycatcher; 222 Corn Bunting; 223 Yellowhammer; 234 Reed Bunting; 293 Great Spotted Woodpecker; 299 Lesser Spotted Woodpecker; 302 Green Woodpecker; 306 Wryneck; 307 Kingfisher; 324 Brown Owl; 334 Little Owl; 423 Mallard; 498 Coot; 524 Lapwing; 533 Snipe; 553 Redshank; 617 Great Crested Grebe; 621 Dabchick. Other numbers are year observed.

I paid my first visit to Belvide reservoir, which is generally a more exciting bird place than the nearby Gailey Pools, a year or two later, when I had a car to drive. It was a day in early spring, at the beginning of April. Before I was turned away by the waterman (who became my close friend in later years—he was a Cumbrian, who had grown up among the mountains of Lakeland, and he had a directness of speech that I enjoyed) I had seen a crowd of Sand Martins over the water and found both Chiffchaff and Willow Warbler in the copse by the reservoir, whilst the ducks on the water seemed to include all that one could reasonably hope for: Goosanders, Goldeneye, Garganey and numbers of the commoner species. I wrote about this to Duncan Wood, then still at school, and commented: 'It seemed to be rather a good place.' He quoted this understatement back to me on our expeditions there in later years.

One thing became clear to me very early. As the Bittell reservoirs are just under the ridge of the Lickey Hills, far from any river, they do not seem to attract passing migrants in any numbers. Belvide, although it too is near the watershed of England, is in low, nearly flat, country, and birds coming up the Severn valley and continuing north where the Severn bears west might well be attracted to this large lake. Whatever the explanation may be, it is undoubtedly true that Belvide does attract numbers of the early migrants passing north. In all my years of observation at Bittell I believe I never found a March Sand Martin; Belvide can be almost relied on to have them at almost any date after 20th March, and sometimes earlier.

Bittell was not nearly as attractive to strange birds as the larger Staffordshire reservoirs. However, frequent visits over a period of twenty years gave me some surprises. Except in seasons when the water was low and a good deal of mud was exposed, waders were scarce there; but you could never be sure. My two most surprising waders both turned up in 1940, a year of quite high water: a Kentish Plover on 15th July, from its plumage evidently a bird of the year; and on 31st October of the same year a Purple Sandpiper. During these twenty years I never saw a Wood Sandpiper at Bittell.

On a day of high north-westerly wind, 21st October 1936, as John Stephens and I were approaching the reservoir from the farm on the hill to the north, three large dark birds came over our heads, then flew round over the reservoir and soon disappeared to the south. We saw at once that they were skuas, but which species? Luckily one of the three showed the typical twisted tail feathers of a Pomarine. All were in adult plumage and all appeared to be the same size, so presumably all were Pomarine.

In 1939 I contributed a short paper on the birds of Bittell to the annual report of the Birmingham Bird Club (now West Midland Bird Club). This was my summary of the background of knowledge of the reservoirs and their birds. 'Rev. K. A. Deakin, for many years Rector of Cofton Hackett, kept records covering the period from 1860 to 1910. Messrs H. Lloyd Wilson and D. Grubb are among those who frequently visited the reservoirs in pre-war [i.e. before 1914] times.' It would be interesting to know what happened to the Deakin records. How did the birds in 1870 compare with the birds to be seen there in 1970?

Practically all the British ducks occurred at one time or another during my twenty years, except for the Eider. Of the surface feeding ducks, Pintail and Gadwall were much the scarcest. I was only able to give six records of Gadwall and five of Pintail in the course of nineteen years' observation up to 1938. Scoters appeared surprisingly often, in both spring and autumn. The first time I took Wilfrid to the Bittell reservoirs, on 1st May 1920, when he had just returned (temporarily) from Australia, we found a party of six Common Scoters and a drake Velvet Scoter, the only one of this species I ever saw at Bittell and the first he had seen in his life. Goosanders and Smew were much less reliable as winter visitors than they were on the larger Staffordshire reservoirs. In 1938 I was only able to give one record of a Red-breasted Merganser, and one of a Long-tailed Duck. All five grebes had appeared, but Red-necked only three times.

When we look at the status of the gulls in those days, there really are some surprises. Although I had recorded Black-headed Gulls in every month of the year, I stated emphatically, 'It is not a regular winter visitor.' In later years it has surely become that; but just when? Herring Gulls, too, were quite scarce, with only four definite records of adult birds; immature Herring Gulls are of course rarely separable from immature Lesser Black-backs, a species which in those days (as it still is) was a regular passage migrant across the Midlands in some numbers, and so was by far the commoner bird. Herring Gulls began to winter at industrial tips and to roost on some of the reservoirs before I left the Midlands, I suppose in the late forties or fifties. I had no record of a Great Black-back at Bittell in those days, though I had seen them at Westwood Park, Droitwich, and also at Belvide.

The status of the Kittiwake at Bittell was perhaps as surprising as anything. What I wrote in 1937 may stand: 'Recorded about a dozen times in the last twenty years, especially during the last few years, when watching has been more systematic. It begins to look as if there may be a regular cross-country migration in Feb. and March; they have also been seen in May, Oct. and Dec. Only the December record was immediately after stormy weather.'

Looking through the West Midland reports for the past ten years when at least ten times, perhaps twenty times, the number of observers have been involved, I note that Kittiwakes have been recorded in the West Midlands every year, but rarely at Bittell. Indeed, the only Bittell records for these later years are the following: one in December 1961; one in November 1962; one in March 1963; one in February and one in September 1965; and, from 1966 to 1970 inclusive, none at all. On these slight figures there would seem to be some support for my idea of a cross-country migration in February and March; but there is little additional support if all the other records from the three West Midland counties are taken together. All the records for the ten years give the following results month-wise: January 5; February 6; March 7; April 4; May 4; June 1; July 0; August 11; September 4; October 4; November 6; December 9. There is very little to indicate which of these were seen just after severe storms, though this is referred to once or twice. Thus, the one record of a good-sized flock, between 25 and 30, is from Cannock reservoir, on 5th November 1967, after a strong north-west gale (this inevitably reminds me of the three skuas at Bittell on 21st October 1936). I am inclined to think, however, that there are sufficient annual records of Kittiwake appearances in the West Midlands to indicate that, every year, some cross the country on normal migratory flights, which is somewhat unexpected in such a maritime species. I also noted that most of my records of Scoters on Midland pools seemed to be quite unconnected with storms. Again, somewhat unexpected.

A few of the Kittiwake records are of birds that were obviously ailing or even of dead birds (the only time, as far as I recall, that I took Bernard Tucker to the reservoirs, we found a dead Kittiwake). Do maritime birds that are ailing tend to fly inland to die? That they should seek the land, if they are out at sea, seems reasonable; but I can see no reason why an ailing bird should fly a hundred or more miles inland.

When I was young, that is, sixty years ago, any gull seen inland was alleged to be 'storm-driven', though I have no doubt that the passage across the country of Lesser Black-backs is a very old phenomenon. But when Norman Joy first found the passage of waders at Reading sewage-farm he was discovering that gulls also frequently cross the centre of England, and that was something new. In his second article he appealed to observers to visit their local sewage-farms in the next year (1924) to see if they found the same passage in other places. There is little evidence that many did this. As I have said, the discovery of the riches of Northampton and Nottingham, and later of some other such farms, came some years later; indeed, I think Wilfrid may have been one of the first to visit Northampton, when he began to explore from Oxford in and after 1931. How different the picture is today!

Let me compare the records of terns in the Midlands today with the few we recorded year by year in the 1930s. It would be too tedious to give the results statistically, but Common, Arctic and Black Terns are recorded in numbers in the West Midland bird reports every year now; yet I recall that in about 1930 Witherby, having received a report of a Black Tern one spring from a West Midland pool, asked me if it was sufficiently unusual to be worth publishing in *British Birds*. I could only reply that I knew of very few spring records. As I look through the recent reports of the West Midland Bird Club, I find that in both 1966 and 1970 quite a heavy spring passage of Black Terns was observed, with records from many pools and reservoirs in the three counties; but in 1970 none was seen in spring at Bittell, and in 1966 the only observation was of four on 1st May. In other years single birds were recorded in spring. It may be that for some reason Bittell attracts them less than some neighbouring pools—and I do not only mean the large Staffordshire reservoirs. Indeed, what I wrote in 1936 still seems appropriate: 'Fairly frequent in spring, Apr. and May and early June; also in Aug. and Sept.' It is even possible that Bittell is no more frequently visited by people looking for birds than it was in the 1930s. The great differences today are that the big Staffordshire reservoirs are visited by bird-spotters at least five times as often (five is a guess); and a dozen pools in all three counties are frequently visted today which either did not exist or were quite unknown as birding haunts in those days.

The one generalisation that can now be made with assurance is that any good-sized pool or sewage-farm in any part of Midland England, whether near a river valley or not, will certainly attract plenty of birds of passage from time to time, waders, terns, gulls, ducks and others.

Nor is this simply due to the fact that England is a small country with sea-coast a bare hundred miles away wherever you are. Watchers at such inland continental places as Geneva or Delhi have found that migrating seabirds turn up not infrequently, and not only after storms.

CHAPTER IX

Peveril Point, Dorset

During the past ten or twenty years, the pastime of watching birds from some point on the coast has become popular, especially among the younger generation of British ornithologists. In the Dungeness chapter, I have already told how Christopher and I began seabird watching from Dungeness Point, following his great haul of Red-throated Divers one crisp winter's day.

Round about 1955, Wilfrid and I began to discuss where we should go to live in our retirement, he from the Edward Grey Institute at Oxford, I from Birmingham (and Delhi). His first choice was the Scilly Isles, which he had visited once or twice, and had made friends with the local bird people; I said that was too remote. I wanted still to keep up with some of my Quaker interests centring in Friends House, London. Then, said he, 'What about the Devonshire coast?', where I had a sister-in-law and family and he had friends; indeed, Holte Macpherson, whose colleague I had been for many years on the R.S.P.B. Council, and who was also a friend of Wilfrid's, was still living at Exmouth. Why we turned down Exmouth I do not now remember; but Holte Macpherson died about that time. Meanwhile I was advocating the east coast; first of all somewhere in Romney Marsh, easy of access to Dungeness; but that was too flat, said Wilfrid, and we should not be right on the coast. Just then, Bert Axell moved from Dungeness to Suffolk. 'Why not Suffolk?' said I. 'Too cold in the winter,' said Wilfrid. At this stage Bernard Gooch entered into the argument, suggesting that Swanage was the answer. Wilfrid had often visited Studland from Oxford, and had found plenty of good birds. So, in the end, Swanage it was.

It will be seen that we both took it for granted that we wanted to be by the sea, but this did not mean that we had identical enthusiasms to satisfy. For Wilfrid, the birds to be seen round Poole Harbour and in the shallow seas near Studland, one of the few places in England where the 'rarer' grebes are not rare, were sufficient attraction. I also wanted a place where seabirds could be watched. I asked Bernard Gooch if he had ever seen unusual birds from Peveril Point. He said, 'No,' but an Iceland Gull had spent some weeks in Swanage Bay a year or two before, and I recalled that, staying with the Gooches in late May one year, on a day of strong north-west wind when we were sheltering near the lighthouse on Anvil Point, a party of Manx Shearwaters had appeared well out to sea, flying down the Channel. So I hoped that Peveril Point might produce something more than Herring and Black-headed Gulls.

My hopes were fairly well justified. On one of our first visits to Peveril Point one late autumn day, we detected two or possibly three Little Gulls among the Black-headed feeding off the Point. During my first winter in Purbeck a Grey Phalarope turned up at the tiny quay in a very stormy sea, one Sunday morning in December (I never saw one in Swanage Bay again); and it soon became clear that auks, Gannets and Kittiwakes could often be seen from the Point.

Peveril Point is not in fact a promontory jutting out into the English Channel. It is just 'round the corner', so to speak, in Bournemouth Bay. Anvil Point, or Durlston Head, a mile to the south-west, would probably be a better spotting place for birds flying up and down Channel; St Aldhelm's Head, four miles further west, might be better still. None of these can compare with Portland Bill, twenty miles away to the west, which juts right out into the Channel, miles to the south of the main coastline. But at Durlston Head, Anvil Point and St Aldhelm's Head you must watch from the cliff top, and that means missing two-thirds or more of the birds that go by far out. At Peveril, as at Dungeness and Portland, you watch from ten feet or less above the level of high tide, so that every bird that flies past near sea level will pass through the vision of the binoculars or even the telescope. This is almost essential for an effective sea watch.

The so-called Isle of Purbeck has an astonishing geological formation. Half the sedimentary rocks of the south of England, from Purbeck limestone and even the older Portland stone, through the whole succession of Wealden beds which cover many miles from south to north in Sussex and Kent, through the chalk to the various recent sands and clays above the chalk, are all compressed into a north and south distance of some five or six miles; and the sea has broken through this whole strip of rock formation to separate the Isle of Wight, where nearly all occur again, from the mainland of Dorset.

At Peveril Point, one of the lower sections of the Purbeck limestone, including a fine stratum of the dark grey Purbeck marble, disappears under the sea. The house we lived in for twelve years stands on the same geological stratum, but it is nearly two hundred feet above sea-level, though less than a mile west of the Point. Most of the intervening half-mile is open downland (mercifully the local authorities stopped building on Peveril Down just in time); so from our house it was a pleasant walk, taking less than a quarter of an hour to the Point, where a shelter was erected for war-time purposes in 1939 or 1940, with a seat which is very convenient for the birdwatcher (if it does not happen to be pre-occupied by other kinds of seawatcher). The return walk takes longer. If you have not much time and want to spend it all on the seawatch you can drive a car almost to the Point. So it would often happen that I had a short hour to spare, of which three-quarters could be spent gazing out to sea from the Point. And if something strange was to be seen on the sea, I could hasten home and alert the ornithological neighbourhood with little delay. Of course, most of the unusual birds flew past and were gone in a minute or less; so, in case it was a real rarity, it was desirable to have at least one companion, but that was not always possible.

How could a birdwatcher fare better than to have the whole realm of possible seabirds at his back door, so to speak, where he could abandon the affairs of the work-a-day world for an hour and enjoy the bliss of gazing, usually, of course, at nothing but the commoner species of gull? But you could never be sure. It was in mid-June that a Sabine's Gull turned up one year and was on view for several days.

A 'typical' hour's watch at Peveril Point (if there is such a thing) might be something like this. When you arrive, there is nothing to be seen but some Herring and Black-headed Gulls. As you search the sea more carefully, you are likely to find one or more Shags, which may well have been under the water at the first look. If there are none on the sea, one and then another will almost certainly fly past, or come and settle and begin to fish. And then the next, similar-looking bird, proves to be a Cormorant. Looking again at the flock of gulls feeding round the sewage outflow, you notice that a Common Gull, more often immature than adult, has joined the Black-heads; ten minutes later it has disappeared again. Very likely you neither saw it come nor did you see it go. Further, you will notice that the numbers of Herring or Black-headed Gulls varies from time to time—and now a young Great Black-back has joined them.

If it is summer time, suddenly you hear the loud cry of a Sandwich Tern—so loud and frequent are its calls that even my poor ears cannot miss him. Suddenly he rounds the corner from the Bay, swoops down low to catch a fish, misses, flies round again, and may remain for some time: but, like all the terns, he does not settle with the gulls on the water.

Suddenly an auk flies rapidly through the binoculars, far out at sea, too far off to be determined as between Razorbill and Guillemot. As you follow it, a bird—no, two birds close together—come from the opposite direction, a pair of Scoters. It is curious how often, after a gap of perhaps fifteen minutes, several birds appear almost simultaneously. The next may be a far away Kittiwake or, more rarely, one of these oceanic gulls will fly steadily in towards the feeding gulls, close at hand, and settle or feed from the air among the Black-heads for a time. Before you leave, you may have the luck to see a Gannet. These also sometimes come quite close in to feed, plunging from high up with a mighty splash if they detect a shoal of fish, but more often they will pass by at some distance from the shore.

From May till September or even later, we hope for Manx Shearwaters, either singly or in small parties, passing up and down near Peveril Point. I used to say with some confidence that they were most likely to be seen when there was a stiff north-west breeze, that is an off-shore breeze. This is reasonable, as such a wind will cause turbulence in the water, which may have the effect of bringing fish or other seafood near to the surface in the quieter inshore waters. However, during my last two years at Swanage, such observations as I made of

Shearwaters did not fit this theory too well. There must be other factors involved. Some seasons produce far more Shearwater observations than others. Food is no doubt the main factor, at all times. One afternoon I was walking along the cliffs at Durlston Head, the next corner between Peveril and Anvil Point, when my companion and I became aware that there were a number of Gannets fishing a short way out to sea. With them were gulls of several species. As we began to watch the water we noticed a small party of Shearwaters flying to and fro over the sea, not far out but very inconspicuous as seen from the cliff-top against a sea broken by a slight breeze. A single Arctic Skua also appeared—the only skua of any species that I saw that year in the whole area. This was late in June.

Sometimes, from July onwards, the shearwaters can be identified as Balearic, the race that is usually the commoner of the two in the late summer off Portland Bill. Only once I saw, very far out, but visible for some time as it rose and fell, what I had no doubt in my own mind was a Sooty Shearwater—a very long-winged and dark brown bird. They have been recorded in the area by fishermen.*

What are the Manx Shearwaters doing in this part of the English Channel in May and through the summer? British breeding birds reach their breeding grounds in April and May. The breeding season is a long one, and the birds do not leave their colonies till September and October. So the months when they may be seen passing the Dorset coast are exactly the months when they should be on the breeding grounds. Yet the nearest colonies to Dorset are on some of the Welsh islands, at least three hundred miles away all round the coast of Cornwall and up into the Irish Sea. Surely they would not fly so far to get food between their nightly visits to the breeding grounds! Can it be that the birds we see in Dorset seas are non-breeding or first-year birds, which return to the place of their birth with the adult birds in the spring, and then are free to roam the seas?

The Balearic Shearwaters are, of course, even further from their breeding grounds in the western Mediterranean. They too appear in the Channel long before the breeding season is over. Sooty Shearwaters, on the contrary, are birds from the South Atlantic whose breeding season is in the northern winter. They are among those species, far more numerous among birds of the northern hemisphere

* On 26th May 1972 I saw another—again a long way out, but fortunately in sight for a full minute, so that I could see it turn and show its characteristic underside.

than among birds of the south, that like to have two summers each year and no winters ever.

The shearwater tribe have taken me far away from Peveril Point. Our list of frequent visitors to the seas there is not ended. Of the common British gulls, by far the least common at Peveril is the Lesser Black-back. This I cannot explain. It is a common species round Weymouth and abundant in the Bristol Channel. I believe they are plentiful round Southampton Water but I have never seen any large number on any part of Poole Harbour, nor on the coast of Purbeck. Purbeck seems to be just off the migration routes.

Sandwich Terns are much commoner than any other tern species at Peveril, but Common and Arctic Terns are also frequent, especially the former. Often, of course, it is impossible to differentiate between these two; but at low tide they may settle at close quarters on the rocks or among the seaweed, when the colour of the bill and/or the length of the leg can be satisfactorily observed. Little Terns are quite rare.

Of the rarer gulls, I have once seen a Glaucous Gull, which most conveniently came in and settled on the old Swanage pier and stayed for half an hour. Little Gulls occur annually in almost any month and sometimes stay around for a few days. Sabine's Gull has been recorded several times, but the June bird was the only one that stayed to be admired by several observers. I once saw what presumably was a Mediterranean Gull, and this species has been identified at Peveril by George Moule and possibly by others. It is strange that it has not occurred more frequently. Skuas are quite irregular and uncertain, but over the years I have seen Great, Pomarine and Arctic, only the last of the three at all frequently.

In mid-winter, Guillemots and Razorbills may sometimes be seen, especially during stormy weather. Razorbills, more often than Guillemots, may spend some hours or days fishing close to the Point. Both species breed on the Durlston cliffs, Guillemots in some numbers; so also do Puffins, which rarely come close enough to Peveril Point for identification. Moreover, in mid-winter, most Puffins leave British waters and go south. Fulmars also breed, or at least spend the breeding season, on the cliffs; so all through the spring and summer single Fulmars often fly past. Gannets can be seen in any month of the year, but they are most plentiful in the summer, especially in July and August. Probably most of these are from the Channel Islands colony—much nearer than any Manx Shearwater colony.

Common Scoters are the only sea ducks that can be seen with any regularity from Peveril. Velvet Scoters are rare. Eiders sometimes occur in winter, nearly always in immature plumage. Mergansers sometimes fly past; and, much more rarely, Brent Geese. Sheldrakes fly past fairly often.

Finally, divers and grebes. Any time between August and April one may see a diver, or even several, fly past during a Peveril watch. Occasionally one or two may stay and fish in the waters close to the Point for a few days. Of those that can be identified, the majority are Red-throated, but Great Northern are quite frequent. I think I have never identified a Black-throated from Peveril; but they occur in the bays, especially Studland Bay, and in Poole Harbour. In some seasons divers are fairly common, in other years they are rare. The same has been noted, I believe, at Portland.

I have not seen a great movement of divers at Peveril comparable to Christopher's experience at Dungeness, which first aroused our interest in seabird watching. The nearest to it was a brief observation on 9th January 1963, in the early days of the great frost. As far as I recall, our three local bird experts of those days, all young and active, Ilay Cooper, Trev Haysom and Robert Smith, had been to the Tilly Whim caves and had there seen an impressive movement of seabirds; so they came to collect me and we returned there. The east wind was so bitter and shelter so inadequate that after twenty minutes (11.50 to 12.10) we gave up. During that time we saw about a hundred auks, apparently all Guillemots, some ten Gannets, one Great Northern Diver, and at least eleven Red-throated Divers fly west, also three Sheldrakes and a Goldeneye, whilst many gulls were flying east into the wind. A longer watch might well have given us quite a big total. Grebes are much less frequently seen. Most of the few that do occur are Great Crested. This species and both the Slavonian and Eared Grebes are regular winter visitors to Studland Bay and to Poole Harbour; Slavonian also to Kimmeridge Bay, further west, so it is strange that they so rarely show themselves at Peveril. Great Crested sometimes spend weeks in mid-winter in Swanage Bay.

Such are the true sea and ocean birds that may appear from time to time to the sea-watcher who waits at Peveril Point. But he will see some other birds too.

Oystercatchers often fly past and at low tide will settle on the rocks and feed. The only other 'wader' that comes to the rocks to feed is the Purple Sandpiper, and for some reason it has been much less frequent in the late sixties than it seemed to be in the late fifties. At high tide the two lines of rock that jut out into the water from the Point have only enough feeding ground for a few Purple Sandpipers; but in stormy weather all the rocks are awash and there is no good feeding place at all near for the sandpipers to repair to. Turnstones, Ringed Plovers and Dunlins occasionally drop in for a brief visit, especially in the early morning before the human inhabitants of Swanage come out for a morning's blow by the sea. Once only, early August 1968, for several days, I watched a small party of waders, Dunlins, Sanderlings and Ringed Plovers feeding on the scrap of shore just below the Peveril look-out. They refused to be driven off by people who came within a few feet of their feeding ground. At the most they would fly up, settle on the rocks and reappear on the patch of sand and dead seaweed when the intruders had moved on.

During the great frost of winter 1963, I had a strange experience on Peveril Point. But as a prelude to that, something needs to be said about other astonishing things that happened during the arctic spell that kept us frozen and snow-bound throughout January and February. Thus, on 10th January, Trev Haysom took me to see some wild geese that had found an open, windswept patch of grass to feed on west of Langton Matravers. He drove his car as far as we could get along the road from Langton towards Worth Matravers. Then we struck out through the deep snow which sometimes held us up and at other times let us down, over one or two stone walls almost hidden by the snow, till we came to the ridge and could look out towards the sea. Here the strong east wind had driven the snow, and the grass was bare. From behind a wall we were able to approach quite near to the flock of twenty-two Pink-footed and two White-fronted Geese. This is, I think, the only record of Pink-footed Geese in Purbeck. During those days we had such unusual birds as Reed Buntings and Bramblings coming to our garden for food and Long-tailed Tits were joining the other tits at the hanging feeders. One day I encountered a Woodcock trying to find food at the windswept edge of our road. Masses of waders were driven to search for food along the beaches where as a rule none occurred at all. Thus, on 23rd January there were present on Swanage beach, just below the promenade where the persistent east winds had dumped large masses of dead seaweed, four Knot, four or five Redshanks, two Turnstones and two Dunlins. For some days or even weeks, varying numbers of these four species were always on the beach. The most extraordinary assemblage of waders was found by Trev Haysom and myself on the three-mile-long sandy beach to the north of Studland on 7th February. The frost had gone so deeply into the sea that masses of razors and other shell-fish from the shallow seas had been frozen and thrown up dead all along the beach. This had attracted crowds of gulls and waders. The gulls we reckoned at approximately 5000; the waders at about 2000, of which some 1500 were Dunlins. There were many Bar-tailed Godwits, and smaller numbers of Redshanks, Knot, Grey Plovers and Sanderlings, with a few Ringed Plovers. I believe some Ruffs were seen there a day or two later when we had encouraged other local bird people to investigate. It is possible that all these birds were wintering on Poole Harbour, an area that is normally very difficult to explore completely except by boat. At this time most of Poole Harbour was frozen and its muddy shores were also frozen. A number of dead waders were found on its edges. Some also were found dead by the bay, along the Studland beach; so the sources of food thrown up by the tide were not sufficient for the mass of birds that tried to survive there.

Two of my counts of dead birds during the cold spell may be worth giving. On 31st January along a mile of the sandy shore near the Studland ferry I found about ten dead Sheldrakes, three Redshanks, one Velvet Scoter and one Great Crested Grebe. On 10th

February Ilay Cooper and I did a thorough search of the sea-wrack along nearly half a mile of Swanage beach and found the following: one Black-throated Diver, one Red-throated Diver, several Guillemots and Razorbills, a Snipe and a Ringed Plover, gulls of several species including a Kittiwake, Redwing, Rock Pipit, and one or two other small passerine birds, too dead to identify. Which shows how widespread, species and family-wise, the mortality of that disastrous winter was.

Such were some of the highlights, for the ornithologist, of that extraordinary winter; but now we return to Peveril Point. Let me lead up to the strangest bird I saw there by recording what was seen on each visit in January. On the 7th. apart from small passerine birds of various species that were exploring for food on the rocks and the shore, the birds seen out to sea apart from gulls were: two Cormorants, one Shag, about six auks, three Scoters, one Sheldrake, one Gannet: nothing abnormal there, indeed, rather a 'typical' winter day's score. On 13th January I found a Redshank, a Lapwing and a Purple Sandpiper on the rocks, but I saw nothing but gulls on or over the sea. Next day there was a Purple Sandpiper and a Redshank on the rocks; over the sea were three divers, apparently all Red-throated, flying round; and some twenty auks flew past—this during the half-hour from 2.30 to 3 p.m. My next visit was on 23rd January when there were no waders on the rocks but birds on the sea included Cormorant and Shag, Guillemots and a Red-necked Grebe, the only one of this, the rarest of the five British grebes, that I ever saw there. Again, one Sheldrake flew past. Then on 25th January I found my mystery bird. As I arrived on the Point, a small wader flew from the northern reef of rocks to the southern. It showed so much white in the wing that I suspected it to be a Sanderling; but it had the appearance of a Dunlin in winter plumage. It settled close to a Purple Sandpiper; and from time to time they passed each other within inches as they fed on the rock surface. Whenever this happened, I was bewildered to notice that the 'Dunlin' was very slightly the larger, longer bird. According to the measurements given by Witherby in the *Handbook*, the largest Northern Dunlin is only just as long in wing and tail as the smallest Purple Sandpiper. For a Dunlin to look noticeably larger than a Purple Sandpiper seemed incredible. I was so puzzled that I went home and got my wife and my telescope. The birds were still on the same patch of rock. The telescope confirmed the fact that the 'Dunlin' was the larger bird.

When I investigated further, I found one species that seemed to fit, namely the Rock Sandpiper (*Erolia ptilocnemus*) of the north Pacific; and it has a conspicuous wing-bar, and is a rock-feeding bird. It also has a white eye-ring. This I did not see; I did not look for it, as I was not aware of its importance, but the fact that I did not notice it suggests that the bird we saw may not have had one. Anyway, as this species has never, as far as I know, been found any distance from its northeast Pacific home and is less migratory than most waders or shorebirds, it is difficult to believe that one would find its way all across North America and the Atlantic Ocean even in the midst of the strangest winter of my life-time. We looked for it again but neither it nor any ordinary proper-sized Dunlin ever showed up on the Peveril Rocks in the later weeks of the great frost. Next day, for instance, there were two Purple Sandpipers (they were the same size as each other, so if one was the bird of the previous day, it was not an unusually small bird), also a Redshank and a Turnstone. On the 29th the waders on the rocks were one Knot and one Redshank.

The next time I found a Purple Sandpiper on the rocks was on 3rd February, when it was accompanied by one Turnstone. On later visits to Peveril in February, although the cold weather continued, I saw no more waders on the rocks.

We have not quite finished with Peveril and its birds. Indeed, what might well be considered its most characteristic bird has hardly been mentioned—the Rock Pipit. This bird can be found on Peveril Point at all times of the year. One pair, perhaps sometimes two, breed under the steep cliff-like slopes of the down a couple of hundred yards or so from the Point. These may be seen, or at least heard singing, from the Point during the breeding season. At all other seasons several are to be found on the rocks and small patches of sea shore round the shelter. Sometimes in winter the number that can be counted round the Point rises to a dozen, which is a large flock for this very sedentary species. On a stormy day, if you sit quietly in the shelter, it is quite likely that a Rock Pipit will come and settle on the wall within a yard of the silent watcher. Or you will suddenly see a small bird come up the steep side of one of the main rocks, and you think for a moment that you have got a Purple Sandpiper. The two species are, in fact, not far from the same size, and they are not unlike in general colour so that both can be almost invisible as they explore the rock face.

Then there are the small incoming migrants that may appear out of the blue (or the grey) on a spring day. If you have a good pair of ears with you (I must now depend on younger ears than my own) a Yellow Wagtail may declare itself, usually passing over without resting. Or you spot a bird skimming over the water some way out, and wildly hope it is a petrel (I have never seen a petrel from Peveril Point). But it turns out to be a Swallow or Sand Martin; and you can watch it come nearer and nearer till it passes close over your head and disappears inland. Later, in May, Swifts come in during the day, usually flying higher than the swallow tribe.

Peveril Down has its own incoming migrants, too. It is one of the most likely places in Purbeck for providing rest for the incoming Wheatears, any time after the middle of March.

By way of giving me a dramatic last moment, during the last spring that we spent at Swanage, 1969 (and even that is only a quarter true, for we left for America at the end of March), Peveril gave me a final burst of excitement on the morning of 18th March. Up to that date, I had seen no summer migrant, neither Wheatear nor Chiffchaff, though in Dorset you begin to hope for the pioneers of both species by the middle of the month, if not earlier. I got into the car and drove along towards Peveril Point. Suddenly a gorgeous cock Black Redstart flew from the edge of the road into a small bush a few yards up on the Down. I stopped and watched it from the car. As I did so, I saw a small bird flit up into the air for a moment from some low scrub a few yards beyond the redstart—sure enough, a Chiffchaff. Within a minute I had found another in the same patch of scrub. Having watched them for several minutes I drove on to the end of the road. As I was parking the car by the lifeboat house, a flash of white caught my eye. On the grass beyond the end of the road, just above the lookout, a cock Wheatear flew up from the ground and settled on the rail of the seat where people sit to enjoy the scenery on summer days. Breakfast tasted unusually good that morning! In all our seventy years of migrant recording only twice before had we seen these two species on the same date—Wilfrid in 1947 in Thanet on 20th March, and I had both on 24th March at Swanage in 1964. We had them on successive dates in half a dozen years.

I began this chapter with the suggestion that seawatching had become a sport for young ornithologists. Of course, if you are going to spend some time in mid-winter lying down on the open beach at Dungeness, as I did in the twenties and thirties, you need to be young and hardy. But if you can find a convenient shelter, as at Peveril Point, it is the ideal occupation for an ageing ornithologist whose eyes are still good though his ears are poor, and who can no longer cover twenty miles on foot in the day, nor hear the shrill pipings of the small birds in the woods.

CHAPTER X

Winter Birds in the Mid-Atlantic States of North America

If you move from the south of England to Pennsylvania, you naturally compare the bird life of your two homes, especially the birds you may hope to see from your windows during the long winter months when the elderly ornithologist is inclined to stay at home much of the time.

In the 1970s we live in Swarthmore, a suburban place of residence, fifteen miles west-south-west of the great city of Philadelphia. Superficially it is very much like any other residential suburb of a great western city: several square miles of moderate-sized houses, most of them with small gardens back and front. But it is different all the same. This part of Pennsylvania was covered with forest three hundred years ago, and in this particular area when the local authorities planned the development of the town a hundred years ago they decided that (as one rather critically minded inhabitant expressed it) trees mattered more than people. Anyway, they decided that trees mattered. If you

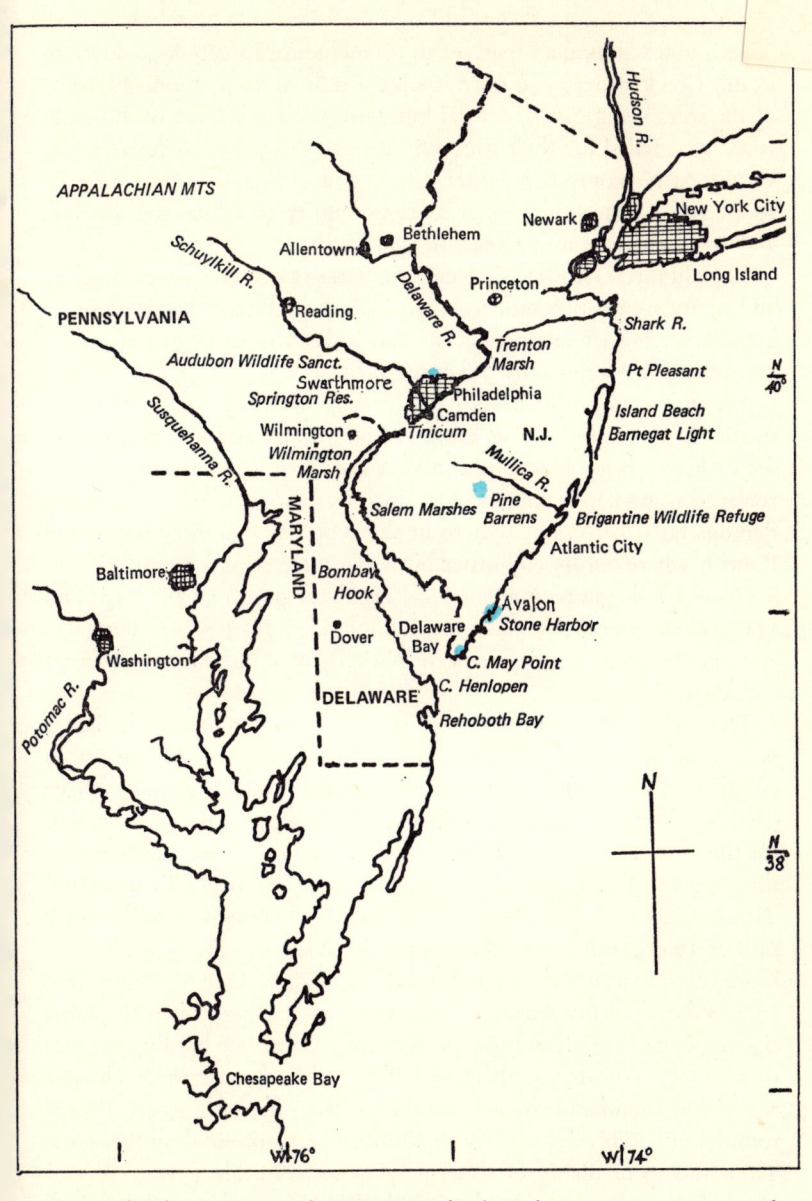

The Mid-Atlantic States of USA—Maryland, Delaware, New Jersey and Pennsylvania.

begin with the local college (and that really was the place where it all began) you will find a superb campus, including a steep slope down to Crum Creek, where you can walk for a mile in deep woodland, some of the trees being giants, several hundred years old. Most of those old trees were felled for their timber in the early days but there are a few survivors. Not only here either, for as you walk about the residential roads you pass numbers of great trees, eighty to a hundred feet tall, and presumably as many years in age, too.

The old forest trees are all deciduous, oaks of several species, beeches, and many more. But modern man here as in Britain has introduced conifers and other evergreens, so that today the variety of species is considerable. All this must affect the bird life.

Yet you may walk through the college woods or along the residential roads for an hour or more in mid-winter, and you may hardly see or hear a bird. The commonest winter bird is the Starling. Has it replaced some native species? Or, since its introduction, has it simply demonstrated here as elsewhere in the world that it can survive and flourish where hardly any other birds can increase and multiply?

However, begin to put out food regularly to attract the birds and you will soon find that there are some hidden away somewhere. On a good day one's garden may be visited by some twenty different species.

The 17th February 1972 was one of my best days in that particular winter, with a total of nineteen species. All but two (or three if you count feral pigeons) were passerines: Feral Pigeon, Mourning Dove (two seen) and Downy Woodpecker (two seen, male and female). Of the crow tribe, two species, a single Blue Jay (sometimes there are three or four) and two Common Crows flying over. Two Tufted Titmice appeared, but not a single chickadee, though in mid-winter one or two Carolina or Black-capped Chickadees are possible, and more often than not they come with the titmice. One Mocking-bird appeared. Of all the American passerine species I think it is the most rigorously territorial; outside the breeding season one hardly ever sees two Mocking-birds together; and if you do, you see them chasing round and round and round until one moves off. Starlings are always round about. This day a party of about twenty appeared on the grass. They also spent plenty of time gorging on suet. There were several House Sparrows, several Red-winged Blackbirds—all in the handsome striped plumage of the female or immature—and three Common Grackles: quite an early date for them, for I have never seen one round

Downy Woodpecker

the garden in mid-winter. This year (1972) one turned up on 12th February, and thereafter I saw one, or occasionally three, on several February days. They seem to come in rather greater numbers from the beginning of March.

A pair of Cardinals showed up as usual; and six Evening Grosbeaks, including two males. These handsome birds, a more brilliant edition of the Hawfinch of Europe, were plentiful in the Atlantic States this winter, but we have rarely seen them in our garden and six at once is our largest number. They did not reappear. As on most days there were several House Finches—I will come back to them later. Several Pine Siskins, also a common bird this winter, though in the previous winter we had none. And several Goldfinches (*Spinus tristis*, of course, not *Carduelis carduelis*), which are amongst our most regular birds. Several Slate-coloured Juncos appeared, two White-throated Sparrows (often there are four or five) and one Song Sparrow—by no means a regular bird in our garden in the winter. It will be noted that all the species in this paragraph, eight different kinds, belong to the large Fringillid family—the finches and buntings and their allies; all are seed-eaters and therefore many of them are able to survive the severe winter of these parts.

During the last two weeks of February I saw several species that had not shown up on the 17th. The 19th brought us the heaviest snowfall of the winter (about nine inches) and the weather remained very cold for most of the succeeding week, so that the snow was deep for some time. One might have expected such a heavy snowfall to bring many birds to the garden, but in fact it did not. However, we did see some that we had not been seeing regularly. A pair of Purple Finches were among the rather few birds we had on the 20th; our only Field Sparrow of the winter appeared on the 21st; and our first Tree Sparrows (*Spizella* not *Passer*) (two) on the 24th. At last, on the 25th, there were two chickadees, on what was otherwise an unusually empty day. I think they were Black-capped, but now that my ears do not help me I find the two species almost impossible to separate. The 26th was an unusually good day for the birds—or rather for the birdwatcher, which is not necessarily the same thing. At one time nearly thirty small finches were on the ground under the feeders together, about twenty of them Goldfinches, the others Pine Siskins. A male Purple Finch, a single Tree Sparrow, and one chickadee were among the less regular species. The crowd of small finches appeared rather before midday. Early in the morning several had come into our trees, looking down at the food but refusing to come down; after a minute they flew away. I went to investigate: was there a cat lurking somewhere near? Apparently not. On several other days about that time I noticed the same curious behaviour: the birds coming into the trees, sitting for a short time, and then flying off again; and this happened early in the morning when it would seem that they would be specially hungry and would come fearlessly to any supply of obvious food.

The more you watch birds at close quarters the stranger, the more inexplicable, their behaviour sometimes seems to be. Normally, for instance, our local Mocking-bird ignores the food that the other birds are eating. The mere presence of a number of birds seems to attract other species, but not the Mocking-bird. He goes his own way, and finds his own food. Berries, sometimes; but what else? Rarely, yes even very rarely, he will suddenly decide that like the Starlings and the Downy Woodpeckers the suet is worth his attention. He is so aggressive that I have been expecting to see him drive the Starlings off. But no; in our garden he has to wait till the Starling has had his fill. I rarely see the Mocking-bird feeding; more often he just sits up in a tree as if meditating on the beauty of the world, or he sits and sings. Sometimes he hops about on the ground, but I do not see him actively feeding there. He has only recently colonised these winter-cold climates, as if the coming of man on his settled habitations had made life possible for Mocking-birds; but if so, what is it that man has brought that he can live by? Possibly berry-bearing bushes cultivated in gardens. I can see no other way in which he shows a clear dependence on the human environment.

Another recent arrival here, so recent that even I can trace it in the years that I have known the Delaware Valley, is the House Finch. This is an interesting story; among other things it seems to throw light on one way that migratory behaviour may begin.

Tufted Titmouse

Some time about 1950 (I cannot find the exact date) some captive House Finches, presumably from Mexico—the true home of the species is California south to Mexico, and neighbouring areas—got loose in New York and soon they spread both east and south. I saw House Finches at domestic feeders in New York State and then in Connecticut in the late fifties and early sixties. Before long they had spread south to the Philadelphia area and were turning up at garden feeders in various suburbs. Since about 1965 they have become quite plentiful; but as they are not in Peterson's *Field Guide* yet, many people still call them Purple Finches. Today (I write in late March 1972) it is almost more remarkable to have no House Finches at the feeders than to have a party of six or ten. But they do not stay all through the year. During the past two weeks their numbers have decreased. On 27th March 1970 I noted in my diary: 'House Finches seem suddenly to have disappeared.' A few nests have been found near Philadelphia, but it seems almost certain that the Philadelphia birds are mostly winter visitors from further north. Banding (ringing) will no doubt soon show the exact nature and extent of this annual movement—perhaps a hundred miles, perhaps less—but the point is that it seems to be a regular annual migration on a small scale, and it is difficult to see how it can be related to the food supply. It looks like an 'unnecessary' migration.

The other new migration in this part of the world, by Cattle Egrets, is no doubt necessary. Within the past thirty years they have spread north right up the Atlantic coast so that today a few are breeding even in Canada. But all the birds from this northern area, down to the Carolinas I suppose, if not even further south, undertake a long southern flight in the autumn. Very few birds of the heron tribe spend the winter as far north as New Jersey: a few Great Blue Herons, a few Black-crowned Night Herons and an occasional egret of one or other species. It is true that on 3rd January 1972 at the famous Stone Harbor sanctuary (where hundreds of herons of several species roost all through the autumn, arriving in amazing numbers at sunset) there were some two to three hundred Snowy Egrets, two or more American Egrets (the Great White Heron of British bird books), over thirty Louisiana Herons, two or more Little Blue Herons and at least six Glossy Ibises. We left before the Night Herons began to stir. Great Blues do not usually roost there. But most of those we did see are classified as only summer migrants in New Jersey. I have little doubt that when, later in January, the marshes began to freeze, most of those we saw flew further south. That is to say, some only fly south when compelled by the weather. On the other hand, it will be seen that we saw no Cattle Egrets. It is possible that we overlooked a few, but I do not think so. We talked with a local observer who had been counting the birds several evenings during the Christmas holidays. She did not mention any Cattle Egrets. It is my belief that they have established a regular migration and that they do not wait for the cold weather to drive them south. If this is true it seems to be a very important truth. This migration is not the result of ice ages or other changes in climatic conditions. It is the response of a very vigorous species to the environment it finds now. Having rapidly established itself over a vast new living space, it has not stayed on in its northern habitat till the cold kills it. It has somehow known that it must fly hundreds of miles south before the cold weather comes—or, in other words, it must undertake a long migration at the time of year when food is still in such good supply that it can fatten itself up for the journey. Yet it has not done this in either Europe or Asia. Only the new, Western Hemisphere, population has adopted this habit.

Well, let us go back to the garden birds. Starlings, for instance. Starlings seem to have brought many of their habits across the Atlantic when they were first introduced to America. The roosting habit for one. At the end of a February afternoon as the light begins to fade I watch their behaviour. One is resting in the top of our hickory tree as if waiting for the moment to come when it must fly off to the roost. Another is in a neighbour's tree. Each, probably, is in its spring territory. Suddenly, the bird from the further tree shoots off, flying south-west towards the roost. Our bird still stays. About a minute later, it goes, flying with equal suddenness and rapidity in the same direction. Ten seconds later, a party of five come shooting past from the north-east. 'My' bird did not wait for them; it did not join up with them. Whatever the force was that finally triggered its departure it was apparently an inner force not connected with the action of others of its species. Yet, as a rule, if I watch at the time the Starlings are flying to their roost, what I see is a series of small parties, three, five, six, rather than individual birds. So, as so often, one is left with what looks like a contradiction. Let us say that some Starlings are carried off to their roosting place by communal action, whilst others go separately. This, of course, fits with many observations of flock behaviour made by Selous and others. A Lapwing flock watched by Edmund Selous suddenly rose from the ground and flew round in perfect unison; but one did not join the flock; it stayed on the ground. Why?

Before leaving the winter birds of the mid-Atlantic States, I must record what was, I think, the strangest happening that has ever occurred to me during over seventy years of bird watching.

On 14th January 1970, we drove over to spend a night with Jack and Tessa Cadbury at their home in the New Jersey Pine Barrens, between Pemberton and Browns Mills. The winter was at its most severe, with much ice on the tidal Delaware River where we crossed it at the Chester ferry, and plenty of snow everywhere. Before dark there was time for a short outing, so Jack drove us round the long, narrow, Browns Mills lake—not a very attractive place for birds, especially when it is all frozen over. Still, we might see something. We saw very little. As we were returning towards Browns Mills we saw a sparrow-like bird on the snowy road in front of us, where for some reason a small stream was unfrozen. We were looking straight into the sun, so the bird appeared quite dark. To my horror, it did not fly up, but I hoped we had not killed it, as it was in the middle of the road, in fact in the middle of our track. When we got to Browns Mills—a mile or so further—Jack stopped to get some 'gas' (petrol). As he raised the 'hood' (bonnet) of the car a bird flew out and right up into a tree. I only saw a bird; he saw a bright-coloured bird which he was convinced could only be a White-winged Crossbill. So, with our tank full, we returned to see if there were any more at the place where we had picked up this one. Now, we had the sunlight behind us. Sure enough there were three, two females and one male; the second male had not yet found its way back. I hope it ultimately did. Part of the time they were feeding or drinking at the open stream; part of the time they were up in pine trees above the road. I suppose the bird we had picked up was feeding on a cone that had dropped from one of these trees.*

How had it survived the ride? The car had a convenient perch under the hood, but that the bird should fly up as the car came over it and that it should find the perch and remain on it for some five minutes waiting to be safely 'released', is so extraordinary as to be almost incredible. Yet it happened.

There are a few more comments that I must make before looking at the winter birds on the sea-coast. Thus, as I watch the small, finch-like birds that come to the garden day by day for food, there is one characteristic of their feeding habits that soon attracts attention. Every member of the 'sparrow' tribe that feeds on the ground in our garden constantly shuffles with its feet, so as to uncover whatever desirable seeds or other food may be buried there. This it does all through the winter; it does it whether or not there are leaves or any other decayed matter on the surface of the earth; it also does it when snow is on the ground. It even does it on the feeder. Presumably before man came on the scene, these sparrows, Song Sparrow, White-throat, Fox

* The Red Crossbill notoriously does not feed on the cones it drops from trees, and it sometimes drops a great many. But my experience of the White-winged Crossbill shows that it often does a lot of its feeding on the ground, at any rate under Hemlock trees (*Tsuga canadensis*). It would be interesting to know if anyone has attempted to interpret this difference in the habits of two closely related species. Bent has, for once, little to say here; he shows that both species eat a great variety of food, apart from seeds of conifers, and that both sometimes feed on the ground; also that both are apt to scatter much seed onto the ground. But it is not clear from his various reports that there is a difference in habit between the two species. So I think the matter needs further exploration.

Sparrow, Junco, possibly some others, were inhabitants of the woods, as indeed they often are still, and there this habit would be of constant value as they foraged for their food among the autumn leaves, or through the winter's snow. Today, they are often accompanied by House Sparrows (called 'English Sparrows' by most of my neighbours). These have been in the country for two hundred years or so, but they have not acquired the leaf-shifting habit. Of course, they are not birds of the woods, and in the gardens where they feed the habit has no great value, though it might help them when the snow is covering the ground. However, they survive the cold remarkably well, so that they clearly have other habits that replace the leaf-shifting by foot. Perhaps the stronger beak, and their incessant use of it to toss everything aside, is the factor that saves them. They do with their beaks what the American 'sparrows', or in Old World terms buntings, do with their feet.

This leads me to another aspect of winter feeding. The one member of the thrush family that can survive the winter in these latitudes is the Bluebird (*Sialia sialis*), surely one of the loveliest creatures in the world. Unfortunately it has become very scarce in many parts of eastern North America in the past twenty years, though there is now some evidence of an increase. Lately I was watching a small party of half a dozen which have been spending this winter (1972)—as indeed they mostly do—in a place where they can roam over an extensive area of uncut grass, with scattered small trees where they sit in the lower branches; every few minutes they drop down into the grass to get some food. What is it? Bent, in his fantastically full account of the life history of American birds, shows that in every month animal food, chiefly insects, predominates, though the Bluebird has quite a wide range of diet. So, even in mid-winter Bluebirds apparently find adequate insect food among these long dead grasses. This specialised feeding habit, so different from the usual ground-hunting of the other American thrushes—such as the Robin (*Turdus migratorius*) and the several brown thrushes—perhaps explains the ability of the Bluebird to survive the severe winter of the eastern seaboard.

There are other things that strike the British birdwatcher when he spends his years among North American birds. In England, almost the last of our small insectivorous migrants to return from the south is the Spotted Flycatcher; most of them do not return till well on in May. Yet here, the Phoebe, which an innocent birder might be pardoned for mistaking for a Spotted Flycatcher (the Tyrannidae are a distinct family from the Muscicapidae, but if ever there was a case of parallel evolution it is here) is the *first* purely insectivorous species to return from the south. It is here in small numbers by the end of March. As far as the ordinary observer can see, it catches its prey by sallies in the air, exactly as our familiar Flycatcher does. It sits on a fence or post or open branch of a tree and returns to the same perch sometimes, though less regularly than the Flycatcher. It even flirts its tail in just the same way. Its plumage is similar, but it has a rather shorter tail. True, it likes to live near water where, I suppose, even on the most dismal day in late March, with raw east winds driving all sensible insects into shelter, it can find the insects that it needs. Anyway, it survives and flourishes.

So too the Chimney Swift, though its habits seem to be closely akin to the Swift of Western Europe, has a surprisingly different cycle of behaviour. But now I am getting among the summer migrants, of which there are many. I had better keep to the winter birds. Let us go to the seashore—we are back in February or January again.

The normal garden birds of the mid-Atlantic States, apart from the introduced Starlings and House Sparrows, are nearly all birds that belong to America only. The occasional woodland bird that belongs to both sides of the Atlantic—the Tree Creeper, the two Crossbills—is hardly a garden bird in the usual sense. But when you go to the sea the position is very different. At any time of year when I walk out on to the sandy beaches of New Jersey the birds I first see do not tell me which side of the Atlantic it is: quantities of Herring Gulls in every kind of plumage; among them, probably, a few Great Black-backs. And in every month of the year—or, let us say, all through the year apart from a few weeks round midsummer—we shall soon find bunches of small waders hurrying along close to the edge of the tide: Sanderlings, exactly as if we were walking along the tide-line in Kent or Dorset or Norfolk or Yorkshire, or wherever there are extensive sands for the Sanderlings to enjoy. Even this is not all. Along the two hundred miles of sandy beach that protect the wetlands of New Jersey from the ocean, there are solid stone breakwaters which are the resort of Purple Sandpipers. Where they spent their winters before man set up these breakwaters it is difficult to imagine; but there they are today, often in numbers that I have never found on any British rocky coast.

In mid-winter waders are scarce in these areas: there are occasional flocks of Dunlins that somehow survive the most severe weather.

Grey Plovers (always called Black-bellied here, however white the belly may be) are to be found throughout the winter in small numbers; otherwise nearly all the waders go further south and avoid the kind of catastrophe that overtook our British waders in the prolonged frost of 1963. So here the picture is quite a contrast: instead of great flocks of waders on all the mud-flats, there is almost nothing except for the two species—Sanderling and Purple Sandpiper—that feed on the very edge of the sea.

When we turn to the sea-ducks, again we find the same species on both sides of the ocean: scoters—but here we have three common species instead of only two, Common, Velvet (called more appropriately White-winged) and Surf. Red-breasted Mergansers are common; Long-tailed Ducks (which are known in America, rather nicely, as Old Squaws) are much commoner than they are in southern British seas; Scaup are present in good-sized flocks (the Lesser Scaup tends to be a bird of freshwater); Goldeneye are here on the backwaters more often than out on the ocean; and two species of Eider, Common and King, turn up along the coast in small numbers almost every winter. Moreover, the Harlequin, a sedentary species in the European part of its range, rarely leaving its Icelandic home waters, is recorded here even as far south as Maryland, almost every winter. These individuals must travel well over a thousand miles from their northern breeding grounds. We end with two small ducks that do not belong to the European coasts at all. In some of the estuaries and tidal rivers the most abundant wintering duck is the Ruddy Duck (*Oxyura*), whose only near relative in Europe is the Pheasant-tail of the west Mediterranean area; so that the Ruddy, escaped from Slimbridge, seems to be finding an unoccupied niche on Midland and south-western reservoirs of England. Remarkably, the feral population survived the 1963 frost, so it ought to survive anything England can do to it.

Our last species is in some ways the most attractive of the whole family, the charming little Bufflehead (*Bucephala albeda*). In female or immature plumage it can be momentarily mistaken for the Ruddy; but the drake is instantly recognised by his brilliant white face and under-parts; indeed, he shows his white as conspicuously as a Goosander or a drake Goldeneye. Buffleheads are usually found in small parties on the backwaters; they constantly dive, so that for a time none is visible; then, as the watcher comes nearer, they rise from the water with a rapid flurry of wings, fly quickly round once or twice and settle a bit further out to begin their diving and feeding again. From

October to the end of April these attractive little ducks are nearly always to be found on our best-known backwater at Avalon, in southern New Jersey.

Most of the freshwater ducks, especially the surface feeders, are species that are familiar in Europe, though several, such as the two species of teal and the Wigeon, are distinct though very closely related. Pintail occur in enormous flocks, much more plentiful than in any part of Britain known to me. The common diving ducks do not so exactly replace the European species: the Ring-neck represents the Tufted, but it seems to be much less abundant. Pochard are represented by two species, the Canvasback and the Red-head, both species of very patchy distribution, the Canvasback being quite abundant in some specially favoured pools.

I began this section with Herring and Great Black-backed Gulls on the New Jersey shore. But what about Common and Black-headed Gulls, the British reader may ask? If you look carefully among the Herring Gulls you may pick out a few Ring-billed Gulls, which here replace the Common Gull of Europe. Apart from the dark ring across the bill it is very much like a Common Gull, though slightly larger, and therefore a little nearer in size to the Herring Gull. One of the oddities of bird distribution is that this species is replaced again on the Pacific coast of North America by the Common Gull, though the people of the western States call it, more sensibly, the Mew Gull (see W.B.A.'s *Birds of the Ocean*).

As to the Black-headed Gull, it may be said that it is replaced by two species, the Laughing Gull and Bonaparte's Gull. Both belong to the quite large tribe of gulls that have dark hoods during the breeding season. Bonaparte's is very much like a Black-headed in appearance. Indeed, apart from its smaller size and the light underside to the wing, the two birds are not easy to distinguish in the field. The wing pattern when the bird is seen from above is practically identical. But if one asks, does it replace the Black-headed on the American side of the Atlantic? I should be disposed to say: no, it does not. Bonaparte's is a winter visitor to the Atlantic coast, but it is not a common bird in this part of its range. I have rarely if ever seen one among the swarms of gulls on the sands of southern New Jersey. If I want to find any I must go to some place where the small New Jersey rivers flow out to the sea. Here, small parties usually congregate; or at least they put in an appearance and then fly off. Look out for Bonaparte's, one might almost say, where in England you would look for Kittiwakes. I believe

I have never seen one at the famous Brigantine Nature Reserve where almost every imaginable water- and sea-bird, to say nothing of eagles, hawks, rare sparrows and many other strange visitors, turn up from time to time. Small numbers appear, chiefly at migration times, in the Delaware river, a few miles below Philadelphia. Further north along the New Jersey shore, off the Shark river area, they seem to be commoner, but in this part of America Bonaparte's is nowhere plentiful, and rarely if ever seen over the fields.*

In the sense of replacing the Black-headed as a bird of open fields and a common breeding species, it is the Laughing Gull that does it in this part of North America. The Laughing Gull looks to be a 'size bigger' than the Black-headed; presumably this is partly because it has a much darker mantle, almost like a British Lesser Black-back, but also I think the wing is broader. The immature Laughing Gull that spent several months at Weymouth a few years ago was often seen in company with Black-headeds, and was seen to be the same length. I should have expected it to look about the size of a Common Gull.

Laughing Gulls are summer migrants to the Delaware Valley and adjacent coasts. When they come, they come in force, and dominate the scene in many places with their loud 'laughs' and boisterous behaviour. Thousands breed in the New Jersey marshes.

There is still the Lesser Black-back to consider. Until recently, it was not admitted to the list of species that have visited America. Now, several occurrences are accepted. I have seen one and only one. I first arrived in America after crossing the Atlantic on a Norwegian freighter in convoy, at the end of March 1945. We docked on the New Jersey side of the Hudson river opposite Manhattan, and there we remained for most of a day before we were able to get ashore. It was a pleasant, sunny day, and I spent the time on deck watching the gulls: quantities of Herring Gulls were frequently flying close round the boat. Twice an obvious Lesser Black-back came past me within a few yards, the orange legs and Herring Gull size showing its identity very plainly. So this rarity was among the first ten species that I saw on the American

---

* Just after I had written this, on 10th April 1972, John Miller and I found a migratory flock of some fifty Bonaparte's Gulls by some large brackish pools just off the busy Industrial Highway, a mile or two from Philadelphia's great airport and close to the tidal Delaware river. This is much the largest assemblage of Bonaparte's that I have ever come across, but I am not suggesting that it is in fact a rare occurrence. My experience is, of course, limited. How birds do love to upset the things you confidently write about them!

side of the ocean! I had Wilfrid's *Birds of the Ocean* with me, so I knew it ought not to be there. But it was. The observation was published in *The Auk*.

There is, I think, a better chance of seeing both Glaucous and Iceland Gulls in this part of North America, certainly the latter species, than in southern England. But Kittiwakes rarely come close inshore.

Both Red-throated and Great Northern Divers are fairly common on the Atlantic coast in the winter, but they are 'loons' not divers; and the Great Northern is the Common Loon, breeding on many lakes in New England and occasionally nearer to this mid-Atlantic coast. But if you want to find a Black-throated Diver on this side of the Atlantic you must begin by calling it an Arctic Loon, and then you must cross the continent and look for it on the north Pacific coast. However, there are some recent records from the Atlantic coast, as far south as Long Island. I believe I saw one on the New Jersey coast on 1st May 1970. It was still in winter plumage, moving north close inshore, diving as it went. I had several close views of it, and the dagger beak was so conspicuous that I should unhesitatingly have called it Black-throated if I had seen it on the Dorset coast. Unfortunately I was alone.

Finally, there are the auks. From time to time a Razorbill is recorded on the New Jersey coast in mid-winter, but I have not seen one. And occasionally Little Auks, here called Dovekies, invade the coast in small numbers: one of those mysterious so-called 'wrecks', though the only one I happen to have experienced did not, as far as I know, result in any casualties. Robert Haines took us to the New Jersey shore on a bitterly cold day, 30th November 1966. First we spotted a small bird flying over the sea some way out, so small that we concluded that it could only be a Dovekie. Then we met some other birders who had been watching several from one of the jetties where a small river flows out to the sea. When we got there we found them, and one was diving close to the stone jetty, so that we could watch it swimming under the water just below us, almost as if it were in a tank in an aquarium. I have watched dozens from Atlantic liners, but I never expected to see one at such close quarters.

Great Black-headed Gull adult and immature

CHAPTER XI

Some Indian Birds

Politics no doubt affects ornithology more than it should do. During the British occupation of India, a number of Britishers, most of them in official positions, spent their leisure time studying and collecting birds. Indian ornithology thus became an important interest to the ornithologists of Britain. In the Introduction to their massive and astonishingly thorough *Handbook of the Birds of India and Pakistan*, Salim Ali and Dillon Ripley give the names of T. C. Jerdon, Brian Hodgson and Edward Blyth as the 'virtual founders of Indian ornithology'. Their work was done in the first half of the nineteenth century; and in 1862 Jerdon published his large two-volume work on the *Birds of India*. Ali and Ripley mention seven other names of men who helped in the pioneer work before Jerdon's book was published.

The next period is dominated by the remarkable personality of Allan Octavian Hume, sometimes called the 'Prince' of Indian ornithologists, or, by those who found him too dominating a character, the 'Pope'. He was a member of the Indian Civil Service, and whilst

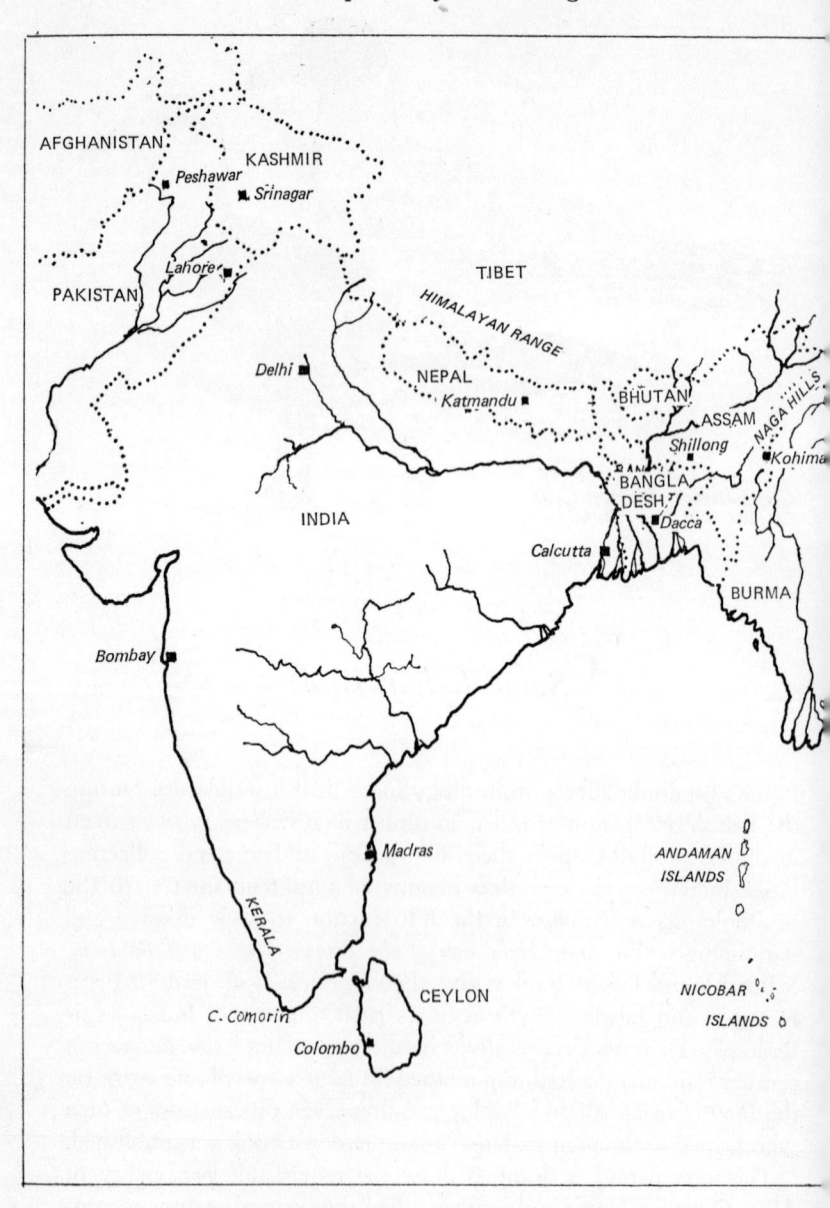

The Indian sub-continent and adjoining countries.

still in official service he was largely instrumental in founding the Indian National Congress. What he might have thought of this body in the days when it was led by Gandhi and by Nehru is perhaps an open question, but his name is still remembered and honoured in independent India, not primarily because of his ornithological activities. Hume founded and edited a journal called *Stray Feathers: A Journal of Ornithology for India and Dependencies*, and this he kept going from 1872 to 1888. Since 1886 the *Journal* of the Bombay Natural History Society has been the paper in which serious contributions to Indian ornithology have appeared. It is still published. Of course, it is what it claims to be—a journal of natural history, not just of ornithology.

Then, in 1889 and succeeding years two men, Oates and Blanford, put together in four volumes all that was known of the birds of all India, including Burma and Ceylon. Some thirty years later this was revised and brought up to date by Stuart Baker, in six volumes—indeed, eight, if you include the synonymy, index, etc. Down to that time and even later, nearly all the contributors to Indian ornithology were British. Of the twelve names given by Salim Ali and Ripley as makers of important contributions to Indian ornithology between the two world wars, only one is Indian—Salim Ali himself.

Now, twenty-five years after independence, the delightful *Bulletin for Bird-Watchers*, produced each month by Zafar Futehally, is mainly written by Indian ornithologists; and the western names that appear among its contributors are not all British. It is, after all, a leading American ornithologist, Dillon Ripley, who is cooperating with Salim Ali in the great enterprise of the *Handbook*, whose sixth, seventh and eighth volumes have lately reached me.

In the 1960s and 1970s transport has become so easy that adventurous young ornithologists think nothing of travelling five or ten thousand miles during their summer holidays. They undertake explorations in Africa, in tropical islands, in many parts of the world, but not any longer in India. There are some good reasons for this. Africa lies directly south of Europe, so that many of the birds familiar to the European ornithologist may be seen in their winter quarters in a totally different kind of habitat. Since Reg Moreau called attention to the special character of the great migration from south Europe over the Mediterranean and the Sahara desert, and since he stirred our interest with his remarkable book *Bird Faunas of Africa and its Islands*, no wonder interest has tended to concentrate on Africa. India, by contrast, has been so much broken up by the huge growth of its human population that problems of altitudinal distribution and even of migration have become difficult to study there. India has regrettably become very remote to British consciousness.

When, some twenty years ago, I spoke to the Oxford ornithologists on 'British Birds in India', Wilfrid made the pertinent and characteristic comment, 'There aren't any.' Literally, that may approach the truth. Yet I should like to encourage a new generation of British and other western ornithologists to consider India as a country with plenty of fascinating problems of bird-life still waiting for closer study. One thing can, I think, be claimed without hesitation for India: its birds are tamer than in any other part of the world. Aldous Huxley, in his travel book *Jesting Pilate*, noted that the first thing that struck him on landing in India was the pervasive presence of birds. The ancient Hindu tradition of respect for all life has prevailed so widely for so long that over all the plains of Hindu India birds are not afraid of man. As you drive along a main road, that lumpy creature on the telephone wire flops lazily down to catch a grasshopper from the roadside and reveals the breath-taking vivid blue wing colour of the Indian Roller. As you rest by the roadside, a pair of small Green Bee-eaters will flash round your head, chasing insects. Go into the village and you may find one or more lordly Peacocks pecking their way round the rubbish-dump, quite unconcerned when some men from the village pass by three feet from them; or one may settle on the roof of a hut and sound his bugle cry. At almost any place you may see vultures and Pariah Kites soaring in the air; if some animal has died, there will probably be thirty or forty vultures of two or three species gorging on the corpse, most unwilling to move off from an approaching human.

Between 1927 and 1955 I spent some twelve years in India, in various bits and pieces. When I was resident, I lived either in Calcutta or in Delhi, but had opportunities to travel widely, and several times spent some days with Salim Ali in some of the wilder unspoilt parts of the country, north-east, west, central and extreme south, not to mention a trek with Dillon Ripley through the Naga Hills. As a result my Indian list is over 800 species—of the twelve hundred or so that are known from the whole area.

My birding in India has been unsystematic and scrappy, so what follows is quotation or gleanings from a few papers I have written or from note-books compiled during some holidays or expeditions.

We may begin with Calcutta. I spent over a year with a section of the Friends Ambulance Unit in Calcutta in 1942-3, and at that time I used to write an occasional bird article for the *Birmingham Post*. So, one day, I wrote more or less what follows (without the scientific names).

'The gardens on the outskirts of Calcutta hold a good variety of bird-life; but apart from the kites and the swifts that are for ever in the skies, and the crows (House Crows, *Corvus splendens*), sparrows (*Passer domesticus*, no other) and Mynahs (*Acridotheres tristis*) that jostle for scraps on the smelly rubbish-heaps, most of them escape observation. For the other species commonly keep to the trees, whose foliage is so dense that the birds remain well hidden. Sometimes I hear the chatter or cry of some bird—a Tailor-bird (*Orthotomus sutorius*), a Grey Tit (*Parus major*, but much less brightly coloured than *Parus major* in Western Europe), a tiny Sunbird (*Cinnyris asiaticus*), a barbet (which in Calcutta means the Blue-throated (*Cyanops asiatica*)) or a dove (either *Streptopelia decaocto*, the famous Collared Dove, or *S. chinensis*, the Spotted Dove)—and I go to the window hoping to see it. But they rarely show themselves. If there is a movement it is likely to be a House Crow, which comes flopping out of the tree to gorge on the latest morsels thrown out by the cook.

'Today I have spent the last hour of daylight on the roof. On most Calcutta houses the roof is flat, and in the house where I am living it is reached by a winding stone staircase. When you climb to the top you can walk about on a level with the upper branches of the trees, so that you feel to be more nearly on equal terms with the birds.

'So much was happening overhead that at first I had little opportunity to attend to the trees. The evening flight of Cormorants and Darters had begun. They kept appearing in ones or twos or larger numbers—sometimes a dozen at once—most of them would be coming from the salt-lakes east of Calcutta to roost on trees near the Hooghly river. The common cormorant of India is the Little Cormorant (*Phalacrocorax niger*). The Darter is a closely related bird, called Anhinga in America, for its scientific name is *Anhinga melanogaster*. The American species is distinct. It is a large bird, with a long tail and a fantastically small head, no broader than its long neck—hence its other name of Snake-bird. One that flew over this evening rather low and near to me had its beak open, so that it looked even odder than the rest of them. As the light faded, occasional herons of some species came over. White egrets of several species are abundant on the rice-fields of Bengal, but these birds were grey, not white. Their rounded wings and rapid wing-beats, dark grey wings and pale grey bodies, showed them to be Night Herons (*Nycticorax nycticorax*)—one of the most widely distributed birds.

'While I was watching the Darters, I heard the clamour of Green Parrakeets (*Psittacula*) from the trees, and two or three flew out, leaving for a roost in some palm trees where scores assemble each evening with great screaming and excitement. At the same time from a thick tree on the other side of the house came the loud chattering call of the Koel (*Eudynamis scolopaceus*), an Indian species of cuckoo. Its loud call is rather like the laughing cry of the female Cuckoo (*Cuculus canorus*). The male is black and the female speckled grey. Both are clamorous, but both tend to remain hidden in the foliage. This evening after a time the speckly female suddenly flew out of the tree and passed close by me to disappear round the corner of another house. But the call came again from the first tree, so I waited in hopes. Actually, the next bird that appeared in the Koel tree was a Red-vented Bulbul (*Molpastes cafer*), a bird the size of a small thrush, with a black top-knot to his head. They are not very common in Calcutta, so one does not often hear the pleasant fluty song in the garden here.

'Then there was another movement in the tree; and I was looking at a fine black male Koel, the satin-black of his body plumage and long tail shot through with a tinge of indigo, his red beady eye and white beak contrasting with the intense black of the plumage. He had found a big berry on the side of the tree nearest to me, and this he quickly pulled off and devoured.

'The light was fading now; the Night Herons were winging their way across the sunset glow; Flying Foxes (which are large bats) flew unsteadily from tree to tree. The Swifts had vanished from the sky; only one or two Kites (*Milvus migrans*) were still soaring on high.

'I was about to turn down the spiral staircase when a familiar call-note caught my ear. It was the note of a Grey Wagtail (*Motacilla cineria*) flying south from its breeding ground somewhere by the rocky streams of Central Asia, to spend the winter somewhere in the Ganges delta—or even, as I soon learnt, round about Calcutta—for I found them coming to roost in surprising numbers on the roof of a house not far from our home in Upper Wood Street. That wagtail call-note at that moment took me very pleasantly across the world, at that time broken in pieces by war, for I could hear the same sound as I stood on my own doorstep in south Birmingham, when the Grey Wagtails come flying south from Scottish burns to the unfrozen streams of southern England. A "British bird in India" in fact!'

When we arrived in India in the summer of 1942 we had expected to be kept busy with civilian relief that might be needed if the Japanese, now in control of Burma, began to bomb Calcutta and other cities in undivided Bengal. But the bombs did not fall, fortunately; instead, Nature intervened with an exceptionally severe cyclone which devastated the coastal parts of south-west Bengal. So we began relief operations there, involving journeys by slow steamer down the Hooghly river. For the ornithologist, one of the virtues of India is that no one is ever in a hurry; you are allowed plenty of time to stand and stare. As the following quotation from another paper I wrote will show.

'I had to spend an hour waiting on a balcony looking out over the broad river, at a place where two parts of it meet. Their confluence is marked by a line of ruffled water, which seemed to provide good feeding for birds. On an earlier visit I had watched a great eagle, the White-bellied Sea Eagle (*Haliaeetus leucogaster*), together with a few of the ubiquitous Kites, fishing here; now it was occupied by some large gulls. Both Black-headed and Brown-headed Gulls (*Larus ridibundus* and *L. brunneicephalus*) I had seen further up the river. Now I was watching a much larger species. There were about a dozen adult Great Black-headed Gulls (*L. ichthyaetus*), and as it was November I was surprised to find that two of them still had the dark hood of summer plumage—the Great Black-head, like other gulls with dark hoods, sheds the dark head feathers in the winter.

'There were also some birds in immature plumage. At first, I thought these must be either Greater or Lesser Black-backed Gulls. On the wing, when the wing and tail colour was what showed, they looked just like them; but closer observation revealed one important difference. Young Black-backs of both species, and young Herring Gulls, are mottled brown all over, with blackish wing-quills and black at the tip of the tail. The under-parts of these birds were almost entirely white. This made them young Great Black-headed Gulls. Even the head, though it has some brown feathers, is largely white in the young "Great Black-heads". Consequently, as they ride on the water, they look very much like adult Black-backs as one may see see them on the sea along the English coast; the white breast and neck contrast with the dark brown mantle and blackish wing-tips.'

There has, I believe, been some controversy about the bill and leg colour of immature Great Black-headed Gulls, so what I saw that day on the Hooghly is of some value. One of the young gulls was carried close past me as it stood on the floating carcase of a dead animal. Its beak was black, and legs and feet pale flesh-colour. Another that I saw, possibly in its second or third year (I believe the first was a first-year bird), had the beak mostly black, with a trace of yellow at the base. The adult birds had yellow beaks, with a red patch at the tip. Neither colour agrees with Witherby's description in the *Handbook* (Vol. V, p. 79). As the species breeds chiefly in Soviet territories, probably the Russian ornithologists have described the colour of the soft parts correctly; but I have no access to their works.

It is odd to turn up this careful account of the largest party of Great Black-headed Gulls that I have ever seen, nearly thirty years after I saw them. In the interval, I have seen occasional single adult birds, in Bombay harbour, near Karachi, and in the Red Sea. During my years in Delhi we had occasional reports of immature Great Black-headed Gulls on the river, but never adults. I myself recorded three together once: they were in the company of Brahminy and Pariah Kites and they seemed enormous—too big for a Lesser Black-back or a Herring Gull; moreover, they had a lot of white at the base of the tail, a feature which is somewhere given as a good identification mark. Yet I now believe that my identification was wrong and they must have been one of the other large gulls. The paler body colour is the most obvious point of distinction for the immature Great Black-headed.

Before we say goodbye to the Hooghly river I will complete the story from that day in November 1942 with some terns that came flying past. There were two birds with pale pearly mantles, and with scarcely a trace of the black cap of summer: these were Gull-billed Terns (*Gelochelidon nilotica*). A larger tern, with steadier flight and blackish wings, also flew round and round over the gulls' feeding ground. This was a Sooty Tern (*Sterna fuscata*). Finally, I was surprised and delighted at the sight of a Pomarine Skua (*Stercorarius pomarinus*) which suddenly appeared on the scene. The gulls showed some agitation as it appeared, but it flew steadily up the river and disappeared.

So much for birds in Bengal in 1942; the common birds of Calcutta gardens and the less common birds of the Hooghly river. During those fifteen months I did very little birding, never even having an opportunity to explore the extraordinary salt-lakes just east of the city. Years later I was to find that if you could tolerate the insects these salt lakes are a paradise for birds, not only water-birds but innumerable warblers. It is (or was) the haunt of what I suppose is the largest *Sylviid* warbler in the world. This is the Striated Bush Warbler (*Megalurus palustris*). It is ten inches long, partly due to a long tail, but nevertheless for a warbler it looks huge as it rises into the air and utters its loud song during a short descent. Once, when later I did visit these salt lakes, I watched at close quarters what to my dying day I shall believe was a wintering *Phylloscopus tibetanus*—it simply was a black Chiffchaff; but as far as I know it has never been found outside Tibet, so it is most improbable. The other day I read in the Bombay N.H.S. *Journal* that some systematic trapping is now being undertaken at the salt lakes; but I do not expect the trappers to find a Tibetan Chiffchaff. If my bird was one, presumably it was something of a real 'vagrant'.

Then, too, in later years, I learnt that Calcutta gardens were a winter haunt of another close relation of the Chiffchaff, the Dusky Leaf or Willow Warbler (*Phylloscopus fuscatus*). This is an unusually tame bird, almost entirely ground-feeding, which will hop about among the flower beds uttering its soft 'chack, chack' call-note. Once you know it you can at once distinguish it from *Ph. collybita tristis*, the Siberian Chiffchaff, which also frequents these gardens, by its rather stouter bill, its darker, slightly richer brown mantle and buffer underside. In east Bengal, now Bangla Desh, round Dacca for instance, it is even commoner than in the gardens of Calcutta.

The Zoological Gardens of Calcutta are full of interest for the ornithologist. Through most of the year there is a large flock of Whistling Teal (*Dendrocygna javanica*) on the large pool, and other wild duck appear there too. In the trees you can discover all manner of wild birds including such a scarce species as the Red-headed Merlin (*Falco chicquera*). Also, some species of wheatear is alleged to have turned up there, far to the east of the normal range of any wheatear.

Before I say goodbye to Bengal I must record one more improbable bird. The White-winged Wood Duck (*Cairina scutulata*) is a scarce bird of very limited range, an unusually large duck, confined to the forest rivers and pools of Assam and Burma, and perhaps north-east Bengal. One day I was travelling by river steamer along the great Padma river on the way from Calcutta to Dacca. I have found this a good route for seeing water-birds and on this occasion we came past a small flock of ducks which did not readily fly up. They were of two sizes. The smaller birds were Spotbills (*Anas poecilorhyncha*), Mallard-size ducks; with them were several larger ducks, with a lot of white in the wing. I had a copy of Smythies's *Birds of Burma* with me, and my companion, an American colleague to whom I had pointed out these surprising birds, agreed with me that they looked exactly like the White-winged Wood Duck as illustrated there. They were too big and too black in the body to be anything else. Later, I somewhere read that an earlier ornithologist had claimed that he saw White-winged Wood Duck in the winter on one of the broad rivers of Bangla Desh. 'He must have been dreaming,' commented C. B. Ticehurst or one of his contemporaries. I suppose I was dreaming too.

The first time I went with Salim Ali on one of his expeditions I happened to tell Mahatma Gandhi that I was going off birding for a week or two. He commented that someone had told him I was interested in birds, and he went on: 'That is a good hobby, provided you do not shoot them.' If I responded at all I suppose I may have said that I could not shoot a bird even if I wanted to. What I did not tell him (as far as I recall) was that, for the first time in my life, I was going with a man who did shoot and presumably would do so. Since that time (1946) I have assisted at shooting quite often on expeditions in Indian jungles, and I must confess that I have been able to identify a number of mystery birds that otherwise would have remained mysteries. Like all other birdwatchers, I like to be able to give an assured name to what I see. And I believe that, in such country as the Naga Hills (which we are about to explore) shooting is still necessary, if you think it important to know just what is there.

Dillon Ripley kindly invited me to join him on an expedition into the eastern area of the Naga Hills, away near the Burma border, in November 1950. I arrived at Kohima on 11th November and found a note from Ripley to say that he and his wife were exploring birds on Mount Japvo, a fine wooded mountain that dominates the scenery above Kohima, and they expected to be back in a few days. Also he told me that his collector, Tony (I forget his surname—a Goan name I think—Tony was proud to claim Portuguese citizenship) would be arriving. This gave me four days by myself and then one day with Tony and his gun, before the Ripleys returned and we set off eastwards.

On 24th November I left them and returned west with the man who carried my baggage, coming back in two days' trek to Phek, where I again waited on my own to be picked up by the District Magistrate, who was on tour, and was now returning to Kohima.

During this expedition I kept a daily diary, written up pretty fully.

In the end I covered ninety pages with records and discussions. Whilst I was with the Ripleys and Tony, of course, there were the specimens at the end of the day to confirm what we had seen. When I was on my own there were none. I propose to quote from the time I spent at Phek on my way back. By that time I had had the opportunity to learn a good deal about some of the commoner birds; my notes will perhaps indicate the kind of troubles that a gunless ornithologist must encounter in thick jungle in a remote part of the world. I do not think any other Westerner has yet wandered about in the jungle near Phek. Phek, let me say, is a highly civilised town—the Governor of Assam had told me that the Naga people are as intensely political as any people in India, and so I found them—not only political but also in all respects highly intelligent. My porter gave me the Meluri names for several of the birds pictured by Hughes in the Smythies book (1940 edition), which I was constantly consulting. For instance: A-kuch-choo for the local Trogon, A-sak-karr for the Hoopoe, Kuch-orra for the Brown Fish Owl.

So, here we are in Phek, waiting for the D.M. to come and pick me up. *Meluri to Phek. 24th and 25th Nov., 1950.* I now have two days' walk to record, most of it dealing with birds that either would not show themselves at all, or else would not stay to be identified properly. Absence of a gun means that occasionally I can stand and watch parties of birds at leisure. Also, it often means that I cannot be sure of the identification of birds that are either high up in trees or are down in the shadow of thick scrub. On the whole, the birds seen were very different from those seen on the other route (I forget now why my guide preferred to go by a different route from our route east).

Here are some details. On the 24th I had unusually good views of a party of Quaker Babblers. They showed no black on the head, whereas one seen today did. But they were conspicuously yellowish from the throat downwards with little grey on the neck. The bird I saw today seemed to be grey on the neck and white or nearly white on the throat. Are some of the birds here *Alcippe fratercula*? I had concluded that birds of this group that I had seen earlier were *A. nipalensis*, but Smythies says in his 1952 edition that the Burmese species and subspecies of Quaker Babbler (*Alcippe*) 'have proved a sore puzzle to the taxonomic scholars'. Now, as I am writing this chapter, comes the seventh volume of Ali and Ripley, so I must follow their findings, as far as I can. They only allow two species of Quaker Babbler, whereas I had wondered if there were three, all mixed up together. The black on the head seems to be one of the surest means of separating *A. nipalensis* from *A. poiocephala*, which is the common species found widely in jungly parts of peninsular India. So these birds would be *A. nipalensis*, and those seen earlier were *A. poiocephala*. *A. fratercula* of earlier authors seems to have vanished, leaving no trace. So, back to my diary: In the low area, from Meluri to the river crossing, which must all be under 2,500 feet, I saw again several parties of Black-chinned Yuhinas (*Yuhina nigrimenta*)—also other things. One of the early parties in this region included Minivets, Spider-hunters and Red-winged Shrike Babblers (*P. flaviscapis*). But the majority were a slightly larger bird—at first I thought a thrush: that size and shape. But as they moved through the tree-tops their single loud guttural 'chur' was very un-turdine. Also they were quite white underneath and looked brown above. They kept moving through the upper branches. The description seems to fit nothing.

I was looking back after them when a bird about seven inches in length came up into a small tree a few yards from me, and for a few moments I had a very good view of it. It sat with its longish tail straight down. Then it decided against me, and dropped down again. It was silent. Colour? Well, plain-coloured. Brown above, streaky, whitish under-parts, slight pale eye-stripe. Beak like a babbler or warbler, not a flycatcher. Large Grass Warbler (*Graminicola*) seems to fit best.

While I was interested in another party of small birds—Grey-headed Flycatchers (*Culicicapa*), *Phylloscopi*, etc.—two large rich-brown owls flew from a tree across the river, followed by many Drongos (they are mostly Bronzed Drongos in these hills—*Dicrurus aeneas*). Brown Wood Owls (*Strix leptogrammica*) I suppose. Another warbler that gave me an unexpectedly good view might well have been the Strong-footed Bush Warbler (*Horeites* or *Cettia fortipes*). I believe it is the author of the 'twee-ee-ee, dirr-tee' that I have heard several times, as also in China in 1943 (I have heard one today, 25th Nov.). But of course it was silent.... (Several more undetermined warblers.) Then: I saw another *Phylloscopus* that looked largish, and fairly long in the tail, compared with an *inornatus* (Yellow-browed) that was near it—in the low branches of open small jungle, a little above me. Its underside looked too yellow for *trochiloides* (Greenish). Then, suddenly, I saw the top of its head—a green occipital streak between blackish head-stripes. It had one distinct wing-bar. This is surely *cantator*. It was silent....

Then the tiniest mouse-like creature whisked across the path and down into slight scrub just below the road. Once I actually saw its little dark form again, it said, 'tic, tic' in the smallest of voices occasionally. Lesser Scaly-breasted Wren-Babbler (*Pnoepyga pusilla*). . . . Leaving out several water-birds, and even a Fairy Bluebird (*Irena puella*)— a lovely creature I have had the good luck to see in both of its Indian homes, the extreme south, the Kerala hills, and in the north-east—we come to another strange creature, the Red-headed Parrotbill (*Paradoxornis ruficeps*). Today (25th Nov.) twice in the first three miles I heard the 'watch-winding' and the sweeter call of the Red-headed Parrotbill. The second time, when they were below me, I saw two or three quite well.

Some dark Laughing Thrushes showed black tails with orange tips, and some red somewhere else. This seems sufficient to identify *Trochalopterum phoeniceum* (which I had already seen at Kohima). It is now put in the same genus as all the other Laughing Thrushes, *Garrulax*. Its English name is Crimson-winged Laughing Thrush. Later I had excellent views on the ground well below me of a party of Rufous-necked Laughing Thrushes (*Garrulax ruficollis*)—very handsome creatures with jet black throat and breast, then the bright rufous patch, another such on the belly, but otherwise grey and brown. Twice today I had good views of Silver-eared Mesias (*Leiothrix argentauris*): gorgeous birds they are, with patches of bright red and yellow scattered over their bodies, mingled with blacks and greys. They have a rich and liquid trill, descending the scale, and also some harsh chatter. In one flock I saw at least one Blue-winged Siva (*Minla cyanouroptera*). Close to one flock was a tree full of tiny *Phylloscopi*, apparently all *proregulus*, and all silent. I noticed today at least three Grey-headed Flycatcher Warblers (*Seicercus xanthoschista*). (This genus is very closely allied to the leaf warblers, and there are at least nine species in the general Himalaya-Burma hill-country. This is the most widely distributed species—or at least its range extends much further west than the others. In the Assam hills, and in winter in parts of low-lying Bengal, one may come across several other species. Most are more brightly coloured than any *Phylloscopus* but in size and shape they are hardly to be distinguished.) I had a fleeting view of a Black-backed Forktail (*Enicurus immaculatus*). (Here again we are dealing with a family of birds that is typical of the Himalayan ranges and adjacent mountains, such as those of West China. Someone—was it Whistler or Dewar?—described the forktails as 'glorified wagtails', but hastily added that such a description is hardly fair on the wagtails. Anyway, they are all black and white birds, with long tails, that haunt the innumerable streams and rivers of this part of the world.) I heard it and its mate calling above and below the road in deep jungle. Other deep jungle birds: another tiny Wren Babbler (*Pnoepyga*) which this time flew above the road, and once or twice I could see undergrowth move two yards from my head. Once I saw it 'run' across a more open patch. It kept saying, 'tic, tic' in a tiny voice.

At the other extreme, a large woodpecker with a fine yellow 'mane' on the back of its head: a big fellow that looked bright green when it flew across some sunlight. It said 'squawk' quite a few times. I think it must have been the Large Yellow-naped Woodpecker (*Picus flavinucha*). . . . By no means the end of the birds of the 25th, but let us go on to the next day.

26th Nov. Phek. I thought there would be less to record today, but there seems to be more than ever. The doctor at the dispensary advised me to go up the path that leads, after some two miles, into high jungle, to the west of Phek. He told me that three kinds of hornbill are found there. It proved to be excellent advice. Even the first two miles, through rather open country, were quite productive. I will begin with narrative, and then proceed to detail on some of the more interesting species. First, the height: approximately 4,500 to 6,000 feet.

A party of Large Cuckoo-Shrikes (*Coracina novae-hollandiae*), a bird of very wide distribution in the oriental region, were in the trees near the Inspection Bungalow in the morning, and I saw them again at 2 p.m.; also a good party of Pied Shrikes (now known as the Bar-winged Flycatcher-Shrike, *Hemipus picatus*), and the usual Minivets (*Pericrocotus*), Chloropsis (or Leafbird, as *Chloropsis* is already the scientific name), White-eye (*Zosterops*), etc. Soon after starting I heard a Jay or Jays (*Garrulus*) above me, presumably the Himalayan Rufous-headed species (but I think today they are all lumped as races of *G. glandarius*, and do not know where I found this Rufous-headed bird, as there is none such in the first edition of Smythies). Early in the walk I had a fine view of a Black Eagle (*Ictinaetus malayensis*) soaring—the long wings, pale bill and legs, showing its identity—and, of course, colour of both upper- and under-parts practically black. A party of Common Rosefinches (*Carpodacus erythrinus*), the majority males, Dark Grey Bush Chats (*Saxicola ferrea*)—a common bird all along the Himalayas—a mixed party of Blue-winged Sivas, Tit Babblers (*Alcippe brunnea*) and various warblers—Wren Warblers (*Prinia*) and

Phylloscopi—one at least *Ph. proregulus*, a Chestnut-bellied Rock Thrush (*Monticola rufiventris*) on a tree-top, an unusually good view of a Blue-fronted Redstart (*Phoenicurus frontalis*) below me, good views of a Spider-hunter (*Arachnothera magna*), Streaked Green Bulbuls (*Microscelis virescens*) and Finch-billed Bulbuls (*Spizixos canifrons*); all these were noted before I got to the thick jungle. And in the early part of the jungle a large party of Chestnut-naped Ixulus (now called Yellow-naped Yuhina, *Y. flavicollis*), and more on the way down. No Black-chinned Yuhina today. Similarly, many Grey Sibias, but no Brown-eared Bulbuls.

Now for some special birds:

Flycatchers. I had good views of two males. One, just below the real jungle, had dull blue, or light blue, head and neck and throat and breast; brown back; much white in base of black tail. At the time, I thought it might be the Slaty-blue Flycatcher (*Muscicapa leucomelanura*), though a bit later I noted in the margin that I thought not: it was too large for this species, which I know well in the western Himalayas. *M. leucomelanura* is one of the smallest blue flycatchers, only 4½ inches long. As I study Smythies in 1972 (second edition) I find *M. concreta*, the White-tailed Blue Flycatcher, the most likely; but from what I saw (it will be noted that I did not get the colour of the underside at all) *M. amabilis*, the Rusty-breasted Blue Flycatcher, cannot be ruled out. The second, at about 6,000 feet, was a gorgeous creature, largish, intense deep blue (perhaps with some black) on upper parts and sides of neck; no white in tail; centre of chin and of throat and most of underparts white; sides bright orange or chestnut. This (I wrote at the time, after consulting Smythies, first edition) seems to be the Rufous-breasted Blue, which might better be called Rufous-sided (*M. vivida*). The similar *M. sapphira* is smaller.(This we found in Sikkim, when I was there a few years later with Salim Ali.)

So to the flycatcher warblers (*Seicercus*). In addition to Grey-headed, I saw two species new to me: several individuals of the Chestnut-headed (*S. castaneoceps*). I should call its cap golden orange, but all other details noted at the time fit well enough: grey head and breast, yellow underparts, white in tail, white or yellow wing-bar. The other was *S. affinis*, the Allied Flycatcher Warbler. White ring round eye, grey head, darker patch behind eye, cap and upperparts greenish, underparts, below throat, yellow. The face markings were peculiar. These were identified among masses of 'tinies', some of which were Golden-headed Babblers (*Stachyrodopsis*, now *Stachyris chrysaea*). One of these that I saw well seemed very orange on the crown; the whole face and neck and throat were yellow; no blackish patch. *Tesias;* Smythies' first edition put these odd little creatures among the wrens, close to *Pnoepyga*, which we met a few pages back; now, in the second edition, they have joined the warblers, which I expect is correct. (Both species are figured, together with several other warblers, on plate 83 of Ali and Ripley, at the end of volume seven. But the warblers are all to appear in volume eight, and apparently these two aberrant little birds will be the first in that book. Hurry up, volume eight; the pictures are fine, but we want the letterpress too! The illustration gives both birds slaty underparts, which does not agree at all with my observation. (Some mystery here, which I cannot at the moment solve.) They are almost tailless. There are two species, living side by side. I had the amazing luck to have close views of one of each species within an hour. The one with gold throat and yellow underparts, grey on neck, came so near me that I could not use the glass: within six feet I think. Luckily, for one moment it came out into the sunlight and I saw its brilliant forehead. Till then I had thought it all dark above. It kept calling a cheerful 'twee, twee'.

The other happened to be in grass just where I stood to watch some barbets. Its dark blue-grey breast contrasted with its golden forehead. It kept calling shrilly: 'twee-di-twee-twee'. In my diary I did not give their names. They are now called Dull Slaty-bellied Ground Warbler (*Tesia cyaniventer*) and Bright Slaty-bellied Ground Warbler (*T. olivea*).*

I ought to mention that, while watching various little birds, I saw a tiny wren-like creature with a long tail creeping up by the boll of a big tree. I think it is likely to have been a Long-tailed Wren (*Spelaeornis*), but I could not be sure of its colour. This too has been reclassified and is no longer treated as a wren at all, but as a genus of babblers (Timaliidae not Troglodytidae); so now we must call it Wren Babbler; the same is true of *Pnoepyga*.

The only woodpeckers I saw during the day were a pair of the Large Yellow-naped (*Picus flavinucha*). Now to the hornbills.

Soon after I got into the high jungle I heard the extraordinary beat

* I had overlooked Smythies's statement that 'both species are dimorphic. white-bellied and rusty-bellied birds being about equally common', so I suppose both mine were *pusilla* or *olivea*, which alone has a bright cap. Even so, what I seem to have seen hardly fits the description of the plumage on Smythies or the plate in Ali and Ripley.

of hornbill wings (like a train starting up, as Ripley says) and saw one come over: white tail, black wings, head and neck looking dark. A few minutes later the sound again, and seven flew over: white tail, white neck and head, black wings for all seven. An hour later one, lower down: casque yellowish, head and neck nearly white, tail white or pale yellow, wings black—no white tips to wings. This seems to make them all Wreathed Hornbills (*Rhuthoceros undulatus*): the first a female, the rest males.

This bit about hornbills seen on the 28th seems to demand quotation before we quit the Naga Hills. 'At one moment I counted 36 in the air; they looked like so many pelicans winging their way solemnly over the jungle. Whether they were all one species I could not be sure; probably mostly Wreathed, possibly some Rufous-necked (*Aceros nipalensis*).'

Barbets: Large blackish plums were dropping so near to my head that I thought monkeys must be in the trees; but no, only barbets, some the Great Barbet (*Megalaima virens*) (which I had been seeing earlier), but more of them were a smaller species, with red forehead and yellow throat and underparts—the Gold-throated Barbet (*Megalaima franklini*).

Now for laughing-thrushes (which, remember, are not thrushes but large babblers, *Timaliids*). Nearly all that I saw were new for me. Here are my descriptions written down at the time, and attempted identifications. (1) Two, seen well, in open scrub, at about 5,000 feet. Two yellowish-white superciliary and moustachial streaks. Throat pale. Underside buff, strongly spotted like a thrush. Upperparts brown, back I think streaked. A chestnut patch in the wing (? secondaries) and possibly another near the tail (? on rump). Tail dark, no pale or bright tips. ? *Garrulax merulinus*, Spotted-breasted Laughing Thrush. If so, presumably the richer-coloured Manipur race, *G. m. toxostominus*. I can find no other laughing-thrush with a spotted breast.

(2) Body plumage largely black or dark, tail black and rather long; yellow in wing (edges to secondaries?). Some rufous on underparts. Head not seen well. Seems to be *Trochalopterum erythrocephalum* (now *Garrulax*), Red-headed Laughing Thrush.

(3) General plumage blackish, head from forehead to nape black. Eye and beak yellow. Some brownish spottings on neck or sides (?). Edges of secondaries blue. Possibly some rufous patches, but no bright red. Tip of tail orange. Tail rather short, or average length. *Garrulax squamatus*, Blue-winged Laughing Thrush.

(4) Body plumage brown. Back and wings nearly uniform colour. Head and throat grey, crown perhaps darker, slight crest. No pale eyebrow or other head-markings. Underparts buff. Tail rather long, dark, with white spots or tips along the underside. Not a large species. A fair-sized party, not shy, but views always very brief.

I offered a tentative identification, doubtfully; happily, two days later I saw some more and saw them better, and realised that they were barwings (*Actinodura*). Indeed, I got some very good views, and found the two species of barwing together in this patch of high jungle. Let me quote: Some of my puzzling laughing-thrushes I was able to turn into barwings. The common bird of the high jungle seemed to be the Hoary Barwing (*A. nipalensis*), with grey head, rufous upperparts, fulvous underparts, tail with white spots below and very slight bars above, and beautiful barring on the grey secondaries. Beak and legs yellow; eye dark. One party was mixed, and included some Spectacled Barwings (*A. egertoni*), a darker species. I saw the streaky neck and breast of one, the white tips to tail feathers, chestnut rump or base of tail, rufous and black in wings: not all on one bird, but all on one or another. Is there any group of birds with just the same fuzzy head that these creatures have? This and the white spots along the underside of the outer tail feathers seem to be important field characters. I saw one or two very well. They are not shy, but they mostly hide away among the greenery. They make many noises: mostly a guttural chatter, but some louder calls.

I have now (1972) consulted Ali and Ripley on the barwings. There seem to be three species, and my first birds were apparently Manipur Barwings (*Actinodura waldeni*) rather than *A. nipalensis*. The two species are very similar, but *waldeni* 'has the underparts entirely rufous-brown'—'fulvous' is my description—whereas *nipalensis* has throat and breast grey, only the lower belly and under tail-coverts rufous-brown. Anyway, *nipalensis* is not known from the hill ranges south of the Brahmaputra. I am not clear why these authors treat them as distinct species, since their ranges do not seem to overlap. I must add that the illustrations on plate 78 do not wholly agree with my descriptions. I did not get the impression of such gaudy birds. *A. nipalensis* is figured by a different artist on plate 76. His more sober colours are, I think, more life-like.

I had two more days at Phek; and it was actually on the last day (28th November) that I discovered what the barwings really were. Somehow, they gave me special satisfaction, partly, no doubt, because

Some Indian Birds

I had such trouble with them; also it was a new genus for me, at the very end of my Naga trip. Those last two days gave me plenty more birds to write about; especially several species of bulbul that I had not satisfactorily identified before. And I saw both those fascinating tailless warblers again—*Tesia*.

So far, in this Indian chapter, I have confined myself to the eastern side of India, Bengal—let us say both Bengals—and Assam with the Naga Hills. I must add something about a few other experiences in quite other parts of the country.

My first long expedition with Salim Ali was in Travancore (now Kerala) from 18th February to 12th March 1947. This was my first experience of birding in thick jungle. We spent some time in each of three different parts of the southernmost hills (or mountains) of India, as well as visiting Cape Comorin and several other areas. Our bird total in three weeks was 193, including some water-birds, but not many. The most productive country proved to be the mountain 'sholas', patches of deep jungle, usually associated with small watercourses. Quoting from my diary, I wrote: 'A number of the species I could not have identified without the authority of Salim Ali, who could recognise almost every sound we heard. N. G. Pillai [our companion from the Trivandrum museum] was if anything even quicker in sight. Their ability to detect birds, even when stationary, in quite thick jungle, amazed me. In Europe of course we have little opportunity or need to acquire this particular art. To me, motion on the bird's part is almost essential among foliage; even so, I found I often lost the bird as it settled.' I have seventy-one pages of notes; with much self-restraint, I refrain from quoting any of them—not even about the status of fourteen warblers, four of them Leaf Warblers, which I discussed at length.

So, we jump two thousand miles or more, to Kashmir. There are two superlative experiences (possibly more) in India: to see the Taj Mahal at Agra and to visit the Kashmir valley. Everyone assumes that they cannot possibly be all they are alleged to be, but nearly everyone, when the great moment arrives, finds with amazement that it is even better than they had been told. That has certainly been my experience of Kashmir, especially the Liddar Valley. I have been in Kashmir several times. My longest holiday there was in 1949, when I stayed there from 30th May to 17th July, well away from the heat of Delhi. From 12th June to 4th July I was at Pahlgam and trekking in the Liddar valley with Leslie and Kathleen Cross. The scenery, the flowers and the birds were as near to heaven as one can imagine. I must add that I trekked up the Liddar Valley to the Kolahoi glacier several years later, in late summer. It was marvellous, but it was not the same. The incredible flowers that rush out the moment the snow goes had finished. Strange accentors were still singing and there were other good birds, and the scenery was still breath-taking, but I knew that June was the perfect month for the Liddar Valley.

I have over sixty pages of notes for the whole Kashmir visit; but I am only quoting one experience, partly because it contains a mystery and also because it was the climax of the walk to the Kolahoi glacier. Just as we were nearing the glacier, on the newly open pasture I saw some strange looking birds; so I excused myself from going right up to the glacier and spent the next hour or more with these birds; they had apparently just arrived on this stretch of ground that had only recently lost its snow-cover after perhaps eight or nine months. This is what I wrote, as soon as we were back at base: 'I spent the best part of an hour on the slopes just below the Kolahoi glacier, 24/6, at c. 11,000 ft., watching the rosefinches, which were almost ludicrously tame. At the time I took the brilliant red big ones and the pale pink, equally large, to be males and females of one species, whilst the very dark, almost black, finches of equal size I took to be a distinct species—suggesting a huge accentor with a finch beak. However, it seems clear (after consulting Stuart Baker's *Fauna of British India*) that these were females of *Carpodacus rubricilla*, and the paler birds were *C. severtzovi*. They were definitely *not* yet in pairs, but the males of the two species consorted together, and the females (I think I saw three or four) kept separate.' When, later, I studied Bates and Lowther's *Breeding-Birds of Kashmir*, I had to conclude that my identification was all wrong. It looks as if I had been watching a large species of *Propasser*, not *Carpodacus* at all! The paler birds would be the males of the Kashmir race of the ill-named White-browed Rosefinch (Pink-browed would be more accurate), whilst the darker red birds were presumably birds of the same species, but a different race: *Propasser thura blythi* is the Kashmir breeding race; *P. t. thura* is a redder bird, that apparently breeds further east. What the latter were doing in the upper Liddar Valley in late June is not very clear. When I revisited the area several years later, in the late summer, I could find no sign of any breeding Rosefinches. *Propasser rhodochrous*, perversely called the Pink-browed Rosefinch, a smaller bird, much less generally rosy in colour, I found at lower elevations in the Liddar Valley.

Red-flanked Bluetail

I must not linger over other Kashmir birds, though one is tempted to mention some of the more exciting, such as the Orange Bullfinch (*Pyrrhula auriantiaca*), and the Black and Yellow Grosbeak (*Perissospiza icteroides*). All these, alas, are birds that will only come in one of the last Ali-Ripley volumes, so I cannot check what they may be able to tell me about rosefinches or other finches. Then one finds such attractive little birds as the Red-flanked Bush Robin or Bluetail (*Ianthia cyanura*)—now a 'British' bird; and the Himalayan or White-moustached Rubythroat (*Luscinia pectoralis*). There was a bird I kept hearing in song in the higher trees, nearly always near running water. The song consisted of five beautiful bell-like notes. For some time I thought it must be some kind of redstart or robin; at last I got a closer view of one that came into the lower branches, and discovered that it was a bird of my favourite warbler genus—the so-called Large-billed Leaf Warbler (*Phylloscopus magnirostris*). I would like to re-christen it the Silver-bell Bird. I do not suppose this name will ever be used in systematic works, but it does deserve a better English name than the one it has tied round its neck today.

I cannot say 'Goodbye' to Indian birds without reference to a few of my bird adventures near Delhi. My suspected Black Tern and Sedge Warbler fall into the chapter on rare birds, but there are a few more incidents that stick in the mind. Several of my best bird memories from Delhi relate themselves very pleasantly with people.

An elderly cousin of mine from Birmingham decided that before she died she wanted to have a look at India. Her nephews tried to persuade her that she would fall ill and be a nuisance to her hosts. She would not listen to them. She came, she travelled all round the country; she was so full of appreciation of all that she saw that she was a most welcome visitor. She did not fall ill. She went home again, much enriched spiritually, and died a year or two later.

When she arrived in Delhi, in January 1951, I naturally offered to drive her out to the famous tower known as the Qutab Minar. While we were gazing up at the tower, suddenly a Wall Creeper appeared, flitting round the wall. I knew one had been seen in Delhi some years before, but there was then only this single record. Happily, the bird remained for several weeks so that most of our small band of Delhi birdwatchers saw it; but, as seems to be usual with this strange and beautiful bird, it sometimes hid itself away.

Several of my bird memories at Delhi are, most naturally, connected with Mrs Usha Ganguli, an outstanding bird observer whose early death is a great loss to Indian ornithology. There was the day when we were driving from Old to New Delhi and noticed a very dark heron beside a pool, somewhere near the present site of the Nehru Memorial. To our amazement it proved to be a Reef Heron (*Egretta gularis*), which one normally associates with the sea-shore. Ali and Ripley say that it 'Occasionally strays a few miles inland to freshwater swamps'. This bird had strayed a thousand miles!

I suppose the last time I saw Mrs Ganguli was when R. and I had a marvellous day's outing with her to the famous Najafgarh Jheel, a huge expanse of water where in those days (ten years ago) there was every prospect of seeing flocks of pelicans and flamingoes, as well as innumerable ducks, geese, storks, herons, waders and other birds. Now, I believe it has been drained. We were eating our sandwiches and trying to identify birds far out over the jheel when suddenly, within twenty yards, two huge Sarus Cranes (*Grus antigone*) came marching into view, wading through a deep pool of water, followed by two downy yellow chicks, happily swimming behind them. I suspect that the chicks were only a few hours old. If ever parents showed their family off to an admiring audience, that was the moment. Parental pride was in every step.

Just before or after this we went to breakfast with Peter Jackson and his family one bright morning, and while we ate our breakfast Peter's rubber boat was being inflated. Then we set off for the river. As R. and I stepped into the boat it seemed as if we were inviting a watery grave. However, it proved river-worthy, even with three aboard; and we found on the large sandbanks a spectacular assembly of Avocets and Stilts, and among them the first Caspian Tern (*Sterna caspia*) recorded for Delhi. In 1954, when General Sir H. Williams compiled a Delhi list, he was able to record over 370 species. My recollection is that by the time we saw that Caspian Tern (in 1963) the list was over 400.

In recent years, many ornithological visitors to India have visited the remarkable Bharatpur reserve, less than a hundred miles south of Delhi. Our last visit to it was on 3rd December 1971, a date that will not soon be forgotten in India, for reasons quite unconnected with ornithology. Our two-day outing from Delhi and back gave me a list of over 100 birds. The highest point, perhaps, was the sight of about twenty Siberian Cranes (*Grus leucogeranus*). This magnificent bird is pure white, apart from black primary wing feathers and a red patch on the face. It seems to have a very restricted breeding range in Siberia—in three widely separated areas; and it occurs in small numbers in north India in winter. One flock visits Bharatpur every winter. Whether they came in the old days, when British Viceroys used to amuse themselves by slaughtering innumerable ducks at Bharatpur, is not quite clear. I have only heard of them as visiting it in the past fifteen or twenty years. This flock was, as usual, remarkably tame. We came upon them quietly feeding in one of the great pools as we drove in the jeep along a bund. It was only when we got down from the car that most of them deigned to fly a short distance. On the wing they look huge and the contrast of the black wing-tips with the white plumage has the same dazzling effect as one gets from the same contrast in a flock of Snow Geese. Some years ago, when we stayed with the Maharajah, he insisted that the Siberian Crane was really the same species as the Whooping Crane (*G. americana*). Systematists do not seem to agree; but the two species are very similar and must surely have a common ancestry.

So, I end my Indian chapter with these enormous fowls. Yet, the truth is that, if I could live my life over again and wander across India, I should be much happier watching and trying to identify warblers in the Liddar Valley of Kashmir, or the Naga Hills or round Darjeeling or even by the salt lakes of Calcutta or in the jungly hills of Orissa, Kerala, Madhya Pradesh or near Bombay, than visiting the pools where strange water-birds occur.

It is a fascinating avifauna and one which will repay close study for centuries to come.

CHAPTER XII

Do Birds Migrate Over the Himalayas?

In 1954 Reg Moreau encouraged me to collect all the material I could find which might show whether large numbers of migratory birds migrate across the high ground of central Asia, especially the plateau of Tibet and the Himalayan mountain ranges. It is known that quantities of birds that breed in Siberia winter in India. How do they travel to and fro? By what main routes?

I spent a week or more at Oxford, reading all the material I could find in the Alexander library that had a bearing on the subject, direct or indirect. I began to put my material together. But then I concluded that there must be further material in the possession of various Himalayan climbers, both published and unpublished. So I began to correspond with some such men and got good help especially from Dr T. G. Longstaff. My material was growing nicely during 1955 and I hoped to get an article in shape for *The Ibis* during 1956. I even gave a lecture on the subject at one or two local ornithological clubs. That was my undoing. A week or two after one of these lectures, when I went to my file, I found that I had left some of my material in the public building where I had lectured. This so discouraged me that I gave up the whole venture.

However, I find that I still have some of the relevant material, so I make this short chapter of it here, hoping that it may be of some value to the next man who attempts to cover the ground.

Inevitably one starts with a quotation from Sir John Hunt's book, *The Ascent of Everest*. He is writing about the South Col, from which the final assault on the peak was launched: 'As I approached the tents, I was astonished to see a bird, a chough, strutting about on the stones near me. At every camp we had been visited by choughs; even at Camp VII there were two or three and I had wondered then whether we should find them on the Col. But here the bird was, behaving in the same way at 26,000 feet as his cousins had at Base Camp. During this day, too, Charles Evans saw what must have been a migration of small grey birds across the Col. Neither of us had thought to find any signs of life as high as this.'

These remarkable observations seem to prove two things: first, that even an altitude of over 25,000 feet does not inconvenience a bird. It does not need to carry oxygen. Secondly, even small birds can migrate at such heights; and they evidently occasionally do so. Even if it is argued that the small grey birds may have been some species of finch that breeds at very high altitudes, and that these birds were not necessarily flying more than twenty miles from one high pasture to another, still they did fly right across this high col, and that in spite of the almost constant stormy weather encountered at such heights; all of which seems very remarkable.

Before summarising some of the observations of birds seen at high altitudes from earlier Everest expeditions, let me give some observations of my own on the tendency of birds to go 'right up and over' when confronted by a mountain, rather than avoiding it and keeping at a lower level over a pass a few miles to east or west. In 1953 I spent some two weeks on holiday at Bakrota, above Dalhousie, where the house I was staying in was more than 8,000 feet above sea-level, quite near the summit of that particular range of mountains. Two or three miles east or west the ridge is much lower.

Here are my migration notes from those days: On 1st June, about 7 a.m., I saw a female Golden Oriole come in from the south, indeed, it flew *up* from the south; it settled in a walnut tree for a time, at the crest of the ridge, and then continued its journey to the north. I saw several warblers that seemed to be birds of passage resting in the trees On 28th May there were one or two *Phylloscopous magnirostris*, my 'Silver-bell Bird', with other small birds in the trees on the ridge. On 29th May there were two *P. affinis* in the highest bushes, at 8,000 feet, at 9 a.m. On 30th May I found one *P. trochiloides* in the scrub at about 7,900 feet; also one *Acrocephalus dumetorum* rather lower, at about 7,600 feet. On 3rd June I found one or perhaps two *P. affinis* in a walnut tree at 8,000 feet about 10.20 a.m.

But the main migration was the passage of various swallows and swifts. Day by day, from 29th May to 10th June, I saw some passage. Several species were involved: *Hirundo rustica*, *H. daurica* and *Delichon urbica* were the members of the swallow tribe; *Apus apus*, *A. paicficus*, *A. melba* and one species of *Chaetura* were the swifts. I kept exact notes of the movements seen each day. These are much too full to quote in detail, but the experience of one day, when I was on the look-out for much of the morning and saw an unusual amount of movement, will give the idea: From 9.15 to 10.30 small numbers of Swallows (*H. rustica*) were flying about over the trees to the north of the ridge (7,700 to 7,900 feet). At 9.15 five House Martins and one Alpine Swift flew past at about 7,700 feet, moving north-east over the trees. At 10.30 some more swallows came right overhead, then flew round, and suddenly dashed down and away to the north. At 10.35 one Alpine Swift and one Red-rumped Swallow came over the trees below, moving to north; then two European Swifts flew to and fro once or twice overhead. Similarly one or two common Swallows a minute or two later. I did not see which way they left. At 11.30 one White-rumped Swift flew over and to the north; immediately after, two House Martins appeared overhead for a minute. The migration was only noted in the mornings up to 11 or near midday and again some days at 6.30 or 7 in the evening. I did not often see the direction of departure; but several times birds suddenly dashed away to the north, down the mountain side.

There is, of course, nothing here to indicate a large migratory movement from India to Siberia over the mountains. What I think is shown is the readiness of some migrating birds, including small warblers, to follow the direct route to their destination even if that takes them over quite high obstacles. Of course, some of these species regularly nest at elevations as high as 8,000 feet in the Himalayas. The swallows were in such numbers—one morning I counted over fifty settled on the wires—that I concluded that a considerable passage must come past this mountain top every spring. Possibly their normal height of flight would be about 8,000 feet, so that the wires on this mountain top would give them a convenient resting place, and the tree tops a good place for stopping to feed on flying insects before continuing their journey.

Now, let us see what evidence there is of migration across the higher mountains. First, the 'Birds of Southern Tibet', by H. J. Walton, in *The Ibis* for 1906. He gives a remarkable account of migration seen at the end of September in the Khamba Jung, some fifteen miles north of the Sikkim frontier, where the mean height is over 15,600 feet. There are no trees, but a few stunted willows, also low scrub and coarse grass; barley was being grown there. He writes of large numbers of migrants, and mentions one species of pipit, three species of wagtail, one lark, one leaf warbler (*P. affinis*), Hoopoes, two species of redstart and one chat: all of these in some numbers; four more small passerines in smaller numbers. Curiously, though they were obviously on migration, they seemed to leave the valley in a northerly direction. He writes of several other migrants: geese and ducks were numerous on lakes in early April and, as he had seen none in the Chumbi Valley, he thought they had probably come along the Brahmaputra river, not across Sikkim. He noted many Red-throated Thrushes at Gyangtse, 12,000 feet, in April, evidently on migration. Among the birds seen near Lhasa itself, which appeared to be on migration, were Wrynecks, pipits and Redshanks.

Birds observed high up in the Himalayas were described both in the chapter on Natural History Notes in *Mount Everest: the Reconnaisance*, published in 1921, and by N. B. Kinnear and A. F. R. Wollaston in *The Ibis* for 1922. Wollaston saw a Lammergeier over the north peak of Everest, at 25,000 feet, not much lower than Hunt's Chough. The highest actual migration that he saw seems to have been a Hoopoe (or two Hoopoes?): 'I twice saw a hoopoe fly over the Kharta Glacier at about 21,000 feet; a small pale hawk flew overhead at the same time.' At 17,000 feet, migrants included a Temminck's Stint (it got no further, poor bird), Painted Snipe, Pintail Snipe, House Martin and several pipits. At night the cries of migrating waders were heard, including undoubted Curlews and probable Bar-tailed Godwits. *The Ibis* article adds to the above: large numbers of Indian Redstarts (*Phoenicurus ochruros rufiventris*) on migration at up to 20,000 feet in September; and large numbers of Indian Stonechats (*Saxicola torquata indica*) were apparently migrating through the Kharta Valley in

September at about 17,000 feet. Richard's Pipit (*A. richardi*) was encountered in numbers at these elevations, from 17,000 to 20,000 feet. There was also evidence of Short-toed Larks (*Calandrella brachydactyla*) and of one species of bunting (*Emberiza cia godlewskii*) migrating, the former at 17,000 feet, the latter at a much lower elevation, 12,500 feet, in the Arun Valley. This, I think, covers the actual migration observed.

Dr T. G. Longstaff in his book *The Assault on Mount Everest*, published in 1922, wrote: 'Noel, during his vigil on the Changla (23,000 feet) (May 24-28) saw a small bird fly above him, borne on the westerly gale.' I corresponded with Dr Longstaff, who I believe gave me some further material from other climbing expeditions, but the material was amongst that lost.

I have also several observations from the Karakorum Mountains. Thus, in *Blank on the Map* Eric Shipton records that he found many skeletons or corpses of ducks and other birds, some of them still in good plumage, on the Crevasse glacier, at 15,000 to 16,000 feet. There are some other records of dead birds, clearly migrants, found on glaciers or in other places high up in the Himalayas. Migrating flocks are obviously sometimes overcome by adverse weather conditions.

Several Himalayan climbers have noted quite large flocks of geese, ducks (Garganey are specially mentioned) and also of cranes, migrating over the high mountains. Mr J. A. Sillem kindly sent me a copy of his paper, 'Ornithological Results of the Netherland Karakorum Expedition, 1929/1930'. One of the most striking paragraphs from the point of view of migration is the following: 'On the 16th August we started eastwards. . . . During the first stages, between the Chip-chap River and the Kara-tagh Pass, very few birds were seen, one day not even a single one. But further on, near some salt lakes which we found at an altitude of about 17,500 feet, several wagtails (*Motacilla citreola werae, M. cinerea caspica, M. alba personata*), different waders (*Tringa nebularia, T. ochropus, T. glareola*), Stints (*Calidris temminckii*) and Garganeys (*Anas querquedula*) were met. After crossing the Kara-tagh Pass we camped near the Lake, in the vicinity of which a number of migrants were observed; besides Horned Larks and Mountain Finches we encountered *Anthus t. trivialis, Monticola saxatilis, Carpodacus e. roseata*, and several of the above-named species. As I approached the lake, a flight of about 200 Garganeys went up, and I saw a Tibetan Tern in the distance.' Once again, we have here a mixture of birds, some of which may have been not very far from their high breeding grounds (some of the wagtails, for instance, are known to breed widely in the highlands of Tibet) and long-distance migrants, such as the waders, most of them undoubtedly from much further north.

Meinertzhagen and others have written on the known height of migrating birds; in an old article in *The Ibis* (1920), he could at that time find very few satisfactory records of flight above 10,000 feet. Even above 5,000 feet the numbers were small. He quotes C. H. Donald, writing in the *Journal of the Bombay Natural History Society*, recording an observation from a point some 14,000 to 15,000 feet up in the Himalayas (the actual place does not seem to be recorded) from which he watched a flight of enormous birds, possibly White Storks or Siberian Cranes, in a very clear atmosphere migrating over the mountains. Meinertzhagen estimates that they might have been 6,000 feet above the observer, i.e. about 20,000 feet above sea-level.

What tentative conclusion, if any, can be drawn from these observations? First, let me quote from *Beyond the Caspian*, by Douglas Carruthers, published in 1949. He writes: 'Two thousand miles from the Arctic Ocean, but only two hundred feet above it, the Aral basin lies like a trough between the Caucasus and the Central Asian highlands, and up it comes the main spring flood of bird-life from India,

Persia, Arabia and far Africa; and back again down it flows the autumn migration from the western half of Siberia.... Even if some birds, such as geese and ducks, take the Himalayas in their southward flight, smaller birds in the main do not; and in order to avoid this mountain barrier, well over perpetual snow-line, which stands like a wall across two thousand miles of middle Asia, the stream of migrants from western Siberia circles round it, and is therefore concentrated into the gap between the central massif and the Caspian Sea.' Other observers have recorded masses of migrants using the 'Aral gap'. Undoubtedly it is a great migrant route.

What, then, does all this amount to? I am not sure that the situation is well enough known, even today, to justify Carruthers' sweeping statements. When you find quantities of wagtails in the upper valleys of the southern Himalayan rivers in the autumn (some of them of Siberian or Chinese races), it is difficult to believe that they have migrated from Siberia or China right round the Himalayan massif, to west or east, and have then turned north again to feed in these stream beds. Such birds as the Brown Shrike (*Lanius cristatus*) which only breed in north and north-east Asia, and are common winter visitors to Bengal, must surely find their way, year by year, in numbers, across Tibet. There are species, such as the Arctic Warbler, which breed in northern Scandinavia but only winter (normally at least) in southern China and Malaya, presumably as a way of avoiding the passage of the central Asian massif, whilst, on the other hand, the eastern forms of the Willow Warbler (*P. trochilus*), which breed in north-east Asia, winter, along with the western forms, in Africa. Not many Siberian passerines regularly winter in India, but some do. Again, the Aral gap is no doubt an excellent place to spend some weeks or months watching the spring or autumn migration. But no one is going to spend a couple of months sitting on a Himalayan glacier counting how many Stints, Hoopoes and trinomial pipits fly over. Considering how little time the mountain climbers have to stand and stare it seems quite amazing that they have seen *any* migrating birds.

Here again we are apparently faced with a paradox. The majority of small birds do use low passes, where they can find them, and probably extend the actual distance of their migration by many miles in order to find such routes. But, all the same, it seems to be true that some birds, when under the migratory urge, will fly as directly towards the breeding ground as possible even if, as in the case of my Dalhousie

Do Birds Migrate Over the Himalayas? 221

birds, this means flying up and over fairly high mountains in preference to a short diversion which would avoid the mountain. And this applies, sometimes, not only to minor heights, under ten thousand feet, on the outer ridges, but even to the very highest mountains, well over twenty thousand feet. This, at least, is the tentative conclusion I have reached. It is possible, of course, that this determination to go straight on is only in control where the birds are fairly near their breeding ground. Thus, a bird making for some area in Tibet might go right over the tops, whereas birds on their way from India to Siberia will use a lower and more circuitous route.

It will be seen that all my evidence is over twenty years old or nearly so. Possibly there is new evidence that I have not seen. It is my impression, however, that much remains uncertain, and that the conclusions of Carruthers and others need to be further examined.

CHAPTER XIII

Rare Birds

The first number of Witherby's magazine, *British Birds*, was published in June 1907. Following an editorial, the first article was by Howard Saunders, author of what was then the standard text-book on British birds, the second edition of which was published in 1899. The article dealt with 'Additions to the list of British birds since 1899'. He listed twenty such species. Of these, several would now be called subspecies and several more have been rejected among the 'Hastings rarities'. But this is not the main point. I go back to this article in order to quote the disarming comment Saunders made about the scientific unimportance of rarities. 'It is true,' he wrote, 'that the scientific study of migration does not consist in the acquisition of new or rare visitants: yet even a severe migrationist may secretly feel a greater pleasure at the occurrence of a Red-rumped Swallow than at the passage of a continuous flight of Starlings or Jays.' Incidentally, that must have been the last thing Saunders wrote, for he died in October of the same year.

I hope the earlier chapters of this book will show that I am not a mere rarity scalp-hunter. Indeed, until at earliest the 1930s I was hardly aware that it was possible to 'hunt' rarities. In spite of the extraordinary birds that were reported from Bristow's taxidermy shop in Hastings during the early years of the century, my impression up to 1930 or thereabouts was that the Norfolk coast around Cley was the only place in England where you could fairly hope to find 'rare' visitors, such as Bluethroats or strange warblers and buntings; and even those would be so skulking that unless you had a gun you could not identify them properly. The only rarities that came my way came by pure chance. I doubt if I saw any 'rare' bird in England as a result of someone else discovering it until Tucker, who as editor of *British Birds* let me into a good number of the 'secrets' that came his way, told me of the Little Ringed Plovers breeding at Tring in 1938.

But rare birds have been quite good in showing themselves to me. On 18th March 1905, when I was under 16, on a school excursion from York to Kirkham Abbey I had gone off by myself for a prowl near the river Derwent, and suddenly found myself watching a family party of Long-tailed Tits. One that came into a bush within a few yards of me had a totally white head. I knew that the continental Long-tailed Tit had a white head and that it had been recorded in England, for Christopher had been given a book by Bowdler Sharpe called *A Chapter on Birds: Rare British Visitors*, where the White-headed Long-tailed Tit was pictured. And here I had one close beside me! I see no reason to doubt that it was in fact a migrant that had crossed the North Sea. The next rarity that happened to come my way was a Woodchat Shrike that I saw on one of my regular Tunbridge Wells walks, at Adams Well close to the county boundary, on 23rd May 1907.

On 4th July 1908 we stayed at a guest-house not far from Ashford, Kent. I rode my bicycle across Romney Marsh to Littlestone. As I was riding past the dunes north of Littlestone, I saw three odd-looking birds on the turf some way off; so I left my bicycle by the road and walked across the grass. I got near enough to identify them as Pallas' Sand Grouse. When they flew they went right away to the west. Christopher went a few days later from Wye, and Claud Ticehurst from Tenterden; but they were not seen again. A few days later the newspapers announced that a fresh invasion of Sand Grouse had taken place—the last of a series beginning in 1863. I knew nothing of the invasion when I found my three birds, and I did not then even possess binoculars. At age nineteen I still relied on my eyes and a small telescope, which I think magnified four times, but its field was very small. Next there was the Siberian Chiffchaff that took up its abode in a sheltered valley near Tunbridge Wells and stayed from 28th November to 17th December 1913, so that several competent ornithologists were able to watch it and hear its characteristic call-note.

From 1907 onwards I often visited Dungeness and wandered over Romney Marsh. I hoped that some of Bristow's rarities might come

my way but they never did. As already recorded, owing to my youthful shyness, I missed seeing C. B. Ticehurst's White Stork at Fairfield Brack. Such 'rare' birds as I did see were Aquatic and Icterine Warblers, and other species that are now seen annually on the autumn migration. The one really rare bird that I saw at Dungeness in those long-ago days was a Cream-coloured Courser on a most desolate part of the beach on 9th September 1916.

On the whole, these rarities of my early days treated me kindly, either waiting to be watched at close quarters or even, like the Siberian Chiffchaff, remaining in one place for some days.

Then there were two rare waders at Cambridge sewage-farm in the 1930s. In those days my wife's parents lived at Cambridge, so we often stayed there for a few days and I was constantly at the sewage-farm. On 23rd October 1932 I visited it with an undergraduate, Alan Hodgkin, destined to become President of the Royal Society. He did not claim to be an expert birdwatcher but he knew the commoner birds well enough. We spotted a strange wader, size of a Redshank, which I was convinced was not a Ruff though it was rather like one. It was on a settling bed, somewhat hidden by the trees; after a short time it flew up and right away. My suspicion was that it was an Upland Plover ('Bartram's Sandpiper' we used to call it in those days). As it flew off, Alan said: 'There was something odd about that—I know: long tail.' I do not think he knew that the Upland Plover is *Bartramia longicauda*, but of course his saying that clinched the matter in my eyes. Later in the day David Lack rang me up to say that Hodgkin had told him of our experience. Lack had seen the same bird earlier in the day and had heard it call (I believe). He too was convinced that it was an Upland Plover. It was not seen again and Witherby was not satisfied. I think I messed up the record, as I had been impressed by the white in the sides of the tail, and Witherby was able to show me that this was just about right for a Ruff. Thirteen years later, when I saw my first American *Bartramia*, I found that my Cambridge description fitted it very well. All of us saw something of the neck-spots, if my memory serves me correctly. The Lesser Yellowlegs of March 1934 was much kinder in its behaviour.

It will be seen that, apart from the Sand Grouse at Littlestone and the Courser at Dungeness, all the rarities that I saw in the first forty years of my life were at inland localities. Rather later, Northampton sewage-farm, not to be outdone by Cambridge, provided me with two more American waders, Pectoral Sandpiper and Buff-breasted Sandpiper: all these four species before I set foot on American soil and before I was free to go to remote Scottish islands at the times of migration.

During my years in the West Midlands, covering the twenties and thirties, I saw nothing there that would count today as a rarity: to be sure, the occasional rarity for the Midlands, such as a Kentish Plover and a Purple Sandpiper, and several Firecrests and Water Pipits; but nothing sensational; and although I usually visited Dungeness some time or other during the year, no real rarity happened to come my way during all those years. Indeed, about 1938 I decided that I should do well if my British bird total reached 250 before I died. It is now well over 300.

During the later fifties and the early sixties I was able to get around to a number of coastal vantage points that I had not visited before—three times to Fair Isle, twice to the Isle of May, several times to the north Norfolk coast, and so on. Then we retired to Swanage, which gave me the advantage of living all the year round on the coast. What Purbeck has done for me in the way of rarities I will come to shortly. But the main point I would emphasise is that, before 1945, the only way to see a rare bird in England was to find it for yourself. The modern practice of rushing off for week-ends to tick off the latest rarity that has turned up somewhere along the coast from Lands End to Dover to Northumberland and beyond to the Isle of Man, to Anglesey to St Ives and Scilly, was out of the question. There may have been fifty ardent ornithologists who would go exploring for rare birds, though I doubt if they numbered even fifty; there were certainly not five hundred or a thousand as there are in 1970. And not many bird-spotters had fast cars.

Of course, in these latter days, at places like Fair Isle you have the inestimable help of trapping. I had the luck to be at Fair Isle when the first British Yellow-headed (or Citrine) Wagtail (*Motacilla citreola*) was trapped in September 1954; and again when the first British Western Sandpiper (*Calidris mauri*) appeared and was duly trapped at the end of May 1956. That bird caused a lot of trouble as its beak was unusually short, so that on measurement it appeared to be a Semi-palmated Sandpiper. At the time I was surprised at this, for the shape of the beak had made me suspect that it was a Western before it was caught. So, when Ian Nisbet pointed out that the colour of the back made it a Western and that the bill-length was possible for either species, I was gratified to find that my original field identification was vindicated. Cley has also been kind to me, although I have not been there at all often. First, there was a fine Rustic Bunting (*Emberiza rustica*), which showed itself well to many observers in September 1958; a few days later my first British Red-footed Falcon (*Falco vespertinus*) was found, and this also waited to be seen by plenty of people. And in October 1961 I was able to help in identifying a Radde's Warbler (*Phylloscopus schwarzi*) that had just been caught; once again, that particular bird must be on a good many 'life-lists'.

By contrast, Dorset has provided me with a series of painfully unsatisfactory rarities, beginning from the first visit Wilfrid and I paid to Portland on 9th September 1955, a few days after our arrival at

Swanage. On this September day we were delighted to find James Monk and Kenneth Rooke with some younger men basking in the sunshine on the Bill, and they whetted our appetites with accounts of a Grey Phalarope they had been watching earlier in the day. After some time on the Bill they suggested looking round the bushes, though they said there seemed to be very few small migrants around. At that time there was only one 'house-trap' in regular working order, by the small stream that flows down just above the Old Lighthouse. We went there and Wilfrid sat in the car just off the road while the rest of us proceeded to drive the trap. I stood near the bushes, in front of our car, whilst the younger men drove the bushes from the place where the stream crosses the road. They had seen one Garden Warbler, but nothing else, earlier in the day; so when they called out: 'One warbler', it seemed reasonable to assume that it was the same bird. It came flying straight towards me and settled, facing me, in a bush which, as I reckoned later, was less than twenty feet from me. It only stopped there for a second, so I could not get my glass on to it. It then flew past Monk who was next in line to me and, disappointingly, just missed the funnel of the trap and went on up the valley to disappear again in the bushes. In that moment when it sat opposite me my eyes had registered an unusually large warbler, much like a Lesser Whitethroat, but the throat perhaps rather less silky white. What British warbler could look like that? I asked myself; and I went up excitedly to James Monk and asked: 'What on earth was it?' 'Oh, just the Garden Warbler again,' was his reply. With my habitual self-distrust, I said weakly: 'I suppose it was.' I ought to have said: 'Sorry, but I really don't believe it. Can't we make sure?' And I should then have told the others what I had seen. Well, I did not do so; and in due course we drove to Weymouth and Radipole, and then left the others and drove back to the hotel in Swanage.

A few minutes after our arrival the telephone rang and Rooke told me that, on their return to the Bill, they had found an Orphean Warbler (*Silvia hortensis*) that had caught itself in the trap during their absence. They were holding it for the night in case we could come to see it. We could not get there till after ten next morning and we searched for it in vain. Had I seen the Orphean Warbler, or had I imagined things? The only thing against it was that none of us had seen the white outer tail feathers as it flew. This really did not surprise me. Both times it flew straight, with no occasion to open its tail feathers; and I know Orphean Warblers sufficiently well in India to appreciate that when they are flying directly away from you the white does not normally show. Indeed, the white in a Whitethroat's tail, which can be very conspicuous, does not normally show when the bird flies directly away from the observer. I made sure that none of the observers had seen it well enough to identify it as a Garden Warbler; they assumed it was the bird they had found in the morning. Could I really be certain that what I had seen was an Orphean Warbler? What I can be quite sure of is that if anyone had said to me 'There has been some rumour of an Orphean Warbler', I should have said 'Of course, that is what I saw'. But until Dr Rooke rang up, the idea of Orphean did not enter my mind, as it is to all practical purposes not a British bird. As far as I know, even with the enormous increase of birdwatching and bird-trapping since 1955, only one more Orphean Warbler has been found (Cornwall, October, 1967).

That was a tantalising beginning for my Dorset bird-spotting. My next rare warbler was no better. On 1st October 1956 I was walking across Peveril Down, at Swanage, when a small warbler came up through some gorse scrub and settled in full view in a dead bush. There it remained for at least half a minute, so that I could watch it at ease with my binoculars. It was a good deal like a Chiffchaff, quite a small brown warbler; but the shape of the bill and the head were both wrong. In recent years I had spent a lot of time at Delhi wrestling with the small brown warblers, especially learning the differences between Chiffchaffs (Siberian there of course) and Booted Warblers (*Hippolais caligata*). Here was a bird which seemed to be identical at every point with the Booted Warblers I had come to know round Delhi. But, of course, there are several very similar species of *Hippolais* that may occur in England, and some of these I have never seen in the field; so that was that.

Two of these troublesome birds showed themselves when I was in the company of Martin Curtler, an ornithologist of considerable experience. On 17th January 1961 we were walking along the path from Holton Heath railway station towards Poole Harbour when Martin called my attention to a bird settled on the telegraph wire, beyond an impassable thicket of gorse. It seemed to be a small thrush, which might have been a Song Thrush, only that it had a very distinct pale wing-bar; and this showed on both wings. It soon flew down and disappeared into the scrub. As it did so, I noticed white edges to the outer tail feathers, as in a Mistle Thrush. But this was no Mistle Thrush; it was much too small, and the colour of its upper back and wings was too warm a brown: the lower back was paler. What could it be? I had no idea of any such thrush—till I happened to open Dresser's *Birds of Europe* at the picture of the Siberian Thrush (*Turdus sibiricus*). The female looked just right. However, we had not seen the pale eye-stripe, nor yet the striking under-wing pattern (the latter we could hardly have expected to see, I think). Two further attempts were made to find the bird again. Both Mistle and Song Thrushes showed themselves, but their presence and what I saw of them even on the wires only served to convince me that the bird we saw was neither the one nor the other. As the Siberian Thrush is essentially a 'ground-thrush' the chance of seeing it again on the wire seemed slight, and the scrub was impassable, at least to anyone of my years.

On 1st May 1961 we were driving along the road between Arne and Ridge. There had been much rain; indeed, it was raining that day. As we came to the open meadows towards Ridge we noticed some Curlews on a flooded field, walking about quite close to the road. We stopped to look at them and found that there were several Whimbrels among them. Then, to our surprise, we saw one bird, slightly larger than a Whimbrel but paler than a Curlew. It was walking about in the long grass quite near to the road; probably some twenty yards from the car. I wondered if Slender-billed Curlew (*Numenius tenuirostris*) was a possibility; I got out my copy of the *Field Guide*, and read: 'Note heart-shaped spots on sides.' The bird was so near that we could easily see the spots on the sides—except when they were hidden for a moment by the long grass. There was no sign of any heart-shaped spots. In the *Field Guide* neither the picture of the bird nor the caption opposite to it gives any idea that the Slender-billed Curlew is specially pale, though the main text does. I doubt if we looked that up. We were told to look for heart-shaped spots; we did so; there seemed to be no such spots; so we concluded that the bird was not a Slender-bill. As it did not have the head-markings of a Whimbrel, we assumed that it must be a small and pale common Curlew. We watched it for some time. We did not get out of the car to make the birds fly up, but left them there. I wrote to James Ferguson-Lees to ask if he knew of any reported variants in Curlew plumage—not to mention size. He replied that apparently there were not. So our bird remained as a mystery until, a few years later, K. D. Smith, having watched many Slender-bills in north-west Africa, reported that the heart-shaped spots are *not* a conspicuous feature in the field. So, our bird may have been one. Who knows?

On 16th September 1966 I was alone at home in the afternoon, feeling rather specially lonely, for my wife was in hospital for a few days and at that very moment a much-loved brother-in-law was being 'laid to rest', to use the old expression, on the other side of the Atlantic. As I sat in the garden, drinking tea and feeling sad, a Kestrel came into view, flying over against a grey sky away towards the cliffs. As I looked, suddenly it made a queer twist in the air and I instantly registered: 'Nighthawk'. (It was a little later that I recalled sitting on the platform of a suburban station on the outskirts of Philadelphia, with my brother-in-law, waiting for our wives to arrive from the city, and we were delighted and diverted by a Nighthawk that dashed around in the air after its insect food.) Two minutes later the bird reappeared, this time from above the house, again hawked around for half a minute and then vanished towards the town of Swanage. For the next hour I was frantically telephoning all over Purbeck in search of some local birdwatcher who might turn his eyes to the skies. They were all out or away. My own search all round the town was equally in vain. The bird refused to come back again. Could it have been something else? I had not seen the white on the wing (I rarely do see this, even when Nighthawks (*Chordeiles minor*) fly right above our house in Swarthmore). There is a very similar Lesser Nighthawk (*C. acutipennis*), but it is said to fly about catching its insect food much nearer the ground. As far as I know, all other possible 'nightjars' have less pointed wings. My Swanage bird had pointed wings all right.

One day I was walking along the Peveril Down with my niece when we saw two gulls on the sea below us. One was larger and the other smaller. A Herring Gull and a Black-headed, no doubt. Then the larger bird flew and proved to be a Black-headed. So what could the smaller one be but a Little Gull? But when it flew up, its wing-pattern from above was that of a Black-headed, not a Little. No other bird smaller than a Black-headed has that wing-pattern, except a Bonaparte. I had to leave for London; first I rang up one or two local observers but no one found my small gull. I had no opportunity to see the underside of the wing.

Oh Meiklejohn! Why do so many of your Hoodwinks (*Dissimulatrix spuria*) insist on crossing my path? Can't you stop them? What did you say? You have had just as many crossing your own path! No, I do not believe it. Or perhaps what you really said was: Half of them were your own fault. If you had behaved more rationally, all would have been well. And this is true enough of my final example, a certain white heron which nearly ruined several of my ornithological friendships. If I had been careful to put all the facts together in the first place, it should not have been too difficult to convince the Rarities Committee that there had in fact been two birds (indeed, fantastic as it may seem, possibly even three), one of which was indeed a Great White Heron (*Egretta alba*), whilst the other one (or two) was (were) albinistic Grey Herons.

Possibly the story is still worth telling in all its detail. On 17th September 1961, as it was a beautiful day, my wife and I decided that we would take our afternoon tea by Poole Harbour or rather, to be exact, by Brands Bay. So, off we set. After we had had our tea I walked off looking for birds—only a few yards—and I met a man and woman wearing binoculars. Being English, we did not accost one another. I assumed that they might be interested in anything but birds; presumably they thought the same. I did not see much. That evening, Helen Brotherton rang up to say that she had just had a phone call from a couple who were staying in Studland, and who had seen by Poole Harbour what they believed must be a Great White Heron. She had arranged to meet them the next morning. Could I come too? So we all met. Sure enough, they were the couple I had seen the day before; and they were then just coming from their view of the white bird, and had not then had a chance to look it up in a book. They did not claim to know much about birds; but their bird seemed to fit the book's account of the Great White Heron. They had seen the bird at very close quarters, so they had seen the yellow bill and glistening white plumage. We went ahead and when we got opposite Brands Bay we looked across and there, in the trees far away, were several grey Herons and a white one. So it seemed that we had found the bird. It would not move from its tree, so we drove around to a nearer spot. By then it had, of course, gone from its tree, nor could we find it on the muddy creeks of the Bay (the tide was low). So, for the moment, we gave it up. I then went to tell Wilfrid and took him on a second attempt to see the bird. When we reached Brands Bay, there it was, up in the tree. Again it refused to move; so in the end we came away. On our way back, as we passed through Studland village, we overtook the first discoverers of the bird. We stopped and talked to them, Wilfrid cross-examining them as severely as ever any lawyer cross-examined a witness in court. All their answers satisfied him. As we left them, he said to me: 'So I suppose we have seen a Great White Heron.' I agreed. But we had not—we had seen the wrong bird.

Next day we searched again, and once more the white heron was in the trees among the other Grey Herons, but this time even further off, partly hidden by the foliage. I thought we had better go along to the ferry and hope that the white heron might have come nearer when we came back after an hour or so. But Wilfrid wanted to wait, so we did. I was rather impatiently training my telescope on various birds on the mud (the tide was very low) when suddenly Wilfrid said: 'There it is!' And how right he was! The real Great White Heron had suddenly appeared in the nearest channel below us. It had been so low down on the mud that it was hidden from us until it moved across the creek. For the next ten minutes or so we had perfect views of it; I even got it into the telescope at the highest magnification and noted the curious fact (which I had read in the *Handbook* description but which I had never noticed in the hundreds I had watched in both India and America) that the legs are less black on the sides than on front and back (or is it the other way?). The bill was bright yellow, a colour that no Grey Heron ever achieves.

Finally it flew. Now, it happened that Arthur Bull had rung me up the previous evening. He had found a white heron in Brands Bay, in very poor weather conditions. He had thought it looked less pure white than he would have anticipated and in particular, when it flew, it looked grey under the wings. So, of course, when our bird flew I looked carefully and decided that perhaps it did look a little grey, though I should have supposed that this was simply the effect of the strong light. (Have I not watched them going to roost at Delhi when they sometimes look so dark on the underside that I have found it difficult to believe that they were egrets at all?) Wilfrid did not see any dark underside to the wing. To him, the bird looked totally white in plumage, as it certainly did while it was feeding. It flew away out of sight, and that was the last I saw of it. Rebecca and I left for Suffolk and Norfolk a day or two later.

During the next week or ten days a number of people came from far and near to see the rarity. Later I saw all the descriptions sent in. All saw one or other of the albino birds (if there really were two) except for a young couple from Wiltshire, who sent in a perfectly good report of the real bird, and who apparently saw it at almost exactly the time that two excellent ornithologists were watching the albino a mile away.

It is curious that the two birds were never seen at once—except by Wilfrid and myself (and then the albino was a long way away): still more so that they apparently arrived and departed about the same time. Both were seen during a period of about ten days, no more.

If it had not happened to me, could I have believed in such a coincidence? Probably not.

Are these strange things worth telling? Perhaps not, but it may be of some comfort to other observers who have sent in reports which appear to them to be quite perfect to know that the Rarities Committee has turned down the reports of others. Witherby turned down several of my early reports of rarities. In each case I had reason to believe afterwards that he was right. The only one that Tucker turned down—a Brünnichs Guillemot that I saw in perfect conditions in the Irish Sea from a ship going in slow convoy in March 1945—I still believe was genuine.

Purbeck has in fact given me some very satisfactory rarities. In just over ten years, from my own window I have seen Firecrest, Hoopoe, Golden Oriole, Alpine Swift and Serin, even if the Nighthawk must be put in square brackets.

The Alpine Swift was a very satisfactory bird. Late in the afternoon of 2nd September 1963 we had just arrived home when from the bedroom window upstairs I saw two or three Swifts flying round. I called to Rebecca: 'Would you like to see a September Swift?' (Swifts are much scarcer in September in Dorset than they are in Kent or East Anglia.) By the time she arrived with binoculars, I had seen a much larger bird with the three or four common Swifts: an Alpine Swift, in fact. We watched it for some time, then they all moved off westwards, so I hastily alerted Langton Matravers to see if they appeared there. But they were not seen. Just before dusk the next evening, as we were walking up the road to our house, an Alpine Swift (presumably the same bird) appeared again. Some years later another Alpine Swift was observed over the same Durlston area of Swanage.

Apart from two probable views of very skulking Barred Warblers—neither of them good enough to record—I have seen no rare warbler in the Durlston area or along the cliffs since the supposed Booted Warbler. Yet, year by year, I have scrutinised every small warbler in the scrub all through the autumn migration; and all the common species occur plentifully—or perhaps I should say all but Reed and Grasshopper. Year after year we have tried to find a Melodious or Icterine, but so far we have had no success in our corner of Purbeck. Melodious in particular is so often seen at Portland that its absence, or seeming absence, from this part of the coast is surprising. When the *Handbook* was published in 1938 there were only three definite records of Melodious Warblers for the whole of England. Although I am only an occasional visitor to Portland I have seen Melodious Warblers there three or more times. I suppose the total Portland score of Melodious Warblers may well now be over fifty; and in some years perhaps a dozen have been recorded from the trapping stations round the coast of southern England and Wales. Our ideas of 'vagrants', driven off course by storms, have been greatly modified by all these records from the coasts. What are all these Melodious Warblers doing, as they turn up year by year? I suppose their appearance may be due to a tendency of birds to wander in various directions in the late summer, before the full orientation accompanying proper migration has taken hold of them. Indeed, how many inland birds go unnoticed?

Incidentally, this may be the place to record that, about 1940, I talked to Miss Lister (Lord Lister's daughter) then aged over eighty, who was responsible for the record of possible Melodious Warblers singing in the Lyme Regis undercliff in 1897 and 1898. She had listened to the song several times but could never see the birds. From her account of the song it seemed to me probable that the birds were Marsh Warblers, and she agreed that that was possible. However, now that we know that Melodious Warblers turn up on autumn migration in Dorset (possibly also in Devon) most years, and as their breeding range is not very far off to the south, I suppose the possibility of a small colony breeding in England should not be ruled out.

My one and only British Black-winged Stilt was a very well-behaved bird. On 14th May 1959, R. and I were driving from Exeter to Swanage. We were in no special hurry; so we took the coast road and came through Weymouth, and past Lodmoor. In those days it was possible to drive off the road half way along Lodmoor, and gaze across at some of the pools and ditches. We did this; and there was one bird, standing all alone in a ditch. My first idea was a Lesser Black-backed Gull, for it had a dark mantle and a white head and breast (its beak was tucked into its back and it was standing in deep water, so that the length of its beak and legs was not immediately apparent). But a view through binoculars immediately turned it into a Stilt. We quickly drove along to the nearest telephone, rang up Miss Crosby, who was fortunately at home, went to fetch her and on our return found the Stilt at the same place. It stayed for several days and was seen by a good many people. The odd thing was that we, non-Weymouthites, were the first to spot it; but in those days there were fewer bird-spotters at Weymouth than there are today.

This chapter is concerned with rare birds in Britain. Britain (or if you prefer, just England) is a conveniently small and compact area where, with the mass of field observers that now cover the whole country (do they?), we seem to know what we are dealing with. In some parts of the world it is harder to know when you are really dealing with a rarity. The rarity may be something that has been overlooked. Thus, in India I once found myself watching a marsh tern at very close quarters over the river Jamuna at Delhi. It ought to have been Whiskered—the common marsh tern of India; but this one had much too dusky a mantle for Whiskered; and it had the dark feathers on the side of the neck which are usually considered diagnostic of a Black Tern in autumn plumage. So far there is no authentic record of a Black Tern in India. On another day, at a marsh near Delhi, where in those days Moustached Warblers (*Acrocephalus melanopogon*) were plentiful (today the marsh has been eaten up by the vast growth of India's capital city) I found myself looking at a bird which politely sat in full view for at least half a minute and which had the markings of a Sedge Warbler (*A. schoenobaenus*). This also is a bird not at present admitted to the Indian avifauna. If you look at the map of its breeding distribution, you may see that its occurrence there would seem perfectly reasonable.

So, too, in North America a Lesser Black-backed Gull and a Dusky Redshank both came my way before either species was recognised as an official North American bird. Now both are.

Why should these birds be more exciting to see out of their normal range than in it? I cannot say. But we all do like to see 'rarities', so I suppose the sensible thing is to go on enjoying them without bothering to justify our satisfaction in seeing them. Of course, when they are 'lifers' that is even more gratifying. On the other hand, when they are birds that you know well in their normal habitat you feel a greater confidence in your identification: though it must be added that, just because they are familiar, you are tempted not to give so much attention to the nice points of identification as you do if the bird is a total novelty.

I have not attempted here to list all the rarities that have come my way in my seventy years and more of birding. That would be tedious. And, of course, most of my recent rarities have been birds already found by some other observer, which have kindly stayed till I arrived on the scene. My chief concern in this chapter has been to show the ways in which rarities were found in the days before there were fieldguides or mist-nets or the most recent types of binocular and telescope.

Let me confess that, in the main, we were much less thorough in our detailed descriptions than the present generation. On 8th December 1948 I went to Cannock reservoir, in the Black Country of the Midlands, to look for a Lapland Bunting that had been reported at a meeting of the West Midland Bird Club the previous evening. I found two or three younger members of the club, and in due course we found the bird—a ridiculously tame creature, that hopped about (or ran?) in the grass and stunted heather a few yards from us. I had never seen a Lapland Bunting before (I have seen plenty at Fair Isle and elsewhere since); it was in immature plumage, with no striking patch of chestnut on the nape. Yet I knew at once that this was not a Reed Bunting but a Lapland. There was something about the shape and colour of the head and upper back that proclaimed it. One of my companions (was it Mead-Briggs?) asked: 'What features or plumage distinctions would you say are proof that that is not a Reed Bunting?' I hardly knew what to answer. Indeed, I believe he himself found a better answer than I could at the moment propose. I should have had some difficulty in convincing a sceptic that I had seen a Lapland Bunting at all.

In the old days, records of field observation were accepted or rejected mainly because you either believed or did not believe the observer. In the article by Saunders in the first number of *British Birds*, quoted at the beginning of this chapter, he mentions, without accepting it as a valid record, an observation by Mr J. P. Nunn of two supposed Ruby-throats (*Luscinia calliope*) seen at Westgate-on-Sea in October 1900. Presumably Saunders knew something of Nunn, so he thought the record deserved to be mentioned, and it still appears in brackets in Witherby's *Handbook*. I once took the trouble to look up the original record in the *Zoologist* to see what his evidence was. To my surprise (yes, I was surprised) he gave no details at all. So we are left wondering why he thought his two birds were Ruby-throats. Did he see two autumn-plumage Blue-throats, which can look very much like Ruby-throats? Or did he really see some feature that would be diagnostic of a Ruby-throat? We shall never know. That was the way things were in those benighted days. A few days ago, happening to look up a reference in *British Birds* (Vol. XXX, 1936-7) I was gratified and also again surprised (surprised the other way this time) to find the full plumage descriptions that I supplied for a record of a Little Gull seen in May in Warwickshire. We were by then learning the importance of these details.

Partly, I think, because of this 'generation gap' I sometimes found myself in a minority of one when I was a member of the British Birds Rarities Committee. A perfectly good record of a Bee-eater in Sussex was turned down because the observer sent no details. As it happened, I knew who the observer was. He was Dr Frederick Curtis, for many years a busy doctor in Redhill, Surrey, who had retired to a house in Sussex; I had not heard of him for many years and realised that he must be well over eighty. In fact, I saw his obituary a few years later; he had died aged over ninety, I believe. When I knew him, fifty years ago, he was a very competent ornithologist but much too busy to watch birds except on his annual holiday. I knew that if he said he had seen a Bee-eater, he had seen a Bee-eater. But the Sussex experts had never heard of him, so out it went. Saunders-vintage bird watchers were out of date.

As I conclude this chapter, I have just been reading Ian Wallace's fascinating account of his month in St Agnes, Isles of Scilly, in

October 1971. I think Dr Curtis, if he had still been living, would have enjoyed that as much as any younger man. How many of the rare birds mentioned there would he have recognised? Certainly some; almost certainly not all. But the generation gap need not be so wide as it sometimes appears to be.

CHAPTER XIV

Some Problems and Notions

Readers of some of the earlier chapters of this book will realise that I have always been fascinated by the unusual, the abnormal. By this, I do not mean things that are merely erratic, or meaningless: nor am I thinking of albinistic or melanistic plumage, or distorted beaks; but rather of habits that do not fit the accepted pattern.

In this concluding chapter I want to examine some of these unexpected bird habits in some depth, to see if it is possible to find any significance in such behaviour. I begin with bird song.

For many years, indeed, for the fifty years or more from the time when I began watching birds to the time when my ears began to give way, I kept daily notes of the bird song that I heard. As far as British birds are concerned, I have mentioned that much of this work was published in *British Birds* in December 1935. It remains, as far as I know, still much the most complete account of song periods that has been published, though E. M. Nicholson has supplemented it in various ways. I go back to it here because, in the introduction, I discussed the question: 'What is Bird Song?', and what I then wrote still seems to be a useful introduction to the whole subject:

'I know of no definition that is wholly satisfactory. In this table [meaning the table published in *British Birds*] I have included all the Passerine species that inhabit England and Wales, whether residents or regular visitors, provided they have some "song" or call-note that is seasonal in nature; that is to say a song or call that is uttered either much more frequently and intensely, or solely, at particular seasons of the year, in nearly every case spring or early summer.' (I might well have added: 'in fact, during some part of the breeding season.') 'There are very few Passerine species that have no such "song". The trill of the Long-tailed Tit, though very much like some other tit trills that are seasonal, seems to be evoked by sudden excitement—especially by the appearance of a bird of prey—at any season of the year. The crows have no regular song, though Jays and Magpies occasionally indulge in choral chatterings early in the spring, and even the conversation of Jackdaws and Rooks seems to take on a heightened significance at that season. Other borderline cases are illustrated by the Red-backed Shrike, Bullfinch, Tree Sparrow and Wagtails, whose songs are usually feeble affairs, infrequent and spasmodic.'

Some of these 'borderline' cases demand more detailed discussion. Let me begin with a bird I did not even include, the common House Sparrow. When J. D. Summers-Smith published his charming monograph on the House Sparrow, I was surprised to find that he did not recognise the House Sparrow as a songster; apart from communal song, in which considerable numbers of sparrows sometimes join together. I corresponded with him on this and drew his attention to a letter from F. J. Stubbs published in the third volume of *British Birds*, where he wrote: 'The bird sings all through the year with the exception of the period of rearing the young; the season of moult; certain damp, dark or foggy days in winter; and when a heavy fall of snow makes the task of securing food so arduous that there is no energy left for song.' Summers-Smith's reply was to the effect that as the song was quite erratic and infrequent he did not recognise it as true song. Which brings us back again to matters of definition.

If you begin by saying that true song must necessarily, by definition, be regular and seasonal, you then rule out the fairly elaborate songs of such species as the Common (or Barn) Swallow, the Pied Wagtail, the Willow Tit (already discussed in an earlier chapter), Red-backed Shrike and some more. It seems to me that any reasonably elaborate and set series of notes, whether they happen to sound musical to the human ear or not, must be recognised as true song. Summers-Smith calls the Sparrow's communal chirruping 'song', but he seems unwilling to call the very same series of noises 'song' when one bird does it alone. This seems unsatisfactory, though it must be recognised that the persistent chirruping that can occasionally be heard from a single cock Sparrow does not conform to the song behaviour that may be called 'typical' for the mass of song birds. Vocally, it is as good an effort as the song of, let us say, the Reed Bunting. But Reed Buntings typically perch on the top of some bush and there proclaim their territorial rights with great persistence, even though the 'song' only consists of some four wheezy notes repeated scores of times. In this sense it is typical song, though to the human ear it is a poor effort. Round the world one can certainly find plenty of other examples of equally persistent singers with an equally poor ditty.

One further aspect of bird song needs to be considered briefly; this is, that the recording of bird song by human agency is more subject to human fallibility than most other kinds of ornithological observation. In other words, some people, even when quite young, have much better ears than others. I have reason to believe that my ears were unusually good when I was young, so maybe I have been able to hear some song that others would miss. Let me give one or two examples. Long ago Witherbys published a book on bird song by a writer called Stanley Morris. It was clear that he had been a careful student of bird song in the south of England for many years. So I was astonished to read that he had only once heard a Tree Creeper sing. In the woods round Tunbridge Wells where I grew up, and in the Lickey Woods, north Worcestershire, which I constantly visited for over twenty years, Tree Creepers were vigorous songsters with a clearly defined song period. Again, I have heard able ornithologists say that they rarely hear any song from Spotted Flycatchers. It is a feeble song, but not at all infrequent. When I lived at Tunbridge Wells, and again during the twenty-plus years in South Birmingham, I lived close to several Spotted Flycatchers. Indeed, at Selly Oak my daily ten-minute walk to Woodbrooke College took me through several Flycatcher territories; and every morning, in most of May and all June, between 8.30 and 9 in the morning I could be sure of hearing the little squeaky song, usually uttered from the higher branch of a tree with much flicking of wings and tail. So, it may be that the failure to hear such songs is simply a failure of the human ear. It should be added, no doubt, that both Creepers and Flycatchers, like most other species, sing more persistently if other male birds are within range. In any case, such failure of the human ear cannot account for the erratic song behaviour of such species as Pied Wagtail, Willow Tit and Red-backed Shrike.

What evokes typical song? Today's answer, I suppose, would be, first territorial assertion, and second, the seasonal development of the breeding impulse; and these two factors are normally interwoven. This is 'normal'. But much song is abnormal. Forgetting borderline cases, for the moment, let us look at some bird song that does not readily conform to this pattern. Species such as Robins and Hedge Sparrows and Wrens can be heard singing vigorously in almost every month of the year. They are silent during the moult, and during adverse weather. These are birds with a strong territorial sense. Robins, at least, will not tolerate the presence even of one of the opposite sex in their territory during the winter. So this emphasises the close relation of song and territory. A number of other British species also sing strongly in the autumn, after the moult. The Skylark is a good example. Yet Skylarks are apt to congregate in flocks during the autumn and winter. Can it be shown that the individuals that sing in autumn are still holding territories? My impression is that some species, such as Yellowhammers and Chaffinches, may spend part of the day in flocks and part of the day in separate territories. This behaviour is specially conspicuous in early spring. A bird that is singing in its territory on a balmy day in February may still be feeding for part of the day, and perhaps also roosting, with a flock. And occasionally it will sing, probably not very briskly, from the feeding ground of the flock.

Even with these 'typical' songsters, however, song may be evoked in very improbable circumstances. Thomas Hardy's famous poem, 'The Darkling Thrush', illustrates the point.

> I leant upon a coppice gate
> When Frost was spectre-grey,
> And Winter's dregs made desolate
> The weakening eye of day . . .

in more prosaic language, a dismal, raw, December afternoon; but

> At once a voice arose among
> The bleak twigs overhead
> In a full-hearted evensong
> Of joy illimited.

And I add my prosy comment, to underline this strange occurrence. It is possible that the next day the sun shone, or there was a balmy evening and the thrush sang not at all. Anyway, such has been my experience.

I made the following note on 24th September 1929. 'In cloudy weather, a Mistle Thrush sang loudly in an oak-tree near Lower Bittell reservoir at about 11 a.m., for half a minute or more. Then over twenty Mistle Thrushes flew from the tree, all the rest having been completely silent, while this one member of the flock was indulging in its unseasonal outburst of song.' Song, not at dawn, but in the middle of the day; not in a territory, but in a flock; not as a challenge to its neighbours, but apparently not affecting them in any way. Very odd.

Here are a few more examples of song that do not seem to fit the accepted normal pattern. The song of the Swallow, when fully uttered, is a beautiful tune of some fifteen notes—quite an elaborate affair. I have listened to a Swallow resting on the roof of a building, far from its nesting site, late in the summer, singing this sweet song persistently. Or, it will sing from time to time as it flies around over a sewage-farm among others of its kind in early April, just after its arrival from the south and before it has begun to visit its nesting site; again, it may be heard singing as it hawks around in the air with others of its tribe in late September just before the return migration.

The Pied Wagtail has a sweet song, not unlike the Swallow's song, but softer. The difference here is that the Swallow has a regular song period, and sings persistently through the nesting period but with the 'extras' at both ends that I have just described. The Pied Wagtail does not seem to sing regularly in the breeding territory at all. Its quite irregular and occasional song can be heard in almost any month of the year; but in my experience it is usually heard whilst the bird is running about feeding, not necessarily near a nest.

Everyone knows about the dawn chorus, even though few get up in time to go out into the woods to listen to it. From one point of view the dawn chorus of winter is a more remarkable phenomenon than the better advertised chorus of 4 a.m. in May or June. Lie in your bed at dawn on some February day and through the open window listen to the Thrushes and Robins piping up in vigorous song at the first glint of daylight, and meditate on the singular fact that they have not fed for more than twelve hours. Yet they greet the dawn with 'joy illimited' before going after their breakfast. Apparently the 'economic motive' is not always paramount with birds (nor the sexual urge) whatever may be the case with human beings. And I confess I find it difficult to see in this early dawn song a territorial challenge, though most of the song does no doubt come from birds that are holding a territory which they will be defending with energy from challengers in a few weeks' time.

It seems difficult to account for some of this unexpected song without recognising that birds are, in general, so full of well-being that they must express themselves in ways that do not necessarily have any special survival value (I shall be returning to this matter a little later). Or, to put it rather differently, the most 'successful' birds have, even in the dead of winter, an amount of surplus energy, i.e. surplus to the constant business of finding adequate food, that expresses itself in various ways, one of which is song, let us say surplus song. Indeed, when you come to think of it much of the usual song of birds would seem to be 'surplus'. Watch a Willow Warbler, for example. Throughout the early part of the breeding season it will be constantly searching among the leaves for insect food and at the same time constantly singing. It is difficult to believe that its survival depends on its singing so constantly while it feeds. Other common English birds, such as Blackbirds, Thrushes, Chaffinches and Skylarks, feed for a time and then sing for a time. Some of them spend an immense amount of the day singing. Again, it is difficult to believe that they would be endangered if they sang less. Indeed, I cannot resist comparing the English Blackbird with its very close relative the American Robin. In the part of America known to me, Robins are about as plentiful as Blackbirds are in England: both of them are among the most 'successful' birds of their range. Yet the amount of time spent by most American Robins in song must be less than a tenth of the time many Blackbirds spend in song. Why? I can only see this as a difference in the character of the two species. I am even attempted to say in their 'temperament'. Is that too anthropomorphic an expression to use? I do not think so.*

* When I wrote this, I had not seen Professor Charles Hartshorne's remarkable book, *Born to Sing*. Hartshorne has spent much of his life travelling around the world, listening to bird song in all the continents. He is fully satisfied that bird song, beyond its survival value through territorial assertion and other functional characteristics, is an expression of feeling, in fact that birds sing because using their voices gives them pleasure, aesthetic pleasure. And in his prefatory pages

If we turn to migration, again we find on the one hand an amazingly rigid pattern of almost incredible flights undertaken year after year, century after century—and on the other hand all manner of surprising deviations.

Here are a few of the migratory patterns followed, as far as one can see, by the species concerned, for countless generations. We begin with a few well known British birds. First, the Swallows, migrating from north-west Europe to South Africa—why must they go so far for their winter quarters? Then the young Cuckoos, who have never seen their parents, having been reared by birds of other species, following the ancestral route to Africa without fail every autumn. The Greenland Wheatear, some individuals coming up through western Europe from the African winter quarters, but others flying directly across the Atlantic storm-belt to reach their summer breeding grounds. (Don't say, 'Perhaps they wait for a lull between the storms'; it is clear enough that they do not, though these, like other migrating birds, apparently sometimes use the appropriate winds to aid their flight.) The other species that regularly crosses the north Atlantic is the North American population of the Arctic Tern, and these apparently fly directly from New England to West Africa. Among the most extraordinary migrations are those of certain Australian and New Zealand Cuckoos (*Chalcides lucidus* and *Urodynamics taitensis*). These birds migrate north to various Indonesian and Pacific islands, each species or race having a separate winter range. Again, one wonders why they must undertake these migrations; they are at least very rigid in their patterns. These and innumerable other annual migrations seem to justify the argument in Bernard Tucker's letter (see Chapter 2) that there must be some compelling reason that has caused birds to undertake such enormous and perilous journeys, year by year. Yet there are some very puzzling aspects of the matter.

Nearly all the 300 and more species of humming-bird live in tropical America; most are year-long residents, sometimes in very restricted habitat. A few migrate north through Mexico into south-western North America. One, the familiar Ruby-throated Humming-bird

---

he quotes both Julian Huxley and E. M. Nicholson in support: Huxley: 'Very often the creature itself cannot be aware of the biological function.... I believe that deliberate sound will almost always have an emotional basis.' Nicholson: 'Birds are all temperament and emotion . . . [their] language expressing apparently not thoughts but feelings.' So I seem to be in good company.

(*Archilochus*) migrates north across the Gulf of Mexico every year and some individuals breed as far north as Canada. If it was not known to do it, the crossing of the Gulf of Mexico for such a small bird would be thought impossible. Why does it do it? How and when did it begin to do it? One would suppose that it could find some niche in Central or South America that would allow it to survive without undertaking such a perilous journey every year. In the case of the small European passerine birds—warblers and others—that cross the Mediterranean and the Sahara desert twice a year, one may perhaps assume that Europe is their ancestral home, and even that the Sahara was much less desiccated a few thousand years ago. The sudden fall in numbers of at least one species, the Common Whitethroat, in north-west Europe in recent years may even cause one to wonder if some of these species can continue to survive the extreme hazards of the journey. Survival may demand that they find breeding space in tropical Africa. However this may be, the case of the Ruby-throated Humming-bird seems to be different. The humming-bird's ancestral home is presumably tropical; yet somehow this one species has boldly and successfully developed a migratory habit that enables it to 'conquer' North America. I find it very difficult to understand why this should ever have happened. It could not gradually have learnt to cross the Gulf of Mexico. Either you do cross it or you don't, and the Ruby-throated does.

When we consider some of these astonishing sea crossings I suppose we must now bear in mind the possibility, widely accepted today, that the continents have broken apart within the last few million years, so that in the lifetime of some of these species the waters they now cross did not exist. It is not easy to imagine what may have happened over millions of years. Why, indeed, did the birds begin to migrate at all?—either these Australian Cuckoos or the Ruby-throated Humming-birds; and in the case of the two cuckoos, how did their migratory patterns become so rigid and yet so distinct? The drifting continents may seem to solve one problem; but only to confront us with several more. In the end the mind boggles over the possibilities of what may have happened in millions of years when we see some fairly rapid changes of behaviour and of habitat in a hundred years or less. Sometimes the scientists of today invite us to swallow, unquestioningly, things that the mind can cope with no better than with the miraculous assertions of an earlier generation of theologians. Just as the theologians assured us that they knew what God had been up to

Some Problems and Notions

and that we must not doubt their authority, so today some scientists assure us that they know what Nature has been up to; they *know*.*

Whilst we are on the western side of the Atlantic, consider the strange migration of the so-called Mountain Plover (*Eupoda montana*) which actually breeds in the prairies of middle-west America east of the Rockies. It winters in Mexico—not a very long migration for a member of the globe-spanning Limicoline family. But, as Matthiesen points out in his *Shore-birds of America*, it takes a round-about route, involving the crossing of two high mountain ranges. The direct route, in addition to being shorter, would avoid crossing these mountain ranges. A strangely rigid pattern of migration!

Here is one more case of 'unnecessary' migration, from the American side of the world. I have only lately had first-hand acquaintance with the birds of Jamaica. We have visited that beautiful island twice in February. One of the few really common and conspicuous birds of Jamaica is the Loggerhead Kingbird (*Tyrannus caudifasciatus*). It has a close relative, the Grey Kingbird (*T. dominicensis*), described by Bond (*Birds of the West Indies*) as 'The commonest West Indian flycatcher and one of the best-known birds of the West Indies.' But I have not seen one, for the simple reason that it is a migrant, leaving the western Antilles completely for the whole winter. It is difficult to believe (I had almost written 'impossible') that it would not be able to find food all through the winter in Jamaica, just as readily as the Loggerhead. How did such a migratory habit originate?

Why are some birds so rigid in their behaviour, whilst others are so adaptable? Are those of rigid behaviour in danger of dying out?

There are many other things that do not easily fit into one's preconceived ideas of migration as we see it today and as we may imagine it evolving in the past. I venture to look at some of them.

First, there are the numerous cases of birds migrating in the wrong direction. To take a single example: Pallas's Warbler—smallest of the leaf warblers, scarcely bigger than a *Regulus*, whose normal home is in

---

* I do not suggest that scientists in general are any more cocksure than other human beings. In the course of my life I have met a number of professional scientists who have the modesty that befits those who are trying to discover a little more about the endless ramifications of natural processes. They know how little even the wisest man knows. Nor am I doubting that the geologists are at any rate approximately right when they give us dates of terrestrial events millions of years ago: millions, rather than mere hundreds or thousands, no doubt, but when they begin to be exact about the numbers of millions, then my scepticism begins to assert itself.

eastern Asia with winter quarters in north India and south China—has been recorded in Britain thirty-nine times up to the end of 1968, 'all in October and November, and all coastal or insular'. When the first of these was recorded in 1896 it was treated as an 'accidental' occurrence. It can hardly be an 'accident' that several of these birds, almost every year, travel persistently at an average speed of several hundred miles a week to the west, possibly starting in a north-west direction, instead of flying south. To be sure, birds can often be carried many miles off course by winds that suddenly blow them in the wrong direction, but there is clear proof from ringing that such birds can somehow quickly find their way back onto the proper course. It is simply not true that winds blow persistently for weeks on end from east to west all across north Asia and Europe in such a way as to bring such birds, willy-nilly, to the shores of the North Sea and across it. And if in one season such an abnormal meteorological phenomenon did occur, it would presumably bring birds of many different species across the world. Undoubtedly some years bring more of such 'vagrants' than other years. This presumably means that in some years the weather conditions are more favourable than others for birds that are headed the wrong way. 'Headed the wrong way'—that is, of course, in turn a speculation. It has been worked out in some detail by K. B. Rooke in the case of Pallas' Warbler; and whether the whole of his thesis is vindicated or not after further experience, it seems probable that some individuals must somehow, year by year, be impelled in the wrong direction—i.e. in a direction that will not bring them to their normal winter quarters.*

* After I had written this paragraph, I had the luck to receive 'visible demonstration' of such occurrences. On 29th November 1972 my wife and I were walking in a small park less than a mile from our home in Swarthmore, Pennsylvania, when suddenly a fine male Black-throated Grey Warbler (*Dendroica nigrescens*) came flitting past our heads, and we watched it at very close quarters for a minute or two. If you look at a map of its breeding distribution you will see that it is a bird of the extreme west, and mainly the south-west, of North America, well over a thousand miles from Pennsylvania. Fortunately, though it did not spend much time in that park our bird did show itself to several experienced observers during the next ten or twelve days, so that it was well identified. Moreover, there were two or three others recorded from the mid-Atlantic States between October and January (and one, a male, duly photographed, appeared on 10th October in Nova Scotia of all places, surely something like three thousand miles from its breeding range, and possibly further north than any part of that range. Did it then work slowly south, until it reached Pennsylvania at the end of November? Improbable, but I suppose not quite

At one time I was attracted by the idea that some birds were irresistibly impelled to follow the setting sun, setting out for their migration day after day as the sun set, and so flying steadily west night after night. If you live in the British Islands and read, year after year, of small warblers and other insect-feeding birds from eastern or central Asia appearing on the east coast of Britain, this idea has its attractions. But if you then cross the Atlantic to the eastern seaboard of North America and learn that warblers from the west coast are netted by 'banders' along the New Jersey coast, autumn by autumn, the sunset idea falls to the ground. All that one can say is that the migratory urge is a mighty impulse which can carry even the smallest birds immense distances, sometimes in directions that must spell disaster.

Once, when I was crossing the sea from Fair Isle to the mainland of Shetland, I watched a party of Skylarks flying steadily to the west. Both Shetland to the north and Fair Isle to the south were visible; but the larks were not heading for either. If they continued on their course, they would ultimately perish in the Atlantic. Of course some strange instinct may have caused them to change course, so as to reach Ireland. I have never watched migration on the north-west of Ireland; I do not know whether migrants have been seen flying out over the ocean there, but I somewhere read long ago of flocks of Rooks flying out to sea from the west coast of Ireland.

I have occasional first-hand experience of the persistence of the migratory impulse beyond what seems necessary for survival. As already recorded, in the early days of January 1928, when I was on a ship steaming from Colombo to Singapore, I watched a thrush of some species, which at first seemed inclined to settle on our ship but then flew off again. I could not determine the species but it is likely to have been one of the migratory thrushes from Siberia. It must have passed over plenty of land in eastern India or Burma where it could have spent the winter without any danger of being overtaken by snow and frost. It may even have spent three or four months there. But here it was, as late as January, so strongly impelled by the migratory urge that it was making this long, 'needless' journey to spend the winter, let us hope, in the mountains of Sumatra. I wonder what Siberian

---

impossible), so presumably some abnormal weather conditions brought them all across the Continent. Even so, I find it hard to picture just what kind of storm from west to east could have done it; and why just this one species? I cannot see that it was a year of prolific west to east flight.

thrushes, if any, have been recorded from that island. Perhaps some go there every year.

I believe I first began to ponder this problem of seemingly needless or excessive migration when in the old days round Tunbridge Wells I made the curious discovery that there were, on the borders of Kent and Sussex, two distinct populations of Lesser Redpolls. During the winter, parties of Redpolls were normally to be found in the alder trees. These birds disappeared in March. A month later, Redpolls reappeared in the pines and birches and a few of these stayed to breed. Year after year I confirmed the distinctness of these two populations and the gap between the disappearance of the wintering birds and the reappearance of the summer birds. Apparently, food was available throughout the year; so the breeding population might have stayed through the winter. I could not check my observation by ringing but I have no doubt of its truth. The same must surely be true of Song Thrushes. A good proportion of the local Song Thrushes, at any rate from woodland areas, leave England for the winter, but Continental Song Thrushes spend the winter together with Redwings and other species, on the meadow-land of southern and eastern England.

One could go on multiplying examples of what might be called improbable or unnecessary migration. Every year, for instance, some migrants overshoot the mark, such as the Turtle Doves that reach Fair Isle each spring, well to the north of their breeding range. Some find their way back again. There is the curious case of the Pied Crested Cuckoo, which apparently spends the winter in East Africa and then migrates to north India for the summer, although some members of the same species, a distinct race but not separable except in the hand, are resident in south India and Ceylon. And no doubt one could go on with many more examples.

What is the significance of all this? It seems to indicate at the least that in a great many species of birds, at certain seasons of the year, the impulse to undertake long migratory flights is so powerful that it carries them much further than appears to be necessary. Of course, one can always say of any individual case that circumstances may have changed over the millennia of evolutionary time, so that what was a necessary migration at one time to enable the species to survive is no longer necessary today because the environment has changed. But it is very difficult to believe that all the existing cases of 'unnecessary' migration can be so explained. Obviously, migration does enable many birds to survive and make use, during certain periods of the year, of excellent feeding and breeding grounds where they could not survive during the whole year. The masses of waders ('shore-birds') that breed in the high arctic, making use of perpetual daylight and masses of insect food, are the most obvious example. But it looks as if the migratory habit has been so effective that it has gone to excess, both in a tendency for some birds (a whole population in some cases, such as the Swallows going to South Africa), or a section of the population (such as the Turtle Doves that go too far north in the spring), to go further than they need; whilst yet others, such as the Redpolls and Thrushes of south-east England, migrate comparatively short distances each year although usually they could survive without migrating at all.

Incidentally, of course, one must note that regular annual migration may affect some members of a species whilst others are resident throughout the year. Thus, most English Robins are resident; but most Continental (European) Robins migrate, some of them from Scandinavia to North Africa. The migration of Robins across the North Sea and across the Mediterranean is a striking feature of the annual passage over those seas. Similarly, the flocks of Starlings that spend the winter feeding on the fields of England contain, as ringing has shown, huge numbers of winter migrants from central or even eastern Europe; but there are some that go to roost in local buildings, where they will breed next spring, and where they themselves were hatched. So, even where the migratory habit is very strongly developed it does not always apply to all the individuals of a species.

I suppose what I am saying is that birds—or at least many of the commoner, more successful birds—are so full of energy that they have plenty of surplus energy to expend beyond what is strictly necessary for survival. Sometimes this expresses itself in song, sometimes in flight, sometimes (as in the case of the Wren) in excess nest-building, sometimes in very elaborate display (as in the case of the Great Crested Grebe), sometimes in what can best be called 'play'. These are various ways in which this possible superabundant well-being of birds may find expression.

So I come to a matter that has nagged at me for many years. It is often assumed that every established habit of any wild creature must have a survival value. Otherwise, the logic seems to be, the habit would not have persisted. It would have been detrimental to the species, which would accordingly have died out. But why should there not be habits that are neutral, neither beneficial nor detrimental, or even partly beneficial and partly detrimental? It is my conviction that a great deal of bird behaviour is for all practical purposes neutral.

Once again, of course, it is very difficult to prove this, one way or the other. Wagtails and Common Sandpipers, it may be argued, get some advantage by always wagging their tails; the constant motion calls attention to their presence. Other members of the species will easily see them. Very good: but what about other birds, with similar habits, that do not wag their tails? I suppose the answer is that they 'survive' by *not* calling attention to their presence. Predators are less likely to see them. Redshanks are very noisy birds, but the Ruff which has similar feeding habits and an overlapping range (and from its widespread distribution, must be adjudged, like the Redshank, to be a 'successful' species) is nearly always silent. Have both the noisiness of the Redshank and the silence of the Ruff contributed to their survival? Would it not make more sense to suggest that noisiness has both advantages and disadvantages; and so has silence; so that both are, if you like so to put it, more or less 'neutral'?

Herring and Lesser Black-backed Gulls are very closely related species, possibly best regarded as two phases of a super-species. Lesser Black-backs are largely migratory; Herring Gulls almost entirely sedentary. Yet both seem to be very successful species in the present state of the environment in the north temperate zone. The migratory habit (and the 'problems' associated with it) of the Lesser Black-back has not caused it to do much better than its relative; nor has it conspicuously fallen behind in the struggle for survival.

Once, when Wilfrid and I were walking together by Upper Bittell reservoir, we suddenly came round a corner close to a Slavonian Grebe It began dipping its bill into the water. I asked Wilfrid what he thought this curious behaviour meant. Surely it was not feeding. 'No,' he said, 'it is just a nervous habit. I have seen them do it before when they are agitated by the near presence of an observer.' I expected my learned biological brother to explain some abstruse significance of this bill-dipping; Wilfrid, I suspect, would have been uneasy about much that I have written in this chapter. 'Questionable or idle speculation,' he might have called it. But here was *he* accusing a grebe, one of the most 'primitive' British birds, of having 'nervous habits'. I was much reassured. I admit I find it much easier to think of the tail-wagging of wagtails and sandpipers as 'nervous habits', fortunately for them not at all dangerous, than to believe that the species would perish rapidly if they stopped wagging their tails.

Let me take another example, which at least is topical. For some years past, much careful work has been done in Britain on the subject of the flocking of birds during the winter—or indeed, throughout the year outside the breeding season. I have already referred to some aspects of these studies in the chapter on tits. Much of this research revolves round the discussion of survival value of flocking. In other words, the assumption is that there must be some definite survival value or the habit would have died out—indeed, the birds would have died out. Yet, as far as I have seen, this study of flocking omits the other aspect of the subject, which is the fact that some other species living in the same environment do not flock. It seems to me that the wrong question is being asked. It should be not 'Why do some birds spend most of their time in flocks through the winter?' but rather 'Why do some birds flock, whilst others refuse to flock?' Indeed, it is much more complicated than this. Some birds, such as Starlings, Skylarks and various other common British species, spend much of their time feeding and flying in dense flocks. Others form rather loose parties; this includes some of the finches and tits and thrushes; some, such as Robins, Hedge Sparrows and Wrens, do not seem to form into flocks at all (though Wrens sometimes come together for roosting purposes); some, such as Nuthatches and Tree Creepers, do not form flocks of their own species. (Have you ever seen more than two or three Nuthatches or Tree Creepers together, unless it is a family party just out of the nest?) But, all the same, one or two of them will join up with the loose parties of tits that roam the woods in winter and will keep company with the other species, even though they never form flocks of their own species. (There is a species of nuthatch in North America that forms flocks, but at the moment I am considering the European species—and in fact the two common widely distributed nuthatches of the eastern United States have the same habits as the European species; that is, they do not normally form parties of their own species, but they join other, rather loose, parties of woodland birds.) There are species some individuals of which seem to live mostly in flocks, whilst others go about on their own; or, alternatively, they spend part of the day in a flock, and another part on their own. I am writing this in December in the State of Pennsylvania, where day by day a small party of House Finches is coming once or twice a day to our feeders; but it also happens that sometimes one comes alone, having apparently broken loose from the party.

If you study this matter in all its complexity I think you may well conclude that there are both advantages and disadvantages in flocking; and that the main reason for flocking may not be connected with the struggle for survival, but possibly it is due mainly (not totally) to some birds having a stronger sense for company, a stronger social sense let us say, than others. What holds a flock together? It is difficult to say. Some ornithologists have taken the view that once a bird has got caught up into a flock, it has great difficulty in extricating itself. I do not take this view; for I have often seen a flock break up or, more significantly, a single bird drop out whilst all the rest flew on. But certainly when you see a skein of geese or ducks or waders winging their way across the sky in perfect formation, it looks as if it is a very tight formation. And such lines of birds can pull very odd strangers into the line. The oddest I have seen was a line of Bar-tailed Godwits flying past Dungeness Point with a Sheldrake in the middle of the line, spaced equally with the Godwits.

Although birds of almost any kind will act as if they sometimes like to keep in close touch with other birds, not necessarily of their own species, one must also recognise that almost any bird can and does undertake enormous migratory journeys without the 'support' of any other bird. As far as I know, most Humming-birds that cross the Gulf of Mexico year by year do it alone. Whether on migration or when living a more or less sedentary life through the non-breeding seasons of the year, many birds live alone, whilst many others are usually found in the company of others, either of their own kind or else of other species. Indeed, as already noted, there are some species which even outside the breeding season hardly seem to tolerate others of their own kind, but which habitually consort with other birds. It is really very odd and very complex. Tentatively, I would suggest that the presence of other birds in the neighbourhood, preferably birds of approximately the same size, provides some kind of mutual psychological support. If it does not sound too anthropomorphic, one might say that they like each other's company; it is not absolutely necessary to their well-being but it contributes something towards it. So much so that when the Nuthatch, feeding perhaps ten yards away, flies off across the field to another part of the wood, within a minute or two some of the tits have begun to cross the field too; but the Wren that seemed to be in the party for the past five minutes remains in its territory and disappears in the undergrowth. In other words flocks form, disperse, re-form, or rather recompose with different membership, according to the various impulses that control the behaviour of birds from hour to hour through the day; and the more we try to reduce the solution to a matter of 'survival factors' the further we are likely to be from the avian truth.

Robins prosper although they never form flocks. Tits form flocks in the winter and they also flourish. Rooks usually go about in flocks. Carrion Crows usually go about alone. Both species flourish. I suggest that so far as 'survival value' is concerned, for a great many species, flocking or refusal to flock is more or less neutral.

Let me attempt to say again, in a few sentences, what I have been trying to say here. I am not suggesting that the widespread, typical habits of birds—song, migration, flocking, and so on—have no survival value. Of course they have. In this last case, for instance, one can see that the habit of winter flocking of several species of woodland birds in England provides all the members of the flock with some help in the search for food. It enables them to warn one another of the appearance of a predator; and there may well be other beneficial results too. But one can also see some disadvantages. Each is competing for the food that is available. A predator probably likes to find a flock of birds at work. He may miss a solitary bird; but if twenty are together he is almost sure to capture one. So there are disadvantages as well as advantages. Presumably they more or less cancel out. So flocking persists, whilst solitary feeding also persists. But my main point is that I think 'survival value' has recently been turned into something of an obsession: find the 'survival value' and you have solved the whole problem. Whereas it is my impression that 'survival value' is one of several factors that contribute to the persistence of these and other habits.

It seems possible that 'survival value' is one of those important half-truths that has been so indiscriminately accepted that it has become almost a superstition. The prevailing picture of life on this planet is of innumerable organisms engaged in a constant and desperate struggle for existence, which is implicit in every action they take. I think this is an exaggeration. Undoubtedly the struggle for existence is a very important part of life; but it is not the whole of life. Man is not the only creature to have evolved so far that he has time to do plenty of things that are not directly connected with the struggle for survival. In spite of the dangers of using anthropomorphic language, it is difficult not to see flowering plants 'enjoying' the morning sunshine as it causes the buds to open, or similarly 'enjoying' a good shower of rain after a drought. On the other hand, when they look bedraggled from strong winds and rain, in some degree they surely 'feel' miserable. If this is in some degree true of plants, it must surely be much more true of animals: in the first place, of insects; butterflies for instance, as they bask on a wall or bank, opening and closing their wings to get the full satisfaction of the sunshine; more still of birds as they sit contentedly preening their feathers or as they race through the air or soar for hours high above the earth, on up-currents of air. In modern jargon one might say that birds, or animals generally, are supreme existentialists, who live intensely in each passing moment and find life good.

Biologists are, I suppose, very much like other human beings. Many of them like to oversimplify. Just as many economists, following Karl Marx, have seen the economic motive as the explanation of everything in human history; and many psychologists, following Freud, have found that everything that man does springs from the unconscious mind; so biologists, following Darwin, have seen the struggle for existence as explaining the whole of evolutionary development. In each case the 'prophet' has indeed made an immense contribution to a better understanding of the world. But perhaps again in each case—certainly in the case of Darwin—the prophet was wiser, less one-eyed than many of his disciples. I believe it is a good rule, when you are convinced of a broad truth, to look for the places where it does not apply. When closely examined almost every aspect of life reveals surprising paradoxes, even seeming contradictions. Kropotkin long ago showed that mutual aid is as much a law of life as is competition. To this one may add the enjoyment of a sense of well-being. We struggle to survive; we aid one another in the struggle; and for much of our lives, even if we are birds or insects, we cease from struggling, and enjoy life.

Adaptability seems to be the most important single quality in the successful development of a species, including man. I do not always find it easy at the age of eighty-three to adapt myself to the thought forms of the younger generations; but I still find myself trying to adapt to what I see in the world of birds; I am still learning about them. I hope that what I think I have seen in their lives will make sense to others. There is at least some satisfaction in trying to express in words some of the meditations that I have lived with for over fifty years.

Forgetting man, since the comparison of man and the animals is always dangerous—whether it takes the form, so popular among the pseudo-scientific biologists of today, of demonstrating how essentially animal human nature is, or, on the other hand, of trying to discover some of the higher human qualities, such as an aesthetic sense, even a moral sense of a kind, in animals—let us confine ourselves to birds. It appears to me that the life of a bird is composed of several parts, which may be described first as the fulfilment of the sexual instinct—this is clearly dominant, intensely so, during the breeding season—next, the struggle to survive, manifesting itself first and foremost through the struggle to achieve and hold an adequate food supply; this often involves vigorous defence of territory; and, beyond this, much activity (even occasional passivity) of a sort that is more or less neutral from the point of view of the struggle for survival, but which can best be described as enjoyment of the vitality that comes to a bird that is no longer bound every moment by the demands of food and reproduction. A bird's capacity to fly and to sing, especially, give it unusual opportunities for this unnecessary but very satisfying ability to spend its 'spare time' enjoyably. Obviously, both flight and the development of the vocal organs have been of the utmost importance in helping birds to survive (though some survive that are flightless and some survive that are practically silent). Yet there is in fact an enormous expenditure of avian energy that appears to have little obvious 'survival value', though of course it cannot have a 'disaster' value either.

Perhaps I have given too much space to this matter of 'survival values'. In any case, as I have already said, it appears that the most important factor favouring survival is adaptability to changes in the environment; and on both sides of the North Atlantic this means adaptability to the habits of industrial humanity.

This book is to some extent an autobiography. I began with my less-than-eight-year-old self spending a spring morning in southern England listening to an early Chiffchaff. I write this conclusion seventy-six years later, when at nearly eighty-four I am still watching and listening, day by day, for the first insectivorous birds returning from the south—this time in the mid-Atlantic States of North America. When the first Phoebe or Kinglet or Black and White Warbler appears, it gives me just the same thrill that I got from that English Chiffchaff long ago.

My brothers and I have all tried to do some systematic bird observation, hoping to add our quota to the endless accumulation of ornithological knowledge. But for all of us, a day or even an hour spent in total relaxation just watching the birds has meant more than any scientific enquiry. It is never necessary to play one off against the other. We have all had what an earlier generation would have called 'curious minds'. The simple and intense delight in seeing and watching birds was always coupled with the desire to understand what we were seeing. Birdwatching is not only an intense asesthetic experience, but also a stimulus to the mind and to the imagination, as one tries to understand the nature of a bird's world.

I suppose that most men, in all parts of the world, accepted their own place in the world of nature as a matter of course until a few generations ago. Now modern urban man finds himself alienated from the world he lives in. He has tried to bend it to his will and has often made a mess of it. So now he is trying to rediscover or rebuild a relationship with the natural world. There are many ways of doing this. Those who enjoy the study of animals and plants are not, in most cases, consciously setting out to restore the lost relationship; but as they continue to explore, the world of nature takes possession of them and they learn things that cannot be put into words. They then cease to be aliens.

Birds, I am afraid, will still tend to treat us with deep suspicion, owing to the ruthless hunting and killing that has characterised man almost everywhere for thousands of years. But, even though we must accept this condemnation and be punished for both our own sins and those of our ancestors, we can still learn that life on this planet is all one, and we are part of it. When Man's inhumanity to man gets the better of us, we can restore our equilibrium by turning again to Nature, the universal Mother, and by exploring her secrets from the inside.

Index

Alexander, C. J., 13–21, 23, 39, 41–43, 49–51, 68–71, 75–78, 102, 137–139
Alexander, G., 11
Alexander, W. B., 13–16, 18, 95, 153, 163, 232, 233, 252
Ali, Salim, 191, 193, 194, 209
America, North, winter birds in, 176–190
Ash, mapping at, 68
Ashdown Forest, 44, 64, 67
Atlas of the Breeding-Birds of the West Midlands, 79
Auk, Little, 46
Austin, Fred, 108, 125–133
Avocet, 213
Axell, H. E., 73, 145–147, 164

Babbler, Golden-headed, 205
  Quaker, 201
Backhouse, J., 13
Barbet, Blue-throated, 195
  Gold-throated, 207
  Great, 207
Barchem (Netherlands), Willow and Marsh Tits at, 80
Barwing, 208
Bee-eater, Green, 194
Belvide Reservoir, 45, 158
Benenden, mapping at, 55
Bird, behaviour, 251–257
  books, 19–20
  calls (*see* Song)
Birds of Cambridgeshire, 39, 96
Birds of Europe, 13, 16, 229
Birds of Surrey, 19
Bird Watcher in the Shetlands, 34
Birmingham Post, article in, 195
Bittell Reservoir, 45, 93, 155–160
Blackbird, 35, 47
  Red-winged, 178
Blackcap, 52, 55, 63, 64, 68, 69, 108, 110, 150, 152, 156
Blake, A. R. M., 79
Blathwayt, F. L., 95
Bluebird, 185
  Fairy, 203
Bluetail, Red-flanked, 211
Bluethroat, 143
Bootham School, 13
Born to Sing, 244 f
Boyd, A. W., 97, 155
Brambling, 15, 42, 110, 170
Breeding Birds of Britain and Ireland, 79 f
British Birds (journal) *passim*

British Ornithological Club, 24, 34
  Migration Committee, 24, 120
British Ornithological Union, 31
Broadwater Forest, 41
Broomhill, mapping at, 152
Brotherton, Helen, 231
Brown Creeper, 86
Bufflehead, 187
Bulbul, Finch-billed, 205
  Red-vested, 196
  Streaked Green, 205
Bull, A., 232
Bullfinch, Orange, 211
Bunting, 218
  Cirl, 44, 69, 152
  Corn, 44, 64, 68, 69, 149, 150, 152, 153, 156–157
  Lapland 236
  Reed, 53, 56, 64, 149, 150, 152, 153, 156–157, 170
  Rustic, 226
  Snow, 43, 111
Bunyard, P., 32
Burkitt, J. P., 35
Burrows, R. B., 130

Calcutta, 195–199
Camber, 43, 152
Cambridge Sewage Farm, 30, 96, 155, 224
Cardinal, 48, 179
Carruthers, D., 219–221
Chaffinch, 15, 35
Champéry, Marsh and Willow Tits at, 76, 80
Chat, Dark Grey Bush, 204
Chelwood Gate, 64, 66
Chickadee, Black-capped, 82, 91
  Carolina, 82, 91, 176
Chiffchaff 12, 32, 35, 43, 46, 52, 58, 63, 64, 108, 110, 152, 156, 174
  Siberian, 70, 199, 224
Chittenden Woods, 55
Chough, 215
Clarke, W. J. 140
Cley, 226
Coleman's Hatch, 64, 65
Cooper, I., 169, 172
Coot, 45, 153, 156–157
Cormorant, 69
  Little, 195
Corncrake, 15, 53, 63, 67, 107
Courser, Cream-coloured, 145, 224
Coward, T. A., 36, 155

Cranbrook, 55, 72
Crane, Sarus, 210
  Siberian, 213
Crosfield, J. B., 12, 14, 70
Crossbill, 70
  White-winged, 184
Crow, Carrion, 43, 44, 47, 64, 149
  Common, 178
  Hooded, 43, 44, 111
  House, 195
Crowborough, 64
Cuckoo, 109, 148, 245
Cuckoo-Shrike, Large, 204
Curlew, Stone, 133, 135, 137, 150
Curtis, F., 237
Curtler, M., 228

Dabchick, 45, 153, 156
Darter, 195
Delhi, 211–213, 228, 235
Diver, Black-throated, 169, 172
  Great Northern, 104, 169
  Red-throated, 43, 104, 139, 169, 172
Dorset, 74, 103, 105, 148
Dove, Collared, 195, 250
  Mourning, 178
  Spotted, 195
  Turtle, 109, 110, 147
Dowitcher, 114–116
Dresser, H. E., 13, 16, 229
Drongo, 202
Duck, Harlequin, 187
  Long-tailed, 187
  Ring-necked, 188
  Ruddy, 187
  Tufted, 45
  White-winged Wood, 199
Dungeness, 42, 47, 73, 103, 117, 121, 123–153 223
Dunlin, 6, 114, 170, 171, 186
Durlaston, 46, 234

Eagle, Black, 204
  White-bellied Sea, 196
Ecological Isolation in Birds, 88
Ecology, 27
Egret, American, 182
  Cattle, 182
  Snowy, 182
Eider, 169
  Common, 187
  King, 187
Europe, Western, birdwatching in, 80–82
Evans, A. H., 33

Fairfield Brack, 24
Fair Isle, 226
Falcon, Red-footed, 226
Fieldfare, 42, 111
Fighting, territorial, 61

Finch, House, 181, 185
  Purple, 180
Firecrest, 43, 44, 46, 70–75, 111, 146, 225
Flocking, 90, 253, 255
Flycatcher, 205
  Grey-headed, 202
  Spotted, 18, 53, 55, 56, 58, 63, 64, 68, 103, 109, 110, 149, 150, 152, 156–157
Flycatcher-Shrike, Bar-winged, 204
Flycatcher-Warbler, Allied, 205
  Chestnut-headed, 205
  Grey-headed, 205
Forests, *see under* names
Forktail, Black-backed, 203
Fowler, W., 34, 70, 101
Frensham ponds, 14, 44
Friar's Gate, 64, 65
Fulmar, 168
Futehaly, Zafar, 193

Gadwall, 159
Gandhi, Mahatma, 200
Ganguli, Mrs Usha, 212
Gannet, 44, 169
Garganey, 56, 108, 110, 218
Gibb, J., 87, 90
Gill, L., 27
Gillmor, R., 91
Godwit, Bar-tailed, 115, 171
  Black-tailed, 115
Goldcrest, 13, 41, 44–46, 147, 156
Golden eye, 111, 169, 187
Goldfinch, 179
Gooch, B., 164
Goosander, 111
Goose, Brent, 139, 169
  Pink-footed, 44, 170
  White-fronted, 44, 170
Grackle, Common, 178
Grantchester, species recorded at, 157 (map)
Grebe, 141
  Black-necked, 104, 169
  Great Crested, 43, 44, 139, 156, 169, 171
  Red-necked, 172
  Slavonian, 104, 138, 169
Greenfinch, 42
Greenshank, 46, 84
Groombridge Sewage Farm, 41, 42, 43
Grosbeak, Black and Yellow, 211
  Evening, 179
Guillemot, 43, 169, 172
Gull, Black-headed, 47, 142, 188, 197
  Bonaparte's, 188
  Brown-headed, 197
  Common, 47, 128, 150, 166
  Glaucous, 168
  Great Black-backed, 43, 47, 166, 186
  Great Black-headed, 197
  Herring, 41, 43, 47, 159, 186

Index

Gull (contd.)—
  Laughing, 188, 189
  Lesser Black-backed, 168, 189, 236
  Little, 164, 168, 237
  Mediterranean Black-headed, 141, 169
  Mew, 188
  Ring-billed, 188
  Sabine's 165

Handbook of the Birds of India and Pakistan, 191
Handbook of British Birds, 17, 18, 38–39, 94, 97
Hartert, E. J. O., 22, 34, 75
Hartley, 55
Hartshorne, C., 244f
Hastings Rarities, 26, 123
Hawfinch, 43, 45
Haysom, Trevor, 46, 147, 169–171
Heron, Black-crowned Night, 182
  Great Blue, 182
  Great White, 231–233
  Little Blue, 182
  Louisiana, 182
  Night, 196
  Reef, 212
History of the Birds of Kent, 71, 76
Hobby, 109, 110
Holmestone, mapping at, 150
Hoopoe, 108, 146, 233
Hornbill, Wreathed, 207
Howard, E., 60–62
Hume, A. O., 191, 193
Humming-bird, Ruby-throated, 245
Hundred of Hoo, mapping at, 153
Hunt, Sir John, 215

Ibis, Glossy, 182
India, birdwatching in, 83–86, 98, 191–213
Isle of Wight, mapping on, 69
Italy, ornithology in, 36

James, Miss C. K., 42
January 1st lists, 40–48
Jay, 204
  Blue, 48, 178
Johnson, I. G., 97
Jourdain, F. C. R., 32, 34
Joy, N., 155, 161
Junco, Slate-coloured, 179, 185

Kashmir, expedition in, 209–210
Kent, birdwatching as a boy in, 14
  bird population in, 41, 49–69
  Weald of, mapping in, 55
  see also under place names
Kerala, expedition in, 209
Kestrel, 69

Kingfisher, 41, 45, 53, 156
Kite, Pariah, 194
  Red, 143
Kittiwake, 46, 160, 172
Knot, 170, 171
Koel, 196

Lack, D., 39, 87–91, 96, 155, 225
Lammergeier, 217
Lapwing, 53, 56, 64, 156–157
Lark, 217, 218
  Black, 26
  Short-toed, 218
Laughing-Thrush, 203, 207
Leafbird, 204
Lemon, Mrs. F., 128–130
Lickey Woods, 18, 45, 73
Liddar Valley (Kashmir) 209–210
Linnet, 117
List-making, 15, 40–48, 225
Lizard, the (Cornwall), 44
Longstaff, T. G., 214, 218
Loon, Arctic, 190
  Common, 190
Low, C., 144
Lynes, H., 32

Macpherson, H., 163
Magpie, 149
Mallard, 43, 45, 53, 153, 156–157
Manual of British Birds, 19, 71, 75, 91, 128
Mapping, 49–59, 68–69, 148–153
Mapping results
  Ash, 68
  Ashdown Forest, 64
  Benenden, 55
  Broomhill, 152
  Camber, etc., 152
  Chelwood Gate, 64
  Coleman's Hatch, 64
  Crowborough, 64
  Dungeness, 150
  Dungeness to Rye, 152
  Friar's Gate, 64
  Hartley, 55
  Hartley, 55
  Holmestone, 150
  Hundred-of-Hoo, 153
  Isle of Wight, 69
  Kentish Weald, 55
  Lydd, 150
  Nutley, 64
  Rolvenden, 55
  Romney Marsh, 149
  Tunbridge Wells, 53, 63
  Wight, Isle of, 69
  Withyham, 64
  Wych Cross, 64
  Wye, 63

Maps
  Grantchester area, 157
  Indian Sub-Continent, 192
  Mid-Atlantic States of U.S.A., 177
  Tunbridge Wells area 1909, 58
  Tunbridge Wells area 1914, 52–53
  Upper Bittell Reservoir, 156
Marley Wood, 87–88
Martin, House, 102, 109, 216
  Sand, 102, 108, 110, 174
Matthiesen, P., 116
Meiklejohn, M. F. M., 230
Merganser, Red-breasted, 104, 187
Merlin, 44, 111
  Red-headed, 199
Mesia, Silver-winged, 203
Migration, 100–122
  B.O.C. Committee, 24, 120
  causes, 37–38, 246
  discussion, 245–251
  over the Himalayas, 214–221
Migration tables
  Summer Migrants in England (1897–1968), 108–110
  Winter Migrants in England (1897–1968), 111
Minivet, 204
Mockingbird, 180
Monk, J., 227
Moorhen, 42, 45, 53
Moreau, R., 193, 215
Mynah, 195

Naga Hills, expedition in the, 200–209
Naturalists' Diary, 11–12, 20, 101
New Jersey, U.S.A., 186, 188
New Year's Day bird lists, 41–48
Nicholson, E. M., 35, 77, 239
Nicoll, M. J., 92, 97
Nighthawk, 230
Nightingale, 13, 52, 55, 56, 58, 64, 68, 102, 109, 152, 156
Nightjar, 15, 53, 54, 55, 64, 70, 150
Noel-Baker, P., 17
Northampton Sewage Farm, 155, 225
Norway, Marsh and Willow Tits in, 81
Nottingham Sewage Farm, 155
Nunn, J. P., 237
Nuthatch, 41, 44, 53, 156–157
Nutley, 64, 66

Oldham, C., 34, 38
Oriole, Golden, 95, 108, 215, 233
Ortolan, 146
Ouzel, Ring, 70
  Brown Wood, 202
Owl, Brown, 156–157
  Little, 156–157
  Screech, 48
  Short-eared, 44

Oystercatcher, 169

Parrakeet, Green, 196
Parrotbill, Red-headed, 203
Parslow, J. F. L., 79
Pennsylvania, U.S.A., 114, 115, 176–190
Peregrine, 69
Peveril Point, Dorset, 163–175
Phalarope, Grey, 164
Phenology, 20
Phoebe, 185
Pigeon, Feral, 178
Pillai, N. G., 209
Pintail, 44, 159, 188
Pipit, 217
  Chinese Water, 98
  Greenish Water, 98
  Hodgson's Water, 98
  Indian Water, 98
  Meadow, 42, 56, 69, 93, 121
  Richard's, 218
  Rock, 43, 69, 92, 96, 172, 173
  Tree, 53, 54, 55, 63, 64, 98, 108, 110, 156–157
  Water, 91–98, 225
Plover, Grey, 43, 114, 171, 187
  Kentish, 107, 125–137, 151, 152, 158, 225
  Little Ringed, 39, 108, 223
  Ringed, 114, 151, 153, 170–172
  Upland, 225
Pochard, Canvas-back, 188
  Red-head, 188
Poole harbour, 171, 231
Population, observations in Kent, 49–69
Portland, 74, 118, 121, 227, 235
Puffin, 168
Purbeck, 46, 104, 165, 228–234

Quaker ancestry, influence of, 13

Rail, Water, 45
Rana, B. D., 91
Rare birds, 222–238
Raven, 44, 69
Razorbill, 168, 172, 190
Reading Sewage Farm, 155
Redpoll, 45, 250
  Lesser, 53, 67
Redshank, 153, 156, 157, 170, 171, 217
  Dusky, 236
Redstart, 15, 55, 64, 103, 108, 110, 217
  Black, 36, 44, 70, 111, 143, 174
  Blue-fronted, 205
Redwing, 41, 111, 172
Reigate, 12, 14
Reservoirs, Belvide, 45, 158
  Bittel, 45, 93, 155–160
  West Midland, 154–162

Richmond, H. W., 33
Ripley, D., 191, 193, 200, 212
Robin, 36, 47, 185, 242
Roller, Indian, 194
Rolvenden, mapping at, 55
Romney Marsh, 23, 49, 103, 123–154
  mapping at, 149
Rooke, K. B., 248
Rosefinch, 210
Rother Levels, 56
Rothschild, W., 22, 32, 75
Royal Society for the Protection of Birds, 25, 125, 128, 129
Rubythroat, White-moustached, 211
Ruff, 24, 171

Sanderling, 114, 170, 171, 186
Sand Grouse, Pallas', 223
Sandpiper, Buff-breasted, 225
  Common, 109
  Green, 42, 111
  Least, 114–116
  Pectoral, 225
  Purple, 44, 158, 169, 186, 225
  Semi-palmated, 114–116
  Stilt, 115
  Western, 226
Saunders, H., 19, 71, 75, 91, 222, 237
Scaup, 138, 187
Sclater, P. L., 75
Scoter, Common, 43, 159, 168, 187
  Surf, 187
  Velvet, 159, 169, 171
  White-winged, 187
Scott, R. E., 73, 147
Selous, E., 34
Serin, 233
Sewage Farms
  Cambridge, 30, 96, 155, 225
  Groombridge, 41, 42
  Northampton, 155
  Nottingham, 155
  Reading, 155
Shag, 14, 166
Shearwater, 140, 141
  Balearic, 141, 167
  Manx, 166
  Sooty, 141, 167
Sheldrake, 153, 169, 171
Shoveler, 56
Shrike, Brown, 220
  Red-backed, 15, 55, 58, 64, 69, 103, 107, 150, 152, 156–157
  Woodchat, 26, 223
Shrike-Babbler, 202
Sibia, 205
Sillem, J. A., 218
Siskin, 13, 45, 111
  Pine, 179
Silva, 203, 204

Skua, Arctic, 167, 168
  Great, 168
  Pomarine, 158, 168
Skylark, 47, 119, 150, 249
Smew, 111
Smith, R., 160
Snipe, 42, 53, 56, 64, 172
  Jack, 13, 111
  Painted, 217
  Pintail, 217
Snow, D. W., 85, 87
Song
  definition, 240
  discussion of, 239–244
  fallibility of listener, 241
  of Willow Tit, 75–78
  periods of, 35, 77, 88, 242
  published charts, 17
  purpose of, 242, 244
Sparrow, Field, 180
  Hedge, 35
  House, 47, 178, 185, 195, 240
  Song, 179, 184
  Tree, 42, 149, 150, 180
  White-throated, 48, 179, 184
Sparrowhawk, 45
Spider-hunter, 205
Spotbill, 199
Starling, 183
Stilt, 213
  Black-winged, 235
Stint, Little, 46
  Temminck's, 217
Stone Harbor Sanctuary, 182
Stonechat, 43, 45, 52, 54, 64, 68, 69, 150
  Indian, 217
Stork, White, 24, 224
Summer migrants, see Migration tables
Summers-Smith, J. D., 241, 249
Sunbird, 195
Swallow, 12, 102, 108, 110, 174, 216, 243
  Red-rumped, 216
Swanage Bay, 164–175
Swarthmore, U.S.A., 176, 230
Swift, 109, 110, 174
  Alpine, 216, 233
  Chimney, 185
  White-rumped, 216

Tailor-bird, 195
Tart, Jack, 44, 108, 126–137, 140–145
Teal, 153, 188
  Whistling, 199
Tern, Arctic, 134–137, 148, 161, 168, 245
  Black, 135–137, 161, 235
  Bridled, 128, 141
  Common, 109, 110, 134–137, 148, 151, 161, 168
  Gull-billed, 198
  Little, 109, 110, 151, 153, 168